PARAPSYCHOLOGY TODAY: A GEOGRAPHIC VIEW

PROCEEDINGS OF AN INTERNATIONAL CONFERENCE
HELD AT LE PIOL, ST. PAUL DE VENCE, FRANCE
AUGUST 25–27, 1971

PARAPSYCHOLOGY TODAY:
A GEOGRAPHIC VIEW

PROCEEDINGS OF AN INTERNATIONAL CONFERENCE
HELD AT LE PIOL, ST. PAUL DE VENCE, FRANCE
AUGUST 25–27, 1971

EDITED BY

Allan Angoff and Betty Shapin

PARAPSYCHOLOGY FOUNDATION, INC.

NEW YORK, N. Y.

Manufactured in the United States of America

PRE

LIST OF PARTICIPANTS

Eileen Coly
President
Parapsychology Foundation
New York, N.Y.

Frances P. Bolton
Vice-President
Parapsychology Foundation
New York, N.Y.

Allan Angoff
Chairman, Domestic and International Programs
Parapsychology Foundation
New York, N.Y.

Resat Bayer
President
Turkish Society for Parapsychological Research
Istanbul, Turkey

Hans Bender
Institut für Grenzgebiete der Psychologie und Psychohygiene
Freiburg, Germany

H. C. Berendt
President
The Israel Parapsychology Society
Jerusalem, Israel

Piero Cassoli
Director
Centro Studi Parapsicologici di Bologna
Bologna, Italy

Frederick C. Dommeyer
Professor of Philosophy
San José College
San José, California

Yvonne Duplessis
Institut Métapsychique International, Paris;
Centre d'Information de la Couleur, Paris, France

Jarl Fahler
Director
Institute of Parapsychology in Finland, Inc.
Helsingfors, Finland

Jan Kappers
Amsterdam Parapsychological Study Circle;
Amsterdam Foundation for Parapsychological Research, Amsterdam, Holland

Theo Locher
President
Vereinigung für Parapsychologie
Brugg bei Biel, Switzerland

J. Ricardo Musso   President
                                    Instituto Argentino de Parapsicologia
                                    Buenos Aires, Argentina

Soji Otani   The Japanese Society for Parapsychology
                                    Tokyo, Japan

John C. Poynton   Biological Science Department
                                    University of Natal
                                    Durban, South Africa

Jamuna Prasad   President
                                    Indian Institute of Parapsychology
                                    Allahabad, India

Andrija Puharich   Physician, Tel Aviv, Israel

Joseph H. Rush   Physicist
                                    National Center for Atmospheric Research
                                    Boulder, Colorado

Milan Ryzl   Biochemist
                                    San José State College
                                    San José, California

Emilio Servadio   President
                                    Psychoanalytic Centre of Rome
                                    Rome, Italy

Marius F. Valkhoff   University of the Witwatersrand
                                    Johannesburg, South Africa

Donald J. West   Institute of Criminology
                                    University of Cambridge
                                    Cambridge, England

J. M. O. Wheatley   Department of Philosophy
                                    University of Toronto
                                    Toronto, Canada

CONTENTS

Contents

INTRODUCTION

Allan Angoff

On behalf of the President and Trustees of the Parapsychology Foundation, I declare our Twentieth International Conference open. We shall address ourselves to the theme: "Parapsychology Today: A Geographic View."

It is significant, I believe, that the Parapsychology Foundation, now completing its second decade, has reached out to the most distant parts of the world to bring together students of psychical research who will tell us of the national variations to which parapsychology, perhaps more than most sciences, is subject. We deal with a universal, a cosmic study, one with established principles and rules, and yet the patterns of study and discovery vary with each country. It is well, therefore, that we come together and exchange views across a conference table, and provide a common reservoir in which all our colleagues, all men, everywhere, may share.

William James put this far better in one of his last papers on the paranormal. It can well be applied to our deliberations here during the next three days. "Out of my experience," wrote James, ". . . one fixed conclusion dogmatically emerges, and that is this, that we with our lives are like islands in the sea, or like trees in the forest. The maple and the pine may whisper to each other with their leaves, and Conanicut and Newport hear each other's foghorns. But the trees also commingle their roots in the darkness underground, and the islands also hang together through the ocean's bottom. Just so there is a continuum of cosmic consciousness. . . . Our 'normal' consciousness is circumscribed for adaptation to our external earthly environment, but the fence is weak in spots, and fitful influences from beyond leak in, showing the otherwise unverifiable common connection. Not only psychic research, but metaphysical philosophy, and speculative biology are led in their own ways to look with favor on some such 'panpsychic' view of the universe as this. . . ."

That is William James, always a favorite colleague of ours at these conferences, and perhaps emphatically so at this conference which we might well call, to borrow his good word, a panpsychic gathering.

Please permit me to pause here and to note that we meet in the shadow of an incalculable loss. For the first time in twenty years the great and gracious lady who organized these conferences when she established this Foundation, is not with us. Eileen Garrett died here in southern France a year ago shortly after we had concluded our 19th conference and in the midst of her planning for this meeting. Her death is an indescribable loss to the world of learning. It is also a loss which continues to stir deep emotions everywhere in the world. For Eileen Garrett, in her fifty years of unique leadership in psychical research, gave also of herself, of her compassion, as she worked to advance the frontiers of science in such a way that it served mankind's more profound needs. We acknowledge here this morning, here in these hills where she attracted and encouraged the leading figures in modern psychical research, our great debt to this woman whose quest for the truth brought so many of us together in the past, and in a sense brings us all here today.

After the death of Mrs. Garrett the trustees met and agreed, unanimously and enthusiastically, that the obvious choice to succeed her in the Presidency was Eileen Coly, her daughter, her close associate for so many years, her strong co-worker in more recent years. I am glad to present Eileen Coly.

Mrs. Coly: I am glad to welcome you to our Twentieth International Conference. I thank each of you for your cooperation during the months we at the Foundation office in New York planned the conference and corresponded with you. Above all, I must thank you for coming such great distances—in some cases vast distances—to help make this gathering so thoroughly international. I know I shall listen to all of you with the most intense interest because you will be confirming again and again the essential unity of parapsychological work all over the world. I think it fair to say that parapsychology is another one of those great unifying forces that overcome national boundaries and national friction with ease. All of you here today symbolize that unity.

I shall listen to you during the next three days with great interest. I know I shall learn a great deal from all of you. The Parapsychology Foundation and, more important, the world of learning will be the gainer from your deliberation.

May I pause here and note that we began planning this conference just a year ago under the direction of our late President, of my mother, Eileen J. Garrett. I am privileged to succeed her and to welcome you, as she welcomed so many of you in the past. And like her, I will say there is hard work in the days ahead, but it need not all be hard work. There will be freedom. We have a swimming pool. We have beautiful country. We have other facilities which will provide what the Americans call, a change of pace. Please enjoy it all. Again, thank you.

ALLAN ANGOFF: Mrs. Garrett founded this organization with the cooperation of a warm friend, a distinguished American public figure, who found time in the midst of her many official duties in the Congress of the United States and elsewhere, to work with her in making the Parapsychology Foundation a living and vibrant reality. Ladies and Gentlemen, the co-founder of the Parapsychology Foundation, Frances P. Bolton.

MRS. BOLTON: I am glad to welcome all of you and to thank you for coming so far to tell us so much that the world must know about the progress of parapsychology in your lands. My warm friend and colleague of so many years, Eileen Garrett, continues with us as your deliberations proceed. Her vision infuses everything we do here and enables all of us in the Foundation to help advance a better understanding of a subject which can do so much to help all men better understand each other. This is the world outlook of Eileen Garrett and the true objective of this meeting which all of you from all over the world symbolize. Thank you again for your important contribution.

ALLAN ANGOFF: Eileen Garrett worked closely with distinguished scientists. Several of them are with us today in this Twentieth International Conference which she envisioned a year ago. We have asked one of them, and he has kindly consented, to share with you some of his impressions of the Eileen Garrett he knew. I am glad to present Dr. Andrija Puharich.

TRIBUTE TO EILEEN J. GARRETT

ANDRIJA PUHARICH

One of the extraordinary aspects of speaking about Eileen Garrett is that the words go not only to this audience of her friends, but to Eileen. With her characteristic twinkle of skeptical belief, and her equally charming appreciation of blarney she would be the first to say, "But how can you be sure?"

That was perhaps the theme of her life—How can you be sure? She had a fierce integrity about this quest for certitude which she relentlessly pursued all of her life. If she thought that an investigator had any common sense and some small idea for an experiment, she never turned down an offer to be personally investigated. She never really wanted to know about the details of any experiment, and she never broke experimental conditions. Her confidence in her psychic ability made her fearless and she never showed the slightest doubt about the reality of her psychic world in action. But take her out of the arena of doing and place her in the arena of academic discussion, and she became the greatest doubting Thomas of them all—doubtful of her powers, in doubt of her controls and of all other pretenders to psychic powers. Which is not to say that she did not have friends among psychics—she certainly did. It was simply a case of self-doubt at a discussion level being extended to all other psychics.

In 1948 I took two years off from my work in medicine in order to find out if telepathy really existed. I was about to give up my quest when I met Eileen. She willingly offered herself as a subject for my Faraday Cage experiments, and proved to me that telepathy did indeed exist and on my own terms. I owe my subsequent efforts in psychic research in great part to this initial experience with Eileen, and her continuing friendship and encouragement.

She always had heroic qualities in all aspects of living. If she was your friend, it was a bountiful friendship. If you were an enemy you had better beware. Being a great judge of human nature she often became overconfident about the loyalty of her friends. She assumed that her big-heartedness and loyalty would always bring about reciprocation in kind. It was one of life's great cruelties to her to be wounded by a betrayal of trust. I can still see the head-light blue quality of her eyes beseeching me, "Why, why would anyone betray my friendship?"

I give these contradictory aspects of her character because in fact her character was made up of the dynamic tension of many such oppositions, and when summed up became her greatness. I do not for a moment doubt her place in psychic history. But if I know Eileen at all, I know that she did not stop her work when her heart stopped beating. Her indomitable will to aid and elevate humanity through knowledge of the psychical and the spiritual has really just begun. I have never made a prediction before, but I will make one now. Eileen will speak, and her best works are yet to come. Truly, she always lived as if to die tomorrow, but she learned as if to live forever.

RECENT PARAPSYCHOLOGICAL RESEARCH IN THE UNITED KINGDOM

D. J. WEST

The British have made many significant contributions to parapsychological research, especially in the early pioneering days, but in recent years, although popular interest in the subject does not seem to have diminished, the amount of serious work done in the United Kingdom has been small in comparison with developments elsewhere, particularly in the United States. I believe this state of affairs to be due in part to a lack of professional status. Historically, the subject has been left to enthusiastic amateurs, and the dominant organization in the field, the Society for Psychical Research in London, has tended, whether deliberately or otherwise, to foster an amateur tradition.

At the end of the nineteenth century, when the Society was founded (and its output of published work can only be described as prodigious), the amateur tradition worked rather well. Although the Society was open to all and sundry, and there were many spiritualist members, effective control naturally fell into the hands of those who did the work and wrote the research reports. This was a nucleus of energetic and gifted young men who had time, skill and money at their disposal, and support from a number of persons of considerable academic or social prestige.

Times have changed. Research today calls for skill and training in experimental and statistical techniques that are normally only acquired by professional scientists. There is less scope for the dilettante, and the professionals are fully committed to earning their living in orthodox research projects. Wealthy academics, free to pursue unconventional research interests at their own expense, are no longer available. The almost insuperable difficulty confronting the Society for Psychical Research in London is to find investigators who have the time, the interest and the ability to do the work, and to do it without the financial and institutional support customary and necessary for modern research.

Much swifter development could be hoped for if the universities would adopt parapsychology as a proper subject for teaching and research. Rhine, Murphy and others in the United States have had a limited success in integrating parapsychological research into university organization, but in England there has been very little progress in this direction. One reason for this is that American universities are more open to the receipt of private funds for the promotion of all sorts of purposes, whereas the state-funded British universities have not the same independent resources to draw upon.

In England, the limited amount of funds which private donors have produced have found their way to bodies outside of the universities. Even the Perrott-Warrick Studentship in psychical research, although administered by Trinity College, Cambridge, has so far had little connection with the University itself. Holders of the Studentship have worked free-lance, without being provided with research facilities by any university department, and without being members of either the University or of Trinity College. Other ventures into psychical research in Britain, such as Celia Green's Psychophysical Research Unit at Oxford, even though they may be run by graduates, have been set up by private funds independently of any university connection. The Society for Psychical Research itself has a research fund, separate from the general purposes fund, which was set up explicitly for the furtherance of research. Up till now the income from this fund has been used almost exclusively for paying the running costs of projects conducted by self-supporting amateur research workers.

There are signs that this state of affairs is changing. At the instigation of John Cutten, currently Honorary Secretary of the Society for Psychical Research, a new Studentship Trust Fund has been set up to promote and sponsor university studentships for the study and investigation of paranormal phenomena. In connection with this enterprise, two British universities have been approached, and the heads of the relevant departments have agreed in principle to consider the admission of suitable students, financed by the new fund, as candidates for graduate work leading to a submission for a doctoral degree, provided that the proposed program of parapsychological research meets with their approval. Already one such student has been selected for graduate work in a university department of psychology and has been given appropriate financial support from the new fund.

The significance of this development is that it may lead to a number of graduate students being recruited into full-time parapsychological research at different universities. These students will have a great advantage over free-lance investigators in having a recognized university status, in having the advice and supervision of academics appointed for the purpose, and finally, if their work proves of sufficient merit, in having the fact acknowledged by the conferment of a degree. As there are no permanent posts in parapsychology available in Britain, it is important that an individual who devotes some years to parapsychological research should not forfeit his place on his ordinary career ladder. By working at parapsychology and for a higher degree at the same time, this difficulty is overcome.

Of course, the obtaining of a higher degree for parapsychological research has long been theoretically possible. It was done, for example, by Drs. Soal, Bendit, and Hettinger, and in the case of one of my own doctorates certain parapsychological publications were taken into consideration by the examiners. But hitherto these have been exceptional cases of work done more or less as a spare time hobby by persons whose everyday employment had been in some more orthodox pursuit. The new provisions will allow full time professional research to be carried out under proper auspices and to receive proper recognition.

Apart from this particular scheme, there are other indications that British universities are no longer completely opposed to parapsychological studies. At the University of Edinburgh, Dr. J. Beloff, in the Department of Psychology, has been able to pursue an intensive program of parapsychological research for some years, and to recruit research assistants to help. Indeed, his work represents the most important and extensive research effort in Great Britain at present. Another important development is the research unit set up at Oxford University by Sir Alister Hardy, emeritus Professor of Zoology, who is investigating both telepathic phenomena and religious experiences. At the time of writing, Cambridge University has just allowed Dr. Y. Raef, an Egyptian scientist, to submit, for a doctorate in philosophy, a thesis on psychic phenomena among the Islamic mystics. This historical and analytic study, carried out at Cambridge, aroused the interest of the late Professor Arberry, a distinguished Islamic scholar, and the late Professor C. D. Broad, so it is good news that it has been brought successfully to completion.

Another step in bringing parapsychology into the universities was foreshadowed in the Vice Chancellor's Address to the Court of the University of Surrey on January 17, 1970. Referring to stages in the evolution of human consciousness, from individual preoccupations to steadily growing group awareness, Dr. Leggett referred to the need to promote investigation in these fields. He cited, as an example, the work of Sir Alister Hardy, and went on to suggest: "A start could be made with one senior appointment, maybe a research professor of metapsychology." In fact, there is hope now that this development may come about quite soon.

Turning now from the question of the organization of parapsychology in Britain to what work has actually been done recently, it has to be admitted that we have had more negative results, and more critical commentaries, than we have had new developments. Indeed this trend has been noticeable for quite some years. The organizational problems referred to earlier, which make it difficult to carry out new research programs, may be in part responsible. On the other hand, one must not underestimate the difficulty inherent in all parapsychological research. Professor Rushton, in his presidential address to the S.P.R. in November, 1970, put it aptly and concisely: "Paranormal phenomena seem to fade away in the attempt to perfect the techniques for eliciting them. . . . It is clearly false in most cases to believe that sensitives are tricksters, but the history of their performance often resembles strikingly that of a fraud whose tricks are being inspected too persistently and analyzed too closely." Anyway, whether the worse difficulty is the nature of the subject or the lack of organized facilities for research, it is certainly easier to find fault with previous investigations than to produce new and better research.

A recent paper in the critical tradition has unfortunately appeared posthumously. It is "The Origin of the 'Prepared Random Numbers' Used in the Shackleton Experiments," by the late Dr. R. G. Medhurst. This refers to the famous Soal-Goldney experiments in telepathy carried out during the Second World War. Many of you may wonder at the British preoccupation with these ancient experiments, which have long been superseded by American work, but the fact is that Soal's researches represent about the only long-continued series of successful ESP experiments that have been reported in Britain in the last thirty years. They stand out as the great exception to the British tradition of failure to reproduce high-scoring ESP effects. Moreover, the Shackleton experiments were widely acclaimed as not only successful, but also as the most carefully conducted and virtually fraud-proof experiments ever done. Anything which seems to cast the least doubt upon them is quite shocking to the British. Medhurst set out with the idea of locating Soal's randomized target sequences in the Chambers's Logarithm Tables from which they were said to have been taken. His purpose was to show that the allegation by Mrs. Gretl Albert that she had seen Soal altering some target numbers must have been mistaken. He used a high speed digital computer to reproduce the last digits of Chambers's seven-figure logarithms, and devised a computer program to match specimen sequences from the ESP targets against all the sequences that could be obtained from the logarithms by the method described by Soal. He found that none of the sequences matched properly. Medhurst's discoveries have since been confirmed by others. The inescapable conclusion appears to be that however Soal prepared his targets it could not have been exactly in the way he reported.

As far as it goes, this finding does not in itself much affect the validity of the experimental results (since the targets were still sufficiently random), but it suggests that Soal was not so obsessionally accurate in his reporting as one might otherwise suppose. Inevitably it reactivates the doubts and suspicions raised when Soal announced, long after the event, that he had lost the original score sheets on a train, and lost with them all possibility of proving by direct examination that no tampering with the figures had taken place. I predict that Medhurst's contribution will trigger off further examinations and further critical reappraisals of the Soal data. I hesitate to predict the outcome, but one thing at least will be proved, namely, that British parapsychologists will not let a positive result stand if there is the slightest chance of exposing it as fallacious.

As has already been remarked, most of the experimental reports in Britain in recent years have been produced by John Beloff and his collaborators. Despite their industry and ingenuity, their results have been disappointingly negative. In many experiments they have made use of an electronic ESP tester, built for the Department of Psychology at Edinburgh University, which produces a random sequence of targets and registers automatically the numbers of hits and trials. The machine was used for some telepathy tests using pairs of "sweethearts" (i.e., engaged couples and newlyweds) as agent and percipient. It was concluded that "mutual attraction between two people is not sufficient to insure telepathic rapport in a guessing situation such as we have here described." In other experiments, conditions were varied in different ways to try to encourage ESP phenomena. For instance, the effects of giving a percipient immediate or delayed information as to the result of each guess were compared. In another telepathy test, physiological responses charted by a polygraph were scrutinized for indications of unconscious awareness on the percipient's part of emotive stimuli being looked at by an agent. In their report on work during the year 1968-1969, the experimenters concluded that the electronic tester and other guessing techniques had failed to provide any solid evidence for the manifestation of ESP.

During 1969-1970, the Edinburgh workers made a determined attempt to use the ESP tester to replicate, as closely as possible, the re-

markable experiments of Dr. Helmut Schmidt. Schmidt used as subjects a few volunteers who had shown some promise in initial screening tests. In an extensive series of trials, under precognitive and/or
clairvoyant conditions of guessing, Schmidt built up deviations from
chance expectation of enormous statistical significance. The Edinburgh workers failed to reproduce the successes reported by Schmidt.
They concluded: "All we know for the time being is that he found
subjects who gave significant scores; we did not."

This particular failure was specially disappointing. It had been
hoped that the Schmidt technique, which allowed subjects to make
their guesses in their own time, unhampered by clumsy processes of
manual recording and supervision, would prove to be the potentially
repeatable procedure we have all been waiting for. Dr. R. H. Thouless had the idea that the Schmidt machine, by allowing immediate
feedback of the result of each guess, might enable a percipient to improve his performance by learning, in a manner analogous to the
learning of a skilled task by gradual elimination of mistaken moves.
Thouless took the opportunity, during a visit to the Foundation for
Research on the Nature of Man in 1970, to try out the Schmidt
machine himself with this possibility in mind. He did not succeed in
producing statistically significant learning effects, and in his report
concluded, "It is obvious that this is the report of an experimental
failure."

The fact that British experimenters so often report null results in
parapsychological experiments may be due to some essential psychological factor missing from their tests. The more skeptically minded
might suggest alternative hypotheses, for example that the British are
particularly cautious and meticulous in the conduct of their tests, and
thus eliminate spurious results. Personally, I don't believe that explanation. Another more plausible possibility is that the British are
engagingly frank about publishing their failures, whereas in other
places it may be the policy to refrain from publication until something positive emerges. Undoubtedly the British are right to publish
failures. In the present state of our subject it is important for potential
experimenters to know before they begin the difficulties likely to be
encountered.

Recent experimental work in England has not been limited to
guessing tests. J. L. Randall, an enterprising teacher at Leamington
College, has been carrying out, with the assistance of interested students, a series of experiments in which subjects tried to influence by
psi the movement of small animals. In simplicity and elegance of

design his experiments are, in my opinion, superior to various previous attempts of the kind.

In one such experiment he used woodlice. The animal was placed in the center of a circular dish. The subject tried to influence it to climb over the edge of the dish at some point on a particular (randomly determined) sector of the circumference. The results of these experiments have not all been published yet, but it would appear to be a promising line of inquiry.

One line of research which has been giving apparently positive results concerns paranormal physical effects at séances. Mr. Colin Brookes-Smith has constructed various pieces of apparatus for registering the operation of paranormal physical forces. He follows the theories of K. J. Batchelor, according to which paranormal phenomena are likely to grow out of effects that are initially produced by normal means. Owing to some natural psychological resistance to conclusive demonstrations of paranormality, conventional methods of direct control against fraud and artefact are likely to inhibit the phenomena. Hence Brookes-Smith has tried to set up methods of registering effects which are unobtrusive and non-inhibitory. In one such test, he arranged an electric bulb on top of a covered table in such a way that it would light up if a hinged flap, mounted on an extension from the table, were lifted up. The "sitters" found that they could cause the lamp to light and go off in exact response to verbal orders. Their concentration upon the lamp rather than the spot where the paranormal force would have to be applied presumably helped to overcome psychological resistance. The sitters were positioned around three sides of the table well away from the hinged flap, so that it would seem that none of them could have produced the necessary movement by normal means.

Opinions differ, of course, as to the value of Brookes-Smith's approach. Avoidance of direct controls and "crucial tests" may be a necessary condition, just as dim lights and curtain screens have in the past been thought to be necessary for physical phenomena. It is unfortunate, however, that these are also the very conditions to facilitate deception. On the other hand, if the Brookes-Smith approach can be used, as he appears to believe it can, to enable all and sundry to obtain paranormal physical effects, then of course elaborate precautions against deception would no longer be necessary. Proof would come from repetition by others.

I prefer to suspend judgment on this issue. If I understand him correctly, Brookes-Smith hopes to circumvent the inhibitory effects of doubt by building up a psychological atmosphere which is free and informal and conducive to paranormal manifestations. At the same time, by using sophisticated, unobtrusive and adaptable apparatus, he hopes to obtain now and then an objective, and hopefully indisputable record of some of the manifestations. It is certainly an interesting prospect, but it sounds rather like a battle of wits between the experimenter and the phenomena. It remains to be seen which side will win.

So far I have mentioned only S.P.R. publications. Few systematic research projects in Britain are to be found in other periodicals. One exception is the *Journal of Paraphysics,* edited by Benson Herbert and M. Driver, with M. Cassirer as research officer. This covers a variety of phenomena, including both séance room effects and unidentified flying objects.

The journal *Light,* one of the oldest psychic periodicals, still flourishes. It is the organ of the College of Psychic Studies, and has predominantly spiritualistic orientation. Most of the contributions are discursive rather than research reports. A recent issue was devoted to a review of the Raudive voice phenomena, following publication of the book *Breakthrough.* Another journal is the *Quarterly Review of the Churches' Fellowship for Psychical and Spiritual Studies,* but this, too, is discursive and philosophical rather than empirical in content. Finally, one might mention the *Journal of the British Society of Dowsers,* another long-established periodical. This very rarely contains material of interest to the serious empirical scientist.

This brings me to the end of this brief review of recent parapsychological experiments in Britain. It has been a very short review for the simple but sad reason that not very much experimental work has been published recently. Studies of an anecdotal and historical nature are going on. For example, interest in the scripts of the SPR cross-correspondence automatists continues, though half a century or more has elapsed since most of them were produced. G. W. Lambert is still producing papers seeking to establish new meanings to names and allusions taken from the scripts. In my view, these efforts will remain for ever inconclusive, for the reason that we have no way of estimating the likelihood of coincidences occurring by chance in such a vast mass of material. Just how vast the material is we are prevented from knowing, and much of it is thought to have been destroyed. The late W. H. Salter, custodian of the bulk of the unpublished scripts which remain, left the material to Trinity College, with the proviso that they were not to be examined before 1995. By that time there may not be many of us around to pursue the matter.

One outstanding historical study deserves mention. I refer to the paper "Supernormal Phenomena in Classical Antiquity" by Professor E. R. Dobbs (*Proc. S.P.R.* [1971] *55*, 189-237). This work surveys the beliefs and practices of the ancient world in regard to divination, possession, telepathy, automatism and the like. It is an authoritative statement revealing the extraordinarily close analogy between modern spiritualist phenomena and similar manifestations reported by the ancients. One is tempted to conclude, with reference both to the phenomena and to their baffling quality of elusiveness and inexplicability, "Plus ça change, plus c'est la même chose."

CALIFORNIA, THE PSYCHIC STATE

FREDERICK C. DOMMEYER

Parapsychology in the far western United States is concentrated in California, which now has a population of over 18,000,000 making it America's most heavily populated state. And despite its expansive area of nearly 160,000 square miles, the majority of its people live in the Los Angeles area in the south and the San Francisco Bay area in the north—the two basic hubs of activity.

In the Los Angeles area, more than in any other part of the United States, there is what R. DeWitt Miller has called a "heterogeneous occultism." [1] There one finds large numbers of professional seers, astrologers, prophets, unorthodox healers, spiritualists, palmists, mediums, psychometrists, etc. Instability is the characteristic feature of this scene. Witchcraft is momentarily on the rise in Los Angeles, as are interest and practice in biofeedback meditation.

The Bay area is less marked by occultism than is the southern section of California. It can, however, claim leadership in the production of altered states of consciousness by means of hallucinogenic drugs and the new Oriental religions. The Haight-Ashbury area of San Francisco leads in drug use, whereas in many parts of the city devotees of the new religions seek altered states of consciousness by that means.

Professor Jacob Needleman says of California that over it "there broods . . . a strong sense of universal forces." [2] He suggests also that the European intellectualism characteristic of the East Coast United States is widely suspect or ignored in California.

This ground-roots occultism clearly influences California parapsychology and is at certain points supportive of it, even financially. Scientific parapsychology, in its turn, lends to certain segments of occultism in California a degree of prestige and, on occasion, some guidance. But large sections of the occult are, as suggested, indifferent to rationality.

II

There are six California authors who merit notice because of their interest in parapsychology. There is first the famous Upton B. Sinclair, who lived in Long Beach. He was nationally known for scores of books critical of the American social scene and for his frustrated attempts to achieve national and state political offices. He died recently at the age of ninety.

In the late twenties, Sinclair carried out three years of psychical experimentation with his wife, Mary Craig Sinclair, which resulted in his book, *Mental Radio.*[3] The experiments Sinclair did involved drawings "received" telepathically by Mrs. Sinclair. The drawings of both "sender" and "recipient" are reproduced in *Mental Radio.* Some pairs of drawings were remarkably similar; others were less so. Present-day interest in Sinclair's work is evidenced by inclusion of some of the book's drawings in Dr. R. A. McConnell's article "ESP and Credibility in Science." [4]

Aldous Huxley, grandson of the distinguished English biologist Thomas Henry Huxley, was the author of such well-known works as *Brave New World* and *Eyeless in Gaza.* He was deeply committed to parapsychology. Born in England in 1894 he was educated at Eton (1908-1911) and at Oxford (B.A., 1916). Huxley and his wife visited the United States in 1937 and thereupon settled down in the hills above Hollywood. Huxley died in Los Angeles in 1963.

The Devils of Loudun (1952) and *The Doors of Perception* (1954) are non-fiction works by Huxley involving aspects of parapsychology. In 1953, Huxley had taken mescaline, which led to the second book just mentioned. He spoke of his mescaline experience at the International Philosophic Symposium held at St. Paul de Vence in 1954 under the auspices of the Parapsychology Foundation. He wrote an article for *Life* magazine (January 11, 1954) surveying the ESP-PK field. In 1961, he made an extended tour of Europe, attending the Parapsychology Foundation conference in France on experimental parapsychology, where he discussed research in telepathy as related to long-distance hypnosis then going on in the Soviet Union.

Henry Fitz Gerald Heard (Gerald Heard), whose home was in Santa Monica, was another well-known lecturer and writer. British by birth (1889), Heard was graduated from London University and later did graduate work in philosophy at Cambridge University (1908-1913). He died in 1972. Though widely known for his books and articles in history, morals, philosophy, theology and anthropology, he devoted much time to parapsychology. He wrote a number of articles and reviews on parapsychological subjects for *Tomorrow* magazine. He was a Council member of the London Society for Psychical Research. He contributed a paper (in absentia) to the first anniversary (1964) ceremonies of the Foundation for Research on the Nature of Man (FRNM) in Durham, N.C. In 1965, he read a major paper at the large UCLA parapsychology symposium.

Another southern California author interested in psi is the earlier mentioned R. DeWitt Miller, a science fiction writer. He was born in Los Angeles in 1910; he died there in 1958. He was a 1933 graduate of the University of Southern California. He wrote hundreds of articles for *Coronet, Esquire, Pageant, Popular Science, Tomorrow,* etc., many of them popular treatments of psychical phenomena. Some of his books were: *Forgotten Mysteries* (1947), *Reincarnation* (1956) and *You DO Take It With You* (1957).

Two northern (Bay area) writers are Gina Cerminara and Bishop James A. Pike, recently deceased. Gina Cerminara received her A.B., M.A. and Ph.D. degrees from the University of Wisconsin. Her graduate degrees were in psychology and education, but her later interests centered in parapsychology. She is best known for her writings on Edgar Cayce, the Virginia Beach clairvoyant who died in 1945 but whose 14,246 recorded "readings" still interest many. *Many Mansions* [5] was based by Cerminara on Cayce's "life" readings; the book had nineteen American printings and was translated into several foreign languages. This work was followed by two other books: *The World Within* [6] and *Many Lives, Many Loves.* [7] These two latter works are also on psychical research themes.

Bishop James A. Pike, a prolific writer and lecturer, achieved eminence as the fifth Episcopal Bishop of California (San Francisco, 1958). He was later associated with the Center for the Study of Democratic Institutions in Santa Barbara.

His reputation was widespread when, in 1966, his young son committed suicide in a New York City hotel. Following this tragic event, Pike experienced in Cambridge, England, where he was completing a sabbatical leave, a series of poltergeist events, which he was led to attribute to his son's discarnate spirit. Later, he had séances with Mrs. Ena Twigg (England), Rev. George Daisley (Santa Barbara) and Arthur Ford (Philadelphia), the last-named now being deceased, all of whom purportedly brought Pike messages from his son. These experiences led Pike to write his widely read book, *The Other Side.* [8] After writing this book, Pike participated in radio broadcasts, panels (e.g., Esalen Institute panel in San Francisco) and lectured on para-psychological topics. Bishop Pike died in 1969.

III

Turning now to the academic scene, and first to the southern section of California, one finds women in the forefront of parapsychological research.

Thelma Moss (Beverly Hills) is doubtless the most active and productive experimenter, writer, lecturer, teacher and organizer in psi in the Los Angeles area. In 1939, she received a degree in drama from Carnegie Institute of Technology and followed this with a successful twenty-year career in acting and writing in the theater, motion pictures and television. In 1960, she received a second A.B. degree (in psychology) and this was followed by a Ph.D. degree in 1966, both degrees from the University of California (Los Angeles). Her present position is that of Assistant Professor in Residence, Medical Psychologist, the Neuropsychiatric Institute, UCLA. She is a member of the American Society for Psychical Research and the Parapsychological Association; she is a Research Consultant for the Southern California affiliate of the ASPR (Southern California Society for Psychical Research).

Since 1961, Dr. Moss has published eighteen articles, half of them on parapsychological topics. She has presented twenty scientific papers in psi at symposia, conferences, panels, etc., at such separate points as Wiesbaden, Germany (1968), and New Delhi, India (1970). Late in 1970, she made an extensive tour of foreign research centers, especially those of the USSR, Bulgaria and Czechoslovakia. Though her interests in parapsychology are varied, her major concern has been in "emotional" telepathy, a field in which she has devised some original and successful modes of experimentation.

Louise Ludwig, M.A., psychology instructor at Los Angeles City College, is another academic psychologist. At the 1969 symposium at UCLA, she presented with Dr. Moss a paper on the psychodynamics of the occupants of an allegedly haunted house. She has also an interest in the relationship, if any, between visualizing and telepathic ability. Her major interest at present is in unorthodox healing, on which she has lectured at UC (San Diego) and at Pepperdine University. She has conducted a course in parapsychology at UC (Irvine).

Dr. Freda Morris received her doctorate in clinical psychology from Illinois Institute of Technology (Chicago) in 1967. She was Assistant

Professor of Medical Psychology at the Neuropsychiatric Institute at UCLA until this past April (1971), when she moved to Virginia.*

She approaches parapsychology via her professional interests in medical psychology and hypnosis. Some patients, she finds, adapt to psychical experiences neurotically; some people make a healthy adjustment to them. Some therefore need therapy. Dr. Morris believes that "psychic phenomena can be used psychoanalytically like dreams." [9]

Mrs. Eloise Shields is a school psychologist in Torrance Unified School District, Los Angeles County, who is deeply interested in parapsychology. Though her professional work is in public schools, she has twice taught a course in parapsychology in the Extension Division of Pepperdine University. She will offer two additional courses under the same auspices in the fall of 1971 and winter of 1972.

As a school psychologist, Mrs. Shields has had many opportunities to test children for psi capacities. The results of such research have been published in two articles.[10] At present she is inquiring into ESP and rapport between student and teacher; she has found evidence of a correlation between dislike of teacher and psi-missing. She continues work on personality correlates of ESP in children. With Louise Ludwig, she is analyzing twenty-eight psychic readings of Douglas Johnson (not the Britisher). Mrs. Shields has been the Secretary, Vice-President, Research Director and a member of the Board of the Southern California affiliate of the ASPR.

Dr. Barbara Brown of the Veterans' Hospital, Sulpulveda, California, created and headed for its first two years the Bio-Feedback Research Society. It had its first meeting in October, 1969. The Society has concerned itself with scores of projects, some of them related to parapsychology. Perhaps the nature of Dr. Brown's interest, as it concerns psi, may be best understood by describing her banquet address to the Parapsychological Association Convention in New York City, September 10-12, 1970. Its title was "Autocontrol of Consciousness, the Next Revolution." In her address, Dr. Brown asserted that man is subject to many undetermined influences that may affect his psi capacity, e.g., phases of the moon. But, she added, there may be physiological influences such as brain-wave states. Even if the relation between brain-waves of certain frequencies and psi capacities turned

---

* This was the information had by the writer at the time this paper was completed. More recently, he has seen Dr. Morris several times in the Bay area of California, where she has been residing over the 1971-1972 winter on a leave of absence from UCLA. Over these months, she has—jointly with Dr. Milan Ryzl—given two talks on hypnosis and ESP, followed by demonstrations, in the home of Professor Jeffery Smith at the monthly meetings of the Parapsychology Research Group, Inc.

out to be merely probabilistic, it may still, she asserts, serve as a predictor of psi capacity. But there may be more to it than that. According to Dr. Brown, it may become possible for man to manipulate his own brain states through biofeedback methods in such a way that they become sufficient causes of psi states.[12]

Another psi investigator is Shafica Karagulla, M.D., (Beverly Hills), a psychiatrist. She is President of the Higher Sense Perception Foundation. The main interest of this Society, writes Dr. Karagulla, is in energy fields that are around man and their correlations with health and disease. She believes that what has become known as Kirlian photography justifies her earlier conclusions based on her medical experience. Her book, *Breakthrough to Creativity,*[13] is about HSP (higher sense perception) of which there are different kinds, including that of "seeing" these "energy patterns."

Two southern California men who have carried out investigations in the psi field are Dr. Kurt Fantl and Dr. Robert L. Constas. Both are psychiatrists. Dr. Fantl and his wife recently did a short study of Peter Hurkos. Dr. Constas has an interest in unorthodox healing, e.g., in the claims of the "psychic surgeon" Tony Agpaoa of Baguio, Philippines, whom Dr. Constas visited. Dr. Constas participated also as a witness on behalf of ASPR interests in the Phoenix, Arizona court case on the James Kidd will, in which money (now $300,000) was left to an institution or person who would prove that the soul survives death. The case is still unsettled.

IV

In the Bay area (northern California), it is again chiefly in the colleges and universities that one finds psi research operating at its best level. But not every such institution has been friendly to psi.

One case of such "unfriendliness" is Stanford University. What has made this situation anomalous are the gifts in 1911 and 1918 by Thomas Welton Stanford, both of which could have been used for serious psychical research from those times to the present. The earlier gift of $60,000 was for the purpose of setting up a Psychical Research Fellowship at the university; the second sum of $526,000, given at the donor's death, was to be used for psychical or psychological science. The fellowship was established in 1912, with John Edgar Coover as its first recipient. A number of appointees followed him. Most of them were uninterested in psychical research or opposed it; the majority of them were well-qualified psychologists. The only exception in attitude and results was Dr. Charles Stuart, fellow from 1942 to 1944, who achieved positive results in his experimental work and published them. A Stanford spokesman nonetheless publicly denied even this one accomplishment.

Outside the context of the T. W. Stanford monies, there have been some men at this university who have worked independently in the psi field. Dr. Jeffery Smith of the Humanities and Philosophy Department is one such faculty member. Dr. Smith was a prime mover in organizing the California Parapsychology Group, Inc. With Dr. Charles T. Tart, he carried out an experiment on the psychometrical capacities of Peter Hurkos. This research led to an article entitled "Two Token Object Studies with Peter Hurkos." [14]

For the past six years, Dr. Smith has been doing psi research with students—research designed to discover ways whereby psi abilities latent in subjects can be cultivated. He spent a spring, 1971, sabbatical leave writing up this experimental work in book form.

Professor Arthur Hastings, Department of Speech, Stanford University, has investigated carefully a number of Bay area poltergeist cases, his special interest. As a popular and adept lecturer, he has participated in a number of psi symposia, panels and lectures in both sections of California.

The Bay area's most active and productive parapsychologist, permanently associated on a full-time basis with a university, is Dr. Charles T. Tart, Department of Psychology, UC (Davis). He received his degrees through to the Ph.D. at the University of North Carolina.

His scientific papers in psi read at symposia, conventions, panels, etc., number seventeen; all of them were presented between 1964 and 1971. Since 1963, he has published sixteen psi articles in the journals. His book (edited by him) entitled *Altered States of Consciousness: A Book of Readings* [15] has been widely read.

Tart's scientific papers and published articles exemplify a wide range of interests: out-of-the-body experiences; ESP testing and teaching machines; hypnosis and psychedelic drugs in relation to psi capacities; physiological correlates of psi cognition; the aura; models of explanation of ESP; scientific method in relation to psi experimentation. Out-of-the-body experiences have, however, been his major concern.

Tart is convinced that ESP card-guessing tests are "an extinction paradigm" and that reinforcement can be used to teach subjects ESP if the capacity is there latently. He believes further that a changed conception of scientific method may be required for parapsychology, i.e., one different from the present paradigm in science. He has reflected in depth on this latter problem as evidenced by his writing a long and as yet unpublished paper on it.

Tart has been a Council member of the Parapsychological Association and a member of the Board of Directors and Research Director of the California Parapsychology Research Group.

In San José State College, largest in the State College system, there has been some psi research. Professor William M. McBain of the Department of Psychology carried on a year's research that eventuated in the presentation (in absentia) of a paper at the Winter Review meeting of the Institute of Parapsychology (FRNM), January 1-2, 1970.[16] His paper was entitled "Quasi-Sensory Communication: An Investigation Using Semantic Matching and Accentuated Affect." He obtained significant statistical results, but a later replication of the experiment did not provide other than chance scores.

The name of Dr. Milan Ryzl, internationally known parapsychologist, has recently been associated with San José State College through a teaching appointment made in the Spring of 1971 to the Division of Cybernetics, effective in the fall term.

Ryzl has been in the United States since 1967, and in the Bay area of California since 1968. Before 1967, he lived in Czechoslovakia where he earned a doctorate at Charles University, Prague, in physics, chemistry and biochemistry. He was already interested in parapsychology in his early twenties as shown by his first published article in 1953.[17] This was the beginning of a long series of published articles and also of scientific papers presented at symposia, conferences and universities.

Ryzl's main contributions to parapsychology have been: (1) the discovery of a method for developing ESP in subjects by hypnosis; (2) training several ESP subjects by this method, notably Stepanek; (3) performing the first experiment under laboratory conditions which demonstrated that ESP can be used for controlled tranmission of information; (4) providing knowledge on "mental impregnation," or the "focusing effect."

Ryzl spent his first year in the United States at the Institute of Parapsychology of the Foundation for Research on the Nature of Man (Durham, N.C.). Earlier, in 1962, he had received the McDougall Award from the Parapsychology Laboratory (Duke University), predecessor of FRNM. Since coming to San José, Ryzl has written a book entitled *Parapsychology: A Scientific Approach.*[18] He has taught a number of courses in parapsychology in UC and SC throughout the state; he has lectured widely at universities, spoken in symposia, panels, etc. He has also done some research in psi and gambling on a Parapsychology Foundation grant.

Dr. Michael Scriven, Department of Philosophy at the University of California (Berkeley), has devoted considerable attention to parapsychology. His most notable contribution has doubtless been his attempt to relate scientific methodology in other scientific fields to parapsychology. He has published ten or more papers in parapsychology over the last fifteen years. His interest in psi goes back to his Oxford days when he was president (1951) of the Society for Psychical Research at that University.

Scriven's appraisal of parapsychology may be noted in his statement: ". . . psychoanalysis provides us with a great theory without a factual foundation; parapsychology, a factual basis on which there is yet to be built a great theory." [19]

Russell Targ is a Bay area industrial physicist—a specialist in lasers —in the employ of GTE Sylvania. He has worked in psi for twenty years. His long-time interest has carried him to leadership in the Parapsychology Research Group, Inc., and to its presidency over the last several years. Under a recent grant from the Parapsychology Foundation to the PRG, Targ has constructed an ESP teaching machine. Using four pictures and a feedback device to let the subject know when his "guesses" are successful, Targ has in a year's time "taught" his nine-year-old daughter to go from a chance level of performance in ESP to three standard deviations from expected chance results. Another of Targ's interests has been in PK on which he has done considerable reading.

Another Bay area man and, like Targ, an industrial scientist, is a fifty-four-year-old chemist in the employ of IBM's Advanced Systems Development Division in Los Gatos. He is Marcel Vogel.

Vogel became interested in Cleve Backster's work in New York City with a polygraph on the emotions of plants. He has, he believes, obtained evidence of plant responses to human emotions similar to those Backster discovered. Vogel has brought in others to assist him in his research, e.g., Jan Thomas, an electrical engineer, and Dr. John Meyers, M.D., who is Medical Director at the San José I.B.M. plant and who is also a Director in Psychic Research, Inc.

Vogel's work has attracted public attention in northern California through lectures he has given and news articles on his experiments, e.g., a feature article in the *San Francisco Chronicle* (July 27, 1970).

Dr. Thomas H. Weide, a supervising clinical psychologist of Santa Clara County Mental Health Services and a San José resident, has recently become active in the parapsychology field in the Bay area. Last year he organized Psychic Research, Inc., whose aim is to do research and to educate in the psi area. Much concerning his organization is still in the planning stage.

Weide taught two courses in parapsychology in 1970 at the University of California (Santa Cruz) in the Extension Division, one introductory and one advanced. His interests in both parapsychology and psychology have led him to an associate editorship of the new *Journal of Transpersonal Psychology*.

Because there is a relationship between this new movement in psychology and parapsychology, it is necessary to refer to the rise and nature of this new school of psychology. Transpersonal psychology is an outgrowth from humanistic psychology, whose creators rebelled against both behaviorism and psychoanalysis. Abraham Maslow, now deceased and a former professor of psychology at Brandeis University, is viewed as the father of transpersonal psychology through a lecture he gave on September 14, 1967, in the First Unitarian Church of San Francisco under the auspices of the Esalen Institute. A journal soon followed whose editor is Anthony J. Sutich (Palo Alto).

The wide-ranging interests of the transpersonal psychologists may be discerned by noting a statement of their business office in Stanford, California. It asserts that they are concerned with the "publication of theoretical and applied research, original contributions, empirical papers, articles and studies in meta-needs, ultimate values, unitive consciousness, peak experience, ecstasy, mystical experience, B values, essence, bliss, awe, wonder, self-actualization, ultimate meaning, transcendence of the self, spirit, sacralization of everyday life, oneness, cosmic play, individual and species-wide synergy, maximal interpersonal encounter, transcendental phenomena; maximal sensory awareness, responsiveness and expression and related concepts, experiences and activities."

Dr. L. J. Bendit of Ojai, California, believes that transpersonal psychology will supersede parapsychology. His thinking carried the suggestion that one must go beyond scientific method as it is presently employed. Dr. Weide holds a somewhat different view, namely, that the highest forms of both normal and parapsychological experiences *are* transpersonal. The long list of the journal's board of editors reveals the names of several who would also be identified with parapsychology.

As a part of northern California's parapsychology may be mentioned as "honorable opponent," Dr. Raymond T. Birge, professor (emeritus) of physics in the University of California (Berkeley). He has had an eminent professional career: Chairman of his department (1932-1955), President of the American Physical Society (1955) and a member of the National Academy of Science—to mention but a few of his honors.

Birge's reputation in science was based partly on a persistent exposure of errors. In 1958, he began reading extensively in parapsychology and he became thereafter a vigorous critic of psi. His first address of this critical sort was his retiring Vice-Presidential speech at the AAAS meeting in Washington, D.C., December, 1958. He has published articles on parapsychology in *Harper's Magazine* [20] and the *International Journal of Parapsychology*.[21]

V

In addition to the aforementioned *Journal of Transpersonal Psychology*, which is a new northern California literary addition, there is *Psychic*, published by James G. Bolen in San Francisco.

The first issue of this popular magazine appeared in June-July, 1969, and other issues have been published bi-monthly since then. *Psychic*, under the editorship of Mr. Bolen, has not only attracted thousands of "average" readers; it has cultivated interest among the "pros" by its interview articles dealing with well-known parapsychologists and psychics, and by articles authored by parapsychologists of repute. Such articles are interspersed with a more popular variety, making the magazine interesting to a wide audience. Format and photography are especially noteworthy.

VI

Two persons in nearby Colorado, but influential in West Coast parapsychology, are Dr. Jule Eisenbud (Denver) and Dr. Joseph H. Rush (Boulder).

Dr. Eisenbud is a psychoanalyst by training and profession. He has been Associate Clinical Professor of Psychiatry, University of Colorado Medical School, since 1950. He has published some thirty articles on psi. His influence in California has been felt mainly through his frequent and able participation in University of California psi symposia and via his recent book, *The World of Ted Serios*, [22] a striking study in thoughtography, which has been widely read and discussed in California parapsychological circles.

Dr. Joseph H. Rush, a physicist and science writer, as well as a one-time professor of physics, is presently at the National Center for Atmospheric Research. He is a charter member of the Parapsychological Association. Beginning in the early forties, he published several articles in the psi field. An important publication of his is *New Directions in Parapsychological Research.*[23]

In this monograph, which merits wider attention than it has had in California, Rush attempts to indicate the nature of the psi state. He bases his view on some experiments he conducted as well as on his reading. He finds this state to be one of "detachment" in which "association" is a characteristic element and where unconsciously motivated non-random material is not obstructed by rational preoccupation, sensorimotor activity or subjective fancy. One exception to the exclusion of the sensorimotor from the induction of the psi state was discovered by Rush, namely, that perceptions and activities that relate to the theme of psi experience are helpful in inducing it.

VII

There are in California many Cayce (Association for Research and Enlightenment) study groups and there is the annual regional A.R.E. Conference held in Asilomar, California, where approximately 400 meet to discuss the Cayce "readings," hear lectures, attend seminars, etc., for a week. There are doubtless several thousand persons in California seriously interested in the "physical" (medically diagnostic and curative) readings and "life" (past lives) readings of the Virginia Beach seer, even though he has been dead since 1945. There are 14,246 such readings, about 65% of them "physical," which are preserved in the library of A.R.E. at Virginia Beach, Va.

William A. McGarey and Gladys T. McGarey (man and wife M.D.'s) are western leaders in A.R.E. Associated with these two practicing physicians and Arthur F. Wright, M.D., are the A.R.E. Clinic, Ltd., and the Medical Research Division of the Edgar Cayce Foundation, both in Phoenix, Arizona. Both Drs. McGarey are well-known in California Cayce circles because of their active roles in the Asilomar conferences and their medical work in nearby Arizona. Dr. McGarey sees himself in his medical work to be "dedicated to studying the concepts of physiology as they are found in the Cayce material . . . and [to] determine their validity and their usability." The "Cayce material" is, of course, the medical data that Edgar Cayce revealed in his trances through clairvoyance.

VIII

A complete survey of psi societies in California would be unprofitable. I have the names and locations of over twenty-five such organizations scattered all over the State of California, and this list is doubtless incomplete. As might be expected, these societies vary greatly in size, purpose, quality and number of members. Some are very circumscribed in purpose, e.g., the Blavatsky Foundation. Some are very small; others have up to four hundred members. Two societies in the southern part of California and two in the north are worthy of notice.

The California Parapsychology Foundation, Inc., in San Diego, has Kay Sterner as its Founder-President. This society was incorporated in 1957 as a nonprofit educational and research organization. In addition to these functions, it has undertaken to provide personal and family counseling. It now has approximately 400 members, with a number of professionally-trained persons among them. It publishes a bulletin, which is sent out not only to its members but to a very large number of interested persons in both southern and northern California.

The society has done experimental work in psychometry, telepathy, GESP and dowsing; it has also carried on research into the problem of post-mortem survival.

The name of Mrs. Marjorie D. Kern is associated with what may be the most notable psychical research society in the western United States. Through her insightful efforts, members of the ASPR (New York, N.Y.) who lived in the Los Angeles area were brought together to form what eventually became in the spring of 1962 the Southern California Branch of the ASPR. Later its status was changed to that of an "affiliate" in order to gain certain tax exemptions.

This society is solidly organized around Mrs. Kern, its President, with its consultants in psychology, psychiatry, medicine, physiology, physics, engineering, mathematics, psychoanalysis and computer sciences. The society's activities have included a large number of lectures by eminent speakers, e.g., Gerald Heard, H. H. Price, Ira Progoff, Thelma Moss, etc. It has investigated a number of psychics, poltergeist cases, haunted houses, etc. Drs. Joseph Brown and Darrell Harmon (an engineer) have constructed a theoretical model, which would account for telepathy and clairvoyance.

The book by Ostrander and Schroeder [24] on "Iron Curtain" parapsychology has aroused much interest among members, and two engineers in the society, George Schepak and Louis Peters, are translating newly published psi materials from Eastern Europe.

The society has 200 local members and there are 200 "New York" members who pay their dues through the California "affiliate." The influence of this organization beyond the Los Angeles area has been mainly a result of the energy of Mrs. Kern. Her considerable knowledge of psi affairs, and especially her contacts with the parent ASPR in New York City, make her a focal point of information for others all over the State.

The California Society for Psychical Study, located in Berkeley (Bay area), has as its President, Donald W. McQuilling. It is a large society, having among its directors and consultants men with doctorates in medicine and in other fields. While Wilson Reid Ogg, an attorney, was its president (1963-1965), the society was incorporated and its activities expanded to include the establishment of a student chapter at the University of California (Berkeley). As part of this expansion, a number of research projects were set up in cooperation with other societies and a newsletter, *Iridis,* was started. Regular lectures have always been a part of the society's activities. In the spring of 1971, an alpha-wave monitor was acquired, permitting members to pursue new modes of inquiry with the assistance of Hugh McDonald of Stanford who serves as a technical assistant.

A second northern society centering in the Palo Alto area, namely, the Parapsychology Research Group, Inc., evolved out of persons interested in psi research who had been meeting in the Portola Valley home of Professor Jeffery Smith. In 1966, this group began functioning under its legal title and bylaws. Its aim was to bring together scientific and scholarly persons of the region who would be interested in conducting "scientific research, both of an experimental and of a theoretical nature, into those faculties of man appearing to be paranormal in origin. . . ." Among the society's early active members were the aforementioned Dr. Smith, Dr. Charles T. Tart, Professor Arthur Hastings, Mr. Charles G. Schulz (a Palo Alto attorney), Mr. Russell Targ and others. Dr. Milan Ryzl became a member in 1968.

IX

In the sixties there was an increasing number of university symposia and courses in psi made available to students and to the California public. Dr. Thelma Moss has been a key person in the UCLA symposia in southern California.

The first symposium, a direct result of the Southern California SPR, was entitled: "ESP: A Challenge to Scientific Research" and it took place in Royce Hall, UCLA, Sunday, May 3, 1964, under the auspices of the UCLA Committee on Public Lectures. The special guest speaker was the distinguished Gardner Murphy. There was also a panel consisting of Jule Eisenbud, Robert Lynch and John Seward. The symposium was cosponsored by the Department of Psychology. Dr. Sidney Cohen, Associate Clinical Professor of Medicine, UCLA, was moderator.

The second psi symposium took place at the University of California in Los Angeles in 1965 (June 5-6) under the auspices of the UCLA's Continuing Education in Medicine and Health Science. Its title was: "Extrasensory Perception—Fact or Fancy?" Notable speakers were Gardner Murphy, Eisenbud, Schmeidler, Heard, Tart, McConnell, Pratt and Moss. Some 600 persons attended.

In 1969, under the auspices of University Extension UCLA, a third psi symposium was presented. Its active participants were Moss, Schmeidler, Ludwig, Tart, Rao, Krippner, Eisenbud, Ryzl, Van de Castle, Ullman and Gardner Murphy. Some 800 attended. The symposium was televised and later rebroadcast in southern and northern California.

A symposium was held in the Bay area in 1970 (April 25-26) under the auspices of University Extension (UC Berkeley). It took place in San Francisco. Its title was: "ESP and Psychic Phenomena: The Invisible Forces of the Mind." Active participants were Moss, Ryzl, Eisenbud, Krippner, Hastings, Tart and Scriven.

On May 15, 1971, San José City College had a day-long "Psychic Fair." Speakers were Hastings, Tart, Arguelles and Fadiman.

From 1963, California has seen the rise of interest in psi in all units of the University of California, but in their extension divisions. This interest has been exemplified in the symposia, courses and lectures that were presented. Attention may be directed briefly at this point to courses. Most of them were two or three unit credit courses; others were special courses of short duration. All were advertised as parapsychology courses.

The first course was of short duration; it was given July 30-August 1, 1963. It was a seminar entitled "New Frontiers of the Mind," with Jeffery Smith and Dr. Murray Korngold as faculty. It was part of a two-week program of the UC Extension Division's Liberal Arts Conference at Lake Arrowhead.

Moss has been involved in several psi courses at UCLA, with one in 1970 having a registration of some 400 students. Ryzl gave a course in parapsychology at San Diego State College in 1969; he gave courses also at UC (Riverside), UC (Santa Cruz) and UC (Santa Barbara) in

1970 and 1971. Weide gave courses at UC (Santa Cruz) in 1970, one introductory and one advanced course. Steward Robb gave a course (1970) at UC (Irvine) in the history of parapsychology. Shields has given two courses at Pepperdine University Extension in 1970 and 1971. This list is not intended to be detailed or complete but merely to note the significant number of extension courses in parapsychology that have been given in the later sixties and early seventies in California. This is not to be overemphasized, however, for such extension courses are not part of the curricula of regular university departments. Even when Professor Roger N. Shepard, Department of Psychology, Stanford University, gave a course in parapsychology in the winter quarter of 1969-1970 for regular university students, he did so under the title "Psychology." There was no other way to get the course into the Stanford curriculum for a quarter. More frequently, professors in California colleges and universities—if they have an interest in psi—will introduce it as part of a course in their own fields, e.g., parapsychological evidences for survival after bodily death in a philosophy of religion course.

X

There are certain summary statements that may be made about parapsychology in California, some of which are applicable to parapsychology in the United States as a whole and some of which are apparently applicable only to the State.

Parapsychology in California, as in the United States generally, is exemplified in all of its stages of historical development, i.e., at the present time, one can see it in its grass-roots (pre-society) stage, in its society stage and in its university stage. Orthodox science has cast aside its earlier stages as it has moved into a more developed one; parapsychology has not and one wonders why there exists this difference. A corollary of this general remark is that the California parapsychological scene is marked by an almost endless variety of psi societies at many different stages of academic adequacy. This is not true of an accepted university field, e.g., in philosophy, there is only one society in California, namely, the Pacific Division of the American Philosophical Association. The same sort of thing could be said of the United States as a whole. Another California characteristic, which seems general, is that its parapsychologists are not required to have any *specific* sort of training to gain prestige in the field. One may be a psychologist, a psychiatrist, a physicist, a chemist, an industrial engineer, a professor of speech or even a philosopher and manage well in the psi area. Indeed, it is amusing to note that the Thomas Welton Stanford Psychical Research Fellowship at Stanford University, which is at the *postdoctoral level,* does not require of its candidates any training whatsoever in parapsychology. Can one imagine a postdoctoral fellowship in nuclear physics requiring no training in that field? No doubt a partial reason for such facts is that California parapsychologists, with the possible exception of Dr. Milan Ryzl, cannot make a living in this field and must find remunerative work in teaching, in medicine and in other areas of work. All of these aspects of parapsychological work in California and outside of it raise some important questions upon whose answers the future of the field may depend.

Turning now to the features that more particularly mark off parapsychology in California from what it is in the eastern United States, one may note the following facts. Parapsychologists in the western U.S. are no longer concerned with their status or "place" in relation to what goes on in their field in the east. Western parapsychology has become of age and is doing parapsychology on its own, while maintaining a cordial link with eastern parapsychologists and societies. In freeing themselves from this dependence on the east, western parapsychologists have become more avant garde. This maturation, combined with the greater sense in the west of a pioneering and liberal spirit, has led western parapsychologists to mingle more freely with public-oriented psi activities without any fear that such activities will jeopardize their academic or other professional status. It is in this respect that California psi activity can be said to constitute a unified whole, with the academic parapsychologists not apart from the interested public but *a part* of it. In my opinion, this fact has not caused the quality of academic parapsychology to suffer and has served to uplift the quality of the field generally. It is no doubt because of this relationship between the academic and the public in California that newspapers are far more generous in reporting psi events and activities than appears to be the case in the eastern United States.

California parapsychologists seem also to have become disenchanted with a single formalized approach to their subject. Especially, there seems a loss of faith in a psychological approach. In the Southern California SPR, there is currently an interdisciplinary emphasis on approaching parapsychological research, which they implement with their consultants in many different sciences. In the same spirit of a broadening tendency, one finds parapsychology a field of interest in the wider contexts of transpersonal psychology and biofeedback research. This leads one to wonder whether, in California, the subject may not be absorbed in the context of wider interests. There are certain hints in some of the colleges and universities of a similar absorption in areas such as cybernetics and psychobiology. There is no reason to assume that such tendencies constitute a danger to parapsychology. Indeed, just the opposite could be contended.

A further thrust forward toward creativity in the psi area is the ground-roots neo-romantic movement which began in California and is now surging through California culture in a more intense form than elsewhere in the country. Its emphases on the immediacy of experience, on emotions, on altered states of consciousness, on ESP in the hippie communes, on anti-intellectualism and antiscientism, on a return to nature, etc., cannot help having effects on California parapsychology and, in fact, have already had them. It is certainly a movement that provides greater tolerance for psi interests and inquiries of certain sorts, though with its anti-intellectualistic emphasis, it is doubtful if any of those swept up in the movement will pursue "established" psi research. On the other hand, it is fairly certain that rationality is too deeply engrained in the colleges and universities of the State to disappear under these romantic pressures. Indeed, under such pressures, it is probable that the present paradigm of science will be creatively altered in such a way that more, rather than less, knowledge will be forthcoming. The thinking of Tart in the area of such modification of scientific method in parapsychology and psychology is a straw in the wind.

It is difficult to believe that, under the pressure of these creative forces intelligently directed, there will not be more parapsychology getting into the colleges and universities so that, in time, it will become a recognized area of study. It is difficult to suppose that, in California, with its great population and wealth, there will not appear a research foundation comparable to FRNM. With Tart, Targ, Ryzl, Moss, Brown, Eisenbud and Rush in western U.S., one can feel confident that parapsychology is in good hands. Despite some clouds in the sky, one can say that the parapsychological sun is rising in the west.

(When the present paper was completed, the writer had only minimal information about the Academy of Parapsychology and Medicine and nothing was therefore included; the Academy was at the time in a very early stage of organization. Since then it has "surfaced" and has been active in ways that indicate a significant role for it in the Bay area. This organization sponsored, jointly with the Lockheed MSC Management Association, an interdisciplinary symposium on "The Varieties of Healing Experience." It took place over the afternoon and evening of October 30, 1971, at De Anza College, Cupertino,

California. Dr. Jack Holland, Professor of Management at San José State College and a Director of the Academy, served as Moderator. Participants were: Raymond K. Lilley, D.D., also a Director of the Academy; Elmer Green, Ph.D., a Director and head of the Psychophysiology Laboratory in the Research Department at the Menninger Foundation; Henry K. Puharich, M.D., well known in parapsychological circles; William A. Tiller, Ph.D., a Director of the Academy and Chairman of the Department of Materials and Science at Stanford University; William A. McGarey, M.D., long connected with the Virginia Beach Association for Research and Enlightenment; and Robert A. Bradley, M.D., President of the Academy. Though not a participant, Robert F. Mattson, Executive Secretary, has been active in the Academy's organization and program. Approximately 2,500 persons attended the symposium at a nominal charge of $5 per person. The number attending was only a small part of those turned away for want of additional seating space, which gives some idea of the range of influence the Academy is having.)

REFERENCES

1. MILLER, R. DeWitt: "Southern California Riddle," *Tomorrow* 4 (1956), No. 2: 79–87.
2. NEEDLEMAN, JACOB: *The New Religions* (Garden City, N.Y.: Doubleday & Co., 1970), p. 5.
3. SINCLAIR, UPTON B.: *Mental Radio* (Springfield, Ill.: Charles C Thomas, 1930, 1962).
4. McCONNELL, R. A.: "ESP and Credibility in Science," *Amer. Psychol.* 24 (May, 1969).
5. CERMINARA, GINA: *Many Mansions* (New York: William Sloane, 1950).
6. ————: *The World Within* (New York: William Sloane, 1957).
7. ————: *Many Lives, Many Loves* (New York: William Sloane, 1963).
8. PIKE, JAMES A. AND KENNEDY, DIANE: *The Other Side* (Garden City, N.Y.: Doubleday & Co., 1968).
9. MORRIS, FREDA: "Emotional Reactions to Psychic Experiences," *Psychic* 2 (December, 1970): 26–30.
10. SHIELDS, ELOISE: "Comparison of Children's Guessing Ability (ESP) with Personality Characteristics," *J. Parapsychol.* 26 (1962): 200–210.
11. ————: "Academic Achievement as Related to ESP in Children," *Indian J. Parapsychol.* (1963).
12. BROWN, BARBARA: "Autocontrol of Consciousness, the Next Revolution." Paper presented at the Convention of the Parapsychological Association, New York, September, 1970.
13. KARAGULLA, SHAFICA: *Breakthrough to Creativity* (Los Angeles, Calif.: DeVorss & Co., 1967).
14. TART, CHARLES T. AND SMITH, JEFFERY: "Two Token Object Studies with Peter Hurkos," *J. Amer. Soc. Psych. Res.* 62 (1968): 143–157.
15. TART, CHARLES T. (ed.): *Altered States of Consciousness* (New York: John Wiley & Sons, 1969).
16. McBAIN, WM.; FOX, W.; KIMURA, S.; NAKANISHI, M.; AND TIRADO, J.: "Quasi-

Sensory Communication: An Investigation Using Semantic Matching and Accentuated Effect," *J. Parapsychol.* **34** (1970): 66–67.

17. RYZL, MILAN: "Parapsychologische Forschung in der Tschechoslowakei," *Neue Wissenschaft* **3** (1953): 362–367.

18. ———: *Parapsychology: A Scientific Approach* (New York: Hawthorn Books, 1970).

19. SCRIVEN, MICHAEL: "The Frontiers of Psychology: Psychoanalysis and Parapsychology," in *Frontiers of Science and Philosophy*, edited by Robert G. Colodny (Pittsburgh, Pa.: University of Pittsburgh Press, 1962), Chap. 3, p. 104.

20. BIRGE, RAYMOND T.: Reply to the Ian Stevenson article which appeared in July issue, *Harper's Magazine*, October, 1959, p. 8.

21. ———: "Telepathy Experiments in Wales" (a review of *The Mind Readers*, by S. G. Soal and H. T. Bowden), *Int. J. Parapsychol.* **2** (1960), No. 1: 5–23.

22. EISENBUD, JULE: *The World of Ted Serios* (New York: William Morrow, 1967).

23. RUSH, JOSEPH H.: *New Directions in Parapsychological Research*. Parapsychological Monograph No. 4 (New York: Parapsychology Foundation, 1964).

24. OSTRANDER, SHEILA AND SCHROEDER, LYNN: *Psychic Discoveries Behind the Iron Curtain* (Englewood Cliffs, N.J.: Prentice-Hall, 1970).

PAST AND PRESENT SITUATION OF PARAPSYCHOLOGY IN JAPAN

Soji Otani

As you know, the country of Japan is a chain of islands, located at the extreme east of the Asian continent. In prehistoric days these islands were connected with the continent. Since the beginning of their history, the Japanese people living on these islands have been influenced culturally by the continent. For very long, the Japanese tried very hard to assimilate the imported culture.

When we trace occultism or mysticism in Japan to their origins, we can find two sources. One is Shamanism and the other Yoga. Shamanism is monotheism. It originated in the northern part of the Asian continent, Siberia, and was characterized by a séance with a medium called a shaman. On the other hand, Yoga, which has been developed in the foot of the Himalayas, is a technique of meditation to adjust one's own mind and body to overcome distresses in this world. It is said that Yoga has been accompanied by many kinds of mysterious phenomena.

In ancient Japan people's faith was first based on Shamanistic thought. In *Nihonshoki,* which is the first official history book in Japan and was compiled at the beginning of the eighth century, there is a description of a séance which was held by Empress Jingu. This fact tells us that the ancient Japanese people would accept a revelation of God in a séance in order to solve political problems. The method of meditation, called "Chinkon," has been handed down in the shrines in various places. Chinkon means the repose of soul and seems to have orginated from the Shamanistic ceremony and the training of the shaman.

Buddhism was transmitted from India to China, then to Japan by Korean people in the sixth century. Thereafter the Japanese government sent students to China to learn Buddhistic thought and acquire other kinds of culture there. At the beginning of the ninth century a priest called Kukai, transmitted Shingon Esoteric Buddhism to our country. It was a sorcerous religion. Another branch of Buddhism, Zen Buddhism, which has been attracting attention in recent years, was transmitted from China in the thirteenth century and made great progress in Japan. Zazen is a technique of getting spiritual enlightenment and peace of mind. These Buddhistic thoughts and techniques, of course, originated in Yoga.

Both Shintoism and Buddhism had, at an early stage, an aspect of sorcery and it is traditionally said that mediumistic persons often produced supernormal phenomena. But the progress of theoretical investigation and the adherence to formality in these religions had inhibited supernormal function. As a result, these supernormal techniques were handed down only as part of folklore. In these cirumstances, individuals who had supernormal ability emerged here and there, and some of them became objects of worship to many people. Thus, the supernormal phenomena of these mediumistic people were unknown to the secular world.

The first man to give attention to such supernormal phenomena was Atsutane Hirata (1776-1843). He objectively described cases of reincarnation and poltergeist activity and studied stories of fairyland at the beginning of the nineteenth century.

In the middle of the nineteenth century, Chikaatsu Honda (1823-1889) resurrected the technique of Chinkon. When he was twenty-two years old, he saw a girl compose a poem while possessed. He investigated the classical literature of Japan and China, visited various shrines of Shintoism and learned about the method of meditation taught in those shrines. After strenuous efforts, he acquired a mediumistic technique and obtained knowledge of the spiritual world in his mediumistic trance. His technique and knowledge were handed down to Wanisaburo Deguchi (1871-1948) through Katsutate Nagasawa (1858-1940). Deguchi became head of some religious body of Shintoism. Honda's technique, which he called Chinkon Kishin Method, meant a way for the repose of souls and for communicating with spirits. At that time, Wasaburo Asano, a scholar in English literature who had joined Deguchi's religious body, knew about the Honda study of the spiritual world and observed many examples of spirit possession there. He also read many works on psychical research and Spiritualism in Europe and America. At last he became independent of Deguchi's religious body and devoted himself to popularizing Spiritualism and the training of mediums. He thought that modern Spiritualism in Europe and America supported the Japanese traditional thought of Shintoism, and that the beliefs of the Spiritualists had been sufficiently demonstrated by the (British) Society for Psychical Research and by many scientists.

Asano's Spiritualism movement helped many people at that time to learn of the existence of the study of psychical phenomena, although his activities prevented the development of parapsychology in Japan because of his uncritical and credulous attitude toward the phenomena. Owing to this Spiritualism movement, many intelligent people in our country misunderstood psychical research and became skeptical of it.

In 1910, Dr. Tomokichi Fukurai (1869-1952), a professor at the University of Tokyo, began his experiments on clairvoyance and thoughtography. Owing to the troubles caused by his works, Dr. Fukurai had to leave his position as professor at the University. After that he went to Koyasan University, a Buddhist institution, located on the top of Mt. Koya. On Mt. Koya there is a big temple which was set up by Kukai in the ninth century. This is a principal temple of the Shingon Sect of Buddhism, which I mentioned previously. The Koyasan University is one of the Buddhist universities. Dr. Fukurai continued his investigations of psychical phenomena and tried to explain by the theory of Buddhism the facts which he found and other psychical phenomena found by Western researchers. In 1932, he published a book, titled *Spirit and Mysterious World*, that contained an introduction to modern psychical research and his own interpretation of psychical phenomena.

Although Fukurai's idea is difficult to understand without sufficient knowledge of Buddhism, I will try to explain his thought briefly. He said that the ego is divided into two parts: the perceiving self and the desiring self. The perceiving self extends throughout the universe, and one can perceive everything without sense organs and without the nervous system. Our consciousness extends to outer objects and can get information about them. This is demonstrated by the fact of clairvoyance. He insists that the objective existence of consciousness is also demonstrated by clairvoyance. The desiring self is the active principle of the perceiving self and consists of spiritual elements. Everything in the universe is the manifestation of this desiring self. According to Fukurai the infinite space is filled with the perceiving nature and infinite spiritual elements, and both are mingled with each other. When one concentrates his mind on something, infinite spiritual elements embody themselves as one thought them to be. This fact is also demonstrated by present-day psychical research. These ideas were presented in his book, *Spirit and Mysterious World*.

Dr. Fukurai, as his first step in the research, aimed to find out through experiments whether clairvoyance was genuine or not. In later stages he wanted to use these facts as tools for demonstrating the truth of the theory of Buddhism, instead of inquiring further into the characteristics of the phenomena. His attitude was already not a scientific one. It should be said that he had become a Buddhistic Spiritualist.

These stumbles in the early stages of psychical research in our country were overcome by the sound critical spirit inside the academic world. Dr. Enryo Inoue (1858-1919) started the Research Society for Supernormal Phenomena in the University of Tokyo in 1888. He gathered a lot of cases of strange phenomena from everywhere in the country and evaluated them from the scientific point of view. But his main purpose was not the investigation of psychical phenomena themselves; it was to eliminate the superstitious attitude that prevailed in the country then and obstructed the scientific way of thinking. He said that not all the supernormal phenomena were strange, but that their seeming strangeness was the result of our lack of the scientific attitude. And he insisted that normal phenomena, about which we usually do not have any doubt, must be explained scientifically. Although he did not directly contribute to the real progress of psychical research in Japan, his scientific attitude toward mysterious phenomena was a good influence on later psychical researchers.

Inoue's scientific attitude was taken over by Professor Oguma (1888-   ), of Meiji University. He specialized in abnormal psychology and investigated hypnosis and dreams. His achievement was his introduction of Western psychical research to our country. Oguma published two books on this subject, in 1918 and in 1924. He distinguished between reliable and unreliable evidence. He also attended several séances and indicated doubtful points, cooperating with Kokyo Nakamura (1881-1952), abnormal psychologist, and Dr. Shoma Morita (1874-1938), a psychiatrist and originator of the Morita therapy. Because of the critical attitude of this research group, they were said to be opposed to psychical research itself. But they were not; they only tried to be scientific.

In this period, public interest in psychical research increased with the introduction into Japan of European and American studies. Motokichi Hirata, scholar of English literature, published a book, *Secret of Spirit* in 1911, which was a good introduction to the achievements of the SPR. Books written by Sir Oliver Lodge, T. Flournoy and H. Carrington were also translated. For a quarter of a century before World War II, over fifty books on psychical research were published, including some by psychologists.

On subjects closely related to psychical research, there were several academic investigations in the psychological realm. They were *Psychological Investigation of Zen* in 1934 by Chijo Iritani, *Psychological Foundation of Zen and Nenbutsu* in 1941 by Daisetz Suzuki, *Problems of Consciousness and Unconsciousness* in 1935 by Tanenari Chiba, *Investigation of Intuition* in 1933 and 1938 by Akira Kuroda and *Science of Mysterious Experiences* in 1948 by Kanae Sakuma. These investigations were somewhat different from the main current of psychology in our country, which was experimental, but the value of these achievements was well recognized because these subjects were picked up from our traditional culture. The value of these books to our research field was that they gave us some ideas about the function of deeper dimensions of consciousness. Dr. Chiba is still in good health and is giving active support to our research activities.

This was the general situation of parapsychology before 1935, just before Japan entered into war, when psychical research was prohibited as were some other academic activities. Characteristic of this period was chaotic struggle, in which some of the pioneers in this research field were groping for a way to harmonize this Western newcomer of the study of mind to our traditional thought, while others could maintain their scientific attitude but could not find any productive way of inquiry.

When we summarize the general opinion of the scientists who were actively interested in psychical research at that time, we can say that the evidence for clairvoyance was not yet sufficient, telepathy might possibly be demonstrated though more systematic statistical experiments might be needed, and the problem of survival was completely out of the question for scholars with the scientific attitude.

The start of the activity inside the academic world in our country was not at all lagging behind Europe and America. Dr. Inoue's Research Society for Supernormal Phenomena was set up only six years after the foundation of the SPR. But its later course was quite different from that of the SPR. The reason for this difference came from the greater intolerance of our scientists at that time. Nothing was known, before the end of the war, about the activities of the Parapsychology Laboratory at Duke University, in the U.S.A.

In 1945 the war ended. For several years after, Japan was in a period of distress. Under such conditions, we received a strong stimulus from the Duke Parapsychology Laboratory. In 1948, the Japanese edition of the *Reader's Digest* was published, in which appeared a condensed translation of Dr. Rhine's book, *The Reach of the Mind*. It was the first that we knew about Dr. Rhine. After that Aiko Segawa

(1914-1963) translated Rhine's book and it was published in 1950. As a matter of fact, we, who knew only about showy phenomena in séances, could not at first understand the importance of Dr. Rhine's method. But we began to feel the weight of his investigation. Otani (1924-   ) decided to adopt Dr. Rhine's method and started experimental investigation of ESP with the measurement of skin electrical resistance.

But the circumstances surrounding parapsychology at that time were very unfavorable. To continue research in parapsychology was considerably adventurous for a psychologist. A negative attitude toward parapsychology prevailed among psychologists, and the study of parapsychology had been taboo since Dr. Fukurai's work on clairvoyance. Outside the psychological world, the situation was the same. Dr. Ukichiro Nakaya (1900-1965), a famous physicist, declared that parapsychology had to be neglected because the phenomena treated in parapsychology were beyond the limits of natural science.

There was a revival of Spiritualist activities. Spiritualists held séances with mediums and propagated spiritualistic thought. Their position was that psychical phenomena could not be investigated by the scientific method because they were too delicate and sacred to be exposed to scientific inquiry.

In 1958, the translation of Dr. Rhine's book, *The New World of the Mind,* was published. In 1961, Dr. Miyagi (1908-   ), a psychologist, published a book titled *World of Mystery.* It was an introductory book on parapsychology and it gave the public a fair understanding of parapsychology, because it was the first work on the subject by one of the leading psychologists in our country.

In the meantime, Dr. Fukurai moved to Sendai, a city in the northern part of Honshu, our mainland, and set up a research group on parapsychology, including psychologists and engineers of Tohoku University. After his death in 1952, his followers founded the Fukurai Institute of Psychology on the property left by Dr. Fukurai. The purpose of this institute is to house the materials dealing with Dr. Fukurai's experiments and to conduct investigations of psychical phenomena, especially thoughtography. But they have not got any affirmative results to date. About the same time, Hiroshi Motoyama (1925-   ), a philosopher, set up the Institute for Religious Psychology backed by a religious body of which he is the head, and began the research into Yoga and parapsychological phenomena.

The year 1963 was a memorable year in the history of parapsychology in Japan. At the beginning of that year Dr. Pratt, of the Duke Parapsychology Laboratory, visited our country. I notified people who were interested in psychical research and ran a meeting at which Dr. Pratt lectured. The meeting was very successful, attended by leading psychical researchers at that time, both scientists and Spiritualists. As a result of this experience, we made up our minds to establish a research body to be composed of purely scientific researchers. In the same year, Otani and Onda (1925-   ), psychologists, and Kanazawa (1930-   ), a mathematician, founded the Japanese Society for Parapsychology.

The first project of this society was to conduct an opinion survey of psychologists in our country concerning their attitude toward parapsychology. We wanted to know where we stood in the minds of traditional psychologists. We delivered questionnaires to about 1,100 of the members of the Japan Psychological Association. Only 23.8% sent back their answers. This rate of reply, which was very low compared with 60% in the U.S.A. in 1938, seems to reflect the lack of parapsychological interest and knowledge of psychologists in Japan. Among the replies, there were some who said that they could not answer, because of their lack of knowledge about parapsychology. The affirmative answers to our questionnaire came to 46.2% of those replying. This ratio seems to show that persons who were favorable toward parapsychology tended to answer. Anyway this figure revealed to us that at least 11% of the psychologists in our country thought that ESP was established or could be demonstrated. When this result was compared with Warner's result in 1938, we had to recognize that the situation of parapsychology in the early 1960s in Japan was twenty years behind that in the United States. This difference was inevitable because in America there had already been a lot of work done by the ASPR and the Parapsychology Laboratory at Duke University for many years.

Under these unfavorable circumstances, the Society decided, as its first object, to carry out substantial investigations using strictly scientific methods. In the fall of 1963, Otani visited the Duke Laboratory and stayed there for a year. This event had a good influence on the later development of parapsychology in our country. After his return, more psychologists came to understand parapsychology better and we could feel that the psychologists' attitude toward us began to change from suspicious to friendly. In 1964, at the annual convention of the Japan Psychological Association, Onda and Otani presented reports on parapsychology, which were the first reports on parapsychology to be delivered at an official psychological meeting. Kanazawa and Otani published a translation of Dr. West's book, *Psychical Re-*

search Today. Dr. West's critical attitude impressed many with the soundness of present-day parapsychology.

The number of qualified investigators increasing, the Society had its first public meeting in Tokyo in 1967, in which individual reports, a special lecture and a symposium were presented. Professor Oguma gave a special lecture, titled "History of Parapsychology in Japan." The symposium was held under the title of "Problems of Methodology in Parapsychology," and leading psychologists were presented as panelists.

In this symposium, Dr. Indow, Keio University, characterized research in parapsychology as similar to research in such rare phenomena as supernova in astronomy. He said when we were engaged in such a work we had to have a firm faith, because it was a very troublesome investigation, but, at the same time, we had to be careful not to influence the outcome of our studies with this faith. Dr. Ogasawara, University of Tokyo, presented his questions about the methodology of parapsychology and proposed the idea of introducing a new concept to parapsychology, which corresponded to the notion of the threshold in psychology.

Over fifty people attended this meeting, including psychologists and psychiatrists. Among them there was a former president of the Japan Psychological Association. It was the first time parapsychology was discussed by psychologists in an official meeting in Japan. The reports of this meeting were published in the *Proceedings of the Japanese Society for Parapsychology.* As a result of this meeting the existence and scientific nature of parapsychology in Japan became widely known among Japanese psychologists.

The more psychologists came to understand our activities, the closer became the relation between the psychological societies and us. Since 1964, reports on parapsychology have been presented every year at the annual convention of the Japan Psychological Association, and at the annual convention of the Japan Association of Applied Psychology parapsychological reports have been accepted since 1962. This year, 1971, the annual convention of JAAP will be held in November in Osaka, at which a speech titled "Zen Experience and Parapsychology" will be presented at its symposium. When the annual convention of the Japanese Society of Hypnosis was held at Sendai in 1967, we presented reports on the relation between parapsychology and hypnosis and received friendly reactions from psychiatrists and psychologists.

Recently several psychological laboratories in Japanese universities permitted the students to select subjects for their graduation theses from the field of parapsychology. Now at Osaka University, Tokyo Women's University and Myojo University, research relating to parapsychology is going on.

Next, I will explain the general type of investigation undertaken by the members of our society. Most of the research conducted in our society so far has been experimental, using the method developed in the Duke Parapsychology Laboratory. The reports of these investigations were given at the annual convention of our Society, and some of them were presented in the *Journal of Parapsychology* and at the Review Meeting of the Institute for Parapsychology in Durham.

ESP experiments with physiological measurements were conducted at an early stage, as previously mentioned. Otani measured subjects' electrical skin resistance during ESP tests and found some relationships between these two factors. Recently Osada used female subjects and found that their ESP scores fluctuate according to the rhythm of their basic body temperature. We have accumulated a considerable amount of experimental data which show the relationship between the autonomic nervous system and the ESP function. Koide tried to see the relationship between subjects' call intervals and their ESP scores. The general impression was that there is some optimum time interval of call for high ESP scoring, but a conclusive result has not yet been obtained because the results were complicated. Otani examined the subject's call frequency for each target symbol or symbol combination, and found a distinct relation between them. These indexes, call interval and call frequency, were thought to reflect the subject's psychological condition at the moment when he made his call. The effect of environmental conditions on ESP function has been measured. Matsuda observed the fact that a flickering light, which gave subjects unpleasant feelings, inhibited their ESP functions. Otani applied an ESP test and anxiety scale to parachute troops, and found that "high anxious" subjects were in a state of high mental tension about the parachute descent and this mental state had a greater effect on ESP functions than in "low anxious" subjects. There have been a few experiments of PK effect. Takahashi was searching for an effective way of detecting PK effect and tried to use a small piece of colored paper and needles instead of dice. In the theoretical field, Kanazawa is interested in the theory of precognition and concentrates his attention on the concept of time. Onda is specializing in the problem of creativity and Zen Buddhism and is considering the relation between these two and ESP functions.

So far I have been mentioning the past and present positions of parapsychology in our country. I believe that all of you understood that parapsychology in our country has been colored by the geographical and historical conditions. In 1638, Japan closed the door to foreign countries and the national isolation was to continue until the middle of the nineteenth century. The spirit of scientific enlightenment in Japan came about in the seventeenth century. In 1674, Kowa Seki (1642-1708) discovered differential calculus in mathematics, independently of Leibnitz. In the eighteenth century, a book of anatomy was published and experiments with electricity were begun. These were the result of the influence of Western science coming through a narrow channel at that time. But it was in the middle of the nineteenth century that mental science was introduced. The transplanting of Western philosophy and psychology proceeded rather smoothly, because those who took part in the introduction of Western thought to Japan were fortunately influenced by Chinese philosophy, Buddhistic philosophy and Christianity. The later development of psychology in Japan has been influenced by its progress in Europe and America. As I mentioned earlier, academic attention to psychical phenomena in Japan was gained toward the end of the nineteenth century, which was very close to the time when the SPR was founded. But the later development of it in our country was quite different from that in Western countries. Psychical research was started in the leading university of our country, but it could not get a seat in the traditional psychological society.

Dr. Miyagi said in his lecture at the second annual convention of the JSP that Japanese psychology has attached too much importance to the experimental approach. Though it was effective in developing scientific psychology, he said, the subjects which were difficult to treat experimentally were eliminated and rare phenomena have been omitted from its domain. As a result, he said, psychologists in Japan were not aware of the significance of psychical phenomena.

But now parapsychology in Japan, after its long struggle, got rid of these spiritual or religious involvements and established itself as a branch of science. It is getting its seat in the academic world, as the first step in the world of mental science. In the recent membership list of the Japan Psychological Association, we can find the name of the Japanese Society for Parapsychology as its affiliated society.

I think that now parapsychology has come to a turning point and parapsychologists are searching for new directions of inquiry both in scope and method. The main directions in which parapsychology is about to advance, I think, are two: one is to go back to the old problems again and the other is to seek a connection with the latest knowledge in other branches of science. We Japanese researchers are also searching for our own new avenue of approach, but at the same time, it is our main concern to contribute to the progress of parapsychology utilizing our particular traditional cultural background. But in fact it is difficult to find such a way, because the world-wide progress in science makes us concentrate our attention on more general areas. In these circumstances, I think, it is very productive to promote international cooperation in our investigation. In the cooperation of researchers from different traditions and cultures, we can expect to find individual peculiarity, and this will lead us to multi-valued investigations. The Japanese Society for Parapsychology conducted several distance-experiments in ESP with international cooperation. In future we want to join the international projects of research in parapsychology. In this sense, I very much appreciate the invitation of the Parapsychology Foundation at this time. But we have some handicaps. They are the geographical position of Japan and the barrier of language, as you know. As we are always making an effort to overcome these difficulties, we expect more help from your side in order to establish a more complete international cooperation between us.

PARAPSYCHOLOGY IN INDIA

Jamuna Prasad

Parapsychology in India has a long past but a brief history. Belief in paranormal powers and in the occurrence of paranormal phenomena is very ancient, but scientific investigation of and experimental research in the "why" and "how" of the phenomena are of recent origin. The culture and tradition of my country have taken due note of paranormal occurrences. Indeed, the survival of life beyond bodily existence is the core of Hindu religion. These beliefs are so embedded in the lives of the people that no necessity is felt to carry on investigations in this field. Paranormal phenomena in ancient times were therefore taken for granted. Ancient Indian literature and scriptures bear testimony to these widespread beliefs.

The ancient Hindu saints and sages practiced certain rituals as a part of daily worship and acquired various powers which in modern times are explained away as magic, charm, siddhis, etc. There are accounts of saints and yogis who could slip out unnoticed from amongst a crowd, who could remain in the air several feet above the ground, who did not sleep even for a second, who never ate anything and lived only on air, and who performed many other such marvelous feats. Clairvoyance, clairaudience, telepathy, thought transference, thought reading, telekinesis, commanding control over nature such as stopping the rain, or creating a storm, and getting whatever one desires, are all powers that the yogis acquired through their yogic practices, but to the common man they were all phenomena which could not be produced by the objective senses and were therefore taken to be paranormal powers of the mind and even dubbed as occultism.

Several such phenomena have been observed and heard about from time to time but they have not been submitted to scientific observation and study. A few scholars have made a casual study of these phenomena without going into the "why" and "how." Spiritualists took them for granted, philosophers and psychologists influenced by the modern experimental approach to various phenomena of mental activity did try to deal with the problem scientifically, but not much headway could be made until the 50s of this century. In spite of the unquestionable faith in the psychical phenomena and a congenial environment conducive to the study of these occurrences, no scientific investigations, in the field or laboratory, were made until very recent time.

It was only in the beginning of the post independence period that, under the influence of the work of psychical research societies in the West, parapsychology was introduced as a theoretical subject for study in some of the universities. About 1951 parapsychology was included as an optional subject at the postgraduate stage, in the Department of Philosophy and Psychology of Banaras Hindu University through the efforts of Professor B.L. Atreya. But it did not make much headway, and was soon discontinued. Studies of the phenomena in the West, however, attracted several Indian scholars who, as individuals, took up research work in this field. Professor C.T.K. Chari and Professor S. Parthasarthy of Madras, and Professor and Mrs. Akolkar of Poona showed keen interest in the study of psychical phenomena. Professor Chari deserves the credit for giving scientific and statistical treatment to research in the field of parapsychology. His work has been published in the *Journal* of the American Society for Psychical Research, among others. His work, though mostly of a theoretical nature, contains critical studies of researches in ESP. Some of his published contributions are: Statistical and Information Theoretic Models; ESP and Semantic Information; Maximum Likelihood Estimation in ESP Research; Some Disputable Phenomena Allied to Thoughtography; Some Generalized Statistical Models for ESP; EEG Alpha Activity and ESP. Professor S. Parthasarthy has given thought to several paranormal phenomena occurring in Indian culture and environment and has thus been able to give direction and scope to researchers in these phenomena. Professor and Mrs. Akolkar have also contributed some papers on the study of ESP. They are at present studying some subjects who have displayed paranormal powers.

Special mention needs be made of Dr. K. Ramakrishna Rao, Professor and Head of the Department of Psychology and Parapsychology, Andhra University, who is the pioneer of scientific experimental study of paranormal phenomena in India. He worked for several years at Duke University in the tradition of Dr. Rhine and has continued that work in India. Since his return from the U.S. he has been able to establish a full-fledged Department of Psychology and Parapsychology in Andhra University. He organized a seminar on parapsychology in

1966 which was attended by research workers from India and abroad. His valuable contributions to the field have won him international recognition. Dr. B.K. Kanthamani of his department, who was also with Duke University for some time, has collaborated with Dr. Rao in several researches. They have been able to give a lead to scientific investigations of the paranormal in our country.

In North India, Dr. Sampurananand, an eminent educationist and philosopher, also got interested in the scientific study of parapsychology. When he was Education Minister, and later when he became Chief Minister of Uttar Pradesh, he started some work in the study of paranormal phenomena at the University of Lucknow, under Professor Kali Prasad who was the head of the Department of Philosophy and Psychology. But not much could be done in this direction. Later on, when Dr. Sampurananand became Governor of Rajasthan, he got a full-fledged department of parapsychology established in the Rajasthan University at Jaipur. The department was headed by Mr. H. N. Banerjee but unfortunately it has now been closed.

Dr. Sampurananand's interest in this field, however, aroused the interest of psychologists and philosophers in the country and several scholars became active in the study of paranormal occurrences. Lucknow and Agra Universities have recently taken the lead in making a beginning by including parapsychology as a subject of study for the postgraduate degree in psychology or philosophy.

The Bureau of Psychology in Allahabad was the first institution in Northern India to take up a research project in parapsychology. This was in 1962-1963. The problem was to find the extent of ESP in the school-going population. Nearly 2,500 boys and girls of delta class (VIII) drawn from thirty-one Government higher secondary schools, were the subjects of this research. Zener cards were used in group and individual situations. Before the experiment with the Zener cards was started, the students were given a talk on the object and importance of the experiment. This talk was followed by a questionnaire in which the students were required to record any spontaneous paranormal experiences that had come to them without the use of normal sensory channels. The questionnaire was originally meant to be a continuation of the frame of reference generated in the subjects by the talk, so that their interest could be further heightened. A careful scrutiny of their responses revealed a rich variety of ESP material of the spontaneous kind. It was, therefore, decided to take a closer look at the material. Subjects who had recorded personal experiences of ESP were interviewed to verify the correctness of these experiences and to exclude fantasies. Both sexes reported affirmatively wide experiences of spontaneous ESP—the percentage being a little over 36%. A large number of subjects (56.4%) reported only contemporary experiences, and a lesser number (20.2%), precognitive experiences. But a considerable number of subjects (23.4%) reported both contemporary and precognitive experiences. Most of the reported ESP experiences occurred during dreams. As for the themes of the experiences, death was the most frequent, followed by accidents, sickness and theft. The investigation, though purely exploratory, revealed that paranormal experiences are widespread among Indian students. Dr. Ian Stevenson and I have made a comparative study of such spontaneous psychical experiences amongst children in the West and in India on the basis of the data of this project. The study was published in the Autumn, 1968 issue of the *International Journal of Parapsychology*.

In 1964 Dr. Stevenson, who has been studying reported cases of reincarnation, visited India and I assisted him in investigating Indian cases. A few of the cases that have been studied by Dr. Stevenson are such that no other explanation seems plausible except the phenomenon of rebirth. If we accept the theory of rebirth even tentatively, two vital questions arise: firstly, "What is it that is reborn?" and secondly, "What is the mechanism of continuity after death?" During the course of my work with Dr. Stevenson I discussed with him the Hindu concept of *samskara* and their role in human behavior as a possible explanation of the problem "What is it that is reborn?" Dr. Stevenson encouraged me to take up a scientific study of the role of *samskara* in human behavior.

Samskara, according to Hindu philosophy, are residues of the impressions of past experiences that tend to govern and regulate the receptive as well as the reactive pattern of the current personality of the individual in a subtle way. These *samskara* pass on from one life to another and control and determine the behavior and cognitive capacities of the individual. They may be modified, changed or obliterated in successive lives and new *samskara* may be imprinted. The study aimed to determine the quantum, if any, of the personality patterns carried over from one life to another. The study was limited to six well authenticated and established cases of rebirth that were studied by Dr. Stevenson. The tools used in the study were a Specific Trait Questionnaire (STQ) specially designed for the project by Dr. Stevenson and adapted by us, and Cattell's 16 PF (for adults) and C.P.Q. (for children) to assess the degree of similarity in likes and dislikes, habits, specific traits, values and other personality dimensions. Two teams of investigators were formed to collect the data separately and independently with respect to past and present personality for each case to avoid any contamination of data. Regarding the STQ, it was felt that specific likes and dislikes are quite often determined by environment and sociocultural milieu. Therefore if both the previous and the present personalities happen to belong to the same geographical region, the similarity in likes and dislikes does not conclusively and convincingly prove the existence of the influence of a previous life although it does not rule out the possibility of such an influence either. Therefore it was considered necessary to get an idea of the generalized pattern of likes and dislikes with respect to the present personality for each case. For this purpose, data on the STQ were collected on at least ten subjects belonging to the same age group, same sex, same caste, same locality, and roughly the same socioeconomic status as the present personality. The aim was to pick out the points of similarity in likes and dislikes that were specific to the present and past personalities alone. The personality make-up of the present and past personalities obtained on questionnaires was compared to determine the extent of similarity in the two profiles. The percentage of perfect similarity was found to be highest (59%) in two cases and lowest (42%) in another two cases. If the figures for perfect similarity are added to those with similarity with a slight variance, the percentages go up to 93, 84, 81, and 75 in four cases and 50 percent in the remaining two cases. As regards the similarity on the Specific Trait Questionnaire, when the generalized likes and dislikes were eliminated, the maximum similarity was on 5 items out of 12 in one case, followed by 4 items in another case. With a view to getting further confirmation of our results, the data on the STQ were presented to five independent and responsible judges who were requested to correctly identify the present personality (which was mingled with about a dozen personalities) with respect to each past personality. On the basis of the ratings by the judges, it was found that the majority of the judges could identify the personalities correctly. Although it would not be safe to draw any conclusions on the basis of such a limited study and in the absence of any follow-up work, the results do warrant further research on larger samples drawn from different countries and cultures.

I undertook the project on the role of *samskara* as an individual with the assistance of a small group of psychologists who have been engaged in various parapsychological researches working part-time or during vacations. Members of this group have also been assisting Dr. Stevenson in his studies of reincarnation cases in India since 1964.

It was, however, felt that the time had now come to put the program of parapsychological research by this group on a sounder footing and make it a full-time job by establishing an institute. Consequently, on my return from the States in October of last year, the Indian Institute of Parapsychology was formally established and registered. The first research project that this infant institute has taken up, with the generous grant from the Parapsychology Foundation, is "Paranormal Powers Manifested During Yogic Training." The ultimate goal of a yogi is to unite with the Infinite or attain self-realization, but, in the process, he is said to attain powers that go even beyond ESP. The Indian scriptures and Yoga literature are replete with instances of cases in which the yogis have been able to recollect the past, tell the present, predict the future or tell of events taking place at some distance beyond the normal sensory channels. Patanjali, the author of *Yoga-Sutra,* a treatise on Yoga, describes in detail a number of powers which can be acquired during various stages of Yoga. The only danger to a yogi in displaying these powers is that he may develop egoism as a result and ultimately fail to reach the goal of self-realization. It is for this reason that most of them do not want to display these powers or subject themselves to experimentation. *Yogesch citta-vrtti nirodhah* yoga restrains the mind (citta) from acquiring various forms of dispositions (vrttis), says Patanjali. It is the restraint of the senses and the mind. It is a methodical effort to attain perfection through the control of the different elements of human nature, physical or psychological. The physical body, the active will and the understanding mind are to be brought under control.

Raja Yoga is the most ancient and highest form of Yoga. All other forms of Yoga are preparatory to this royal way which has within itself all the ingredients of all other yogas. *Raja Yoga* is a system of psychical mastery that teaches control of the streams of thought and builds up a store of mental energy by setting at rest the movements of the mind and by concentrating scattered energy. By holding the mind steady, the dormant powers are gradually awakened and supra-mental visions appear. The *Yoga-Sutra* tells us, "There are laws governing the acquisition of larger visions and manifestation of latent powers. By following these laws, one can reach higher levels of consciousness through the transformation of the psychic organism which enables it to go beyond the limits set to ordinary human experience."

From the above account, it would be seen that the control and emergence of ESP or, for that matter, other paranormal powers, are possible through the practice of *Raja Yoga*. It only remains to be verified experimentally. In India, Yoga is even now practiced in its various forms by several Sadhaks living in different *ashrams* throughout the country. Although the tenets of Yoga do not permit yogis to demonstrate their powers, it would be worthwhile to seek the co-operation of some young trainees who are in the initial stages, and make an experimental study of the stimulation and control of ESP through Yoga. Our study will aim to find out:

1. Whether yogic discipline helps in acquiring psychic powers such as telepathy, clairvoyance and precognition.

2. Whether it also helps in the control of such powers.

3. Whether any changes occur in the perceptual and personal make-up of the yogi during training.

4. Whether the physiological changes accompany the emergence of ESP powers.

It is proposed to include in the sample only those persons (about 10 in number) who live permanently or most of the time with a Guru in the Ashram and practice *Raja Yoga* regularly, and persons who have been initiated into Yoga practice only very recently. Yogis who have been practicing Yoga for a long time and have acquired ESP powers will not be included in the study. Since it may not be possible to prove conclusively whether they acquired these powers through yogic dis-cipline or had them prior to the training, it is further proposed to divide the experimental group into two subgroups: those who had some spontaneous paranormal experiences prior to the beginning of yogic training, and those who have not had any paranormal experi-ence prior to beginning yogic training.

It is supposed that persons who have had spontaneous paranormal experiences prior to yogic training need only slight stimulation for the emergence of these powers while, in the case of the latter group, such powers may be evoked only through strong stimulation. Thus, paranormal powers in the latter group may become manifest after longer yogic practice while they may appear after a shorter time in the case of the former group. A control group will be formed, of about the same size as the experimental group, of persons who live in *ashrams* or in the neighborhood but do not practice Yoga.

It is proposed to use a case history schedule, Rorschach ink-blot test, Zener cards (ESP Test) and some objective tests for clairvoyance, telepathy and precognition. The objective tests will be devised to assess ESP powers, and the responses on these tests will be checked and verified independently with the help of referees. The Rorschach test will be administered to assess the changes in the perceptual and personality make-up that occur during various stages of yogic training.

The above tests will be administered to the experimental as well as to the control group. Zener card and objective tests will always be given before and after a meditation session. The test will be repeated after suitable intervals. In the initial stages, since progress is likely to be slow, this interval may be of about three months, but may progressively be reduced with the satisfactory progress of the experimental group in yogic practice.

The data, thus obtained, will be treated statistically. The successive test scores of the subjects in the experimental group will be compared and the significance of differences will be noted. Similarly personality profiles prepared on the basis of the Rorschach ink-blot test will also be compared. Comparisons will also be made of the successive scores on ESP tests and objective tests of the two subgroups of the experimental group as well as of the personality profiles and scores on tests for the experimental and control groups.

Another potential field for paranormal research in India is the tantric practices. Tantra is the science of gaining control over *prakriti* (matter) through the powers of the mind. Through tantric practices the devotee can easily attain mysterious powers and realize his aims. *Akarshan* (attracting), *sanmohan* (hypnotizing), *uchchatan* (causing disturbance or imbalance in mind) and *maran* (causing death or destruction) are all attainable through tantric practices. It is for this reason that the common people look upon Tantra with fear and suspicion. Tantra is supposed to be capable of curing bodily diseases, even curing a sick person lying in bed in a hospital at a distant place. It is also possible to communicate with a person at a great distance and make him act as the Tantric wishes; it is even possible to kill at a distance a person not easily accessible physically. Hypnotizing is an elementary form of Tantra. There are many Tantrics who can demonstrate such powers. Tantra is thus a very fruitful field for scientific investigation aimed at bringing to light the crucial fact that the human psyche has unlimited potential which can be utilized in several ways for the good of mankind.

It would thus be evident to a critical mind that Yoga and Tantra are variants of the same psychic powers, unknown but unlimited and stimulated using different methods for their emergence. Unified parapsychological research is needed, not only to reveal their nature and function, but to determine the strata at which they function and the level of stimulation they need to become manifest.

The above bird's-eye-view of the scene in India brings out clearly the conducive environment and fertile field for paranormal studies on the one hand, and limitations imposed on the scientific approach on the other. The paranormal phenomena are taken too much for granted to create a broad-based scientific interest. Modern scientists take an entirely different position. In their enthusiasm for the physical sciences, they forget that the atypical case, the unusual incident, the one fact that does not fit with the rest, is the one that if we look seriously at it, teaches us all about the others. This is the reason why seats of learning are slow to react with enthusiasm to this new branch of human study. In fact there is only one university which has a full-fledged department of parapsychology where scientific researches in ESP are being carried on by a team of workers. Parapsychology has not, therefore, been able to make a mark in our country. Unlike psychology which has, besides education, won its place in defense, industry, medicine, administration and other departments, parapsychology has not secured a place worth the name amongst the other sciences in India. Only some learned yogis have started work in collaboration with medical institutes to study physiological changes during yogic *samyama*.

There are very few organizations and societies that concern themselves with the study and investigation of paranormal phenomena. At present there are only two organizations actively engaged in the study of parapsychological problems. One, the Indian Institute of Parapsychology, is at Allahabad. It is mainly concerned with the investigation of the phenomena of rebirth and reincarnation and yoga and paranormal powers. The Department of Psychology and Parapsychology at Andhra University is another organization which has been doing experimental study of ESP in its various aspects.

Even today literature on the subject of parapsychology and paranormal phenomena is very scanty. There are a number of books on oriental occultism, yoga, rituals and religious practices, particularly of Hindus, both by Indian and foreign authors, but no authoritative work on parapsychological researches in India has so far been produced in the form of a book. Professor B.L. Attreya has written an "Introduction to Parapsychology" which is a collection of his lectures on the subject and gives a brief historical account of paranormal phenomenon and psychical researches, particularly those in the West. However, Professor Attreya's interest in the field continued and he has founded a society for psychical research that brings out two theoretical journals: *Darshan International,* an international quarterly of philosophy, psychology, psychical research, religion, mysticism and sociology and *Psychics International,* an international quarterly of psychic and yogic research. *Parapsychology,* the Indian Journal of Parapsychological Research, was brought out for a while by the Department of Parapsychology, Rajasthan University, Jaipur. This journal contained original articles and research reports of work in the field of ESP and rebirth, by people both in India and abroad, but the Journal has been discontinued with the closing of the Department of Parapsychology in the University. Of late Dr. K. R. Rao, Professor and Head of the Department of Psychology and Parapsychology at Andhra University, has been publishing a newsletter from his department that reports the various activities of the department. In New Delhi there was an Institute of Psychical and Spiritual Research whose activities were limited to research on Yoga and its various aspects. The Institute also brought out a monthly bulletin containing theoretical articles besides reports of its own activities. But in spite of our limitations, it is hoped that very soon several societies will develop in the different parts of the country and function effectively, so that more useful and informative literature will be produced. Consequently scholars from various disciplines will be attracted toward the study of the paranormal.

In conclusion it may be remarked that, though poor in equipment and scientific techniques, India offers a vast potential for paranormal research, specially with respect to Yoga and Tantra which should be utilized to the fullest before too much materialistic influence minimizes such a chance. Here is an opportunity for effective coordination in research between the East and the West that may offer valuable clues for the understanding of the nature of man, and which may yield fruitful results for the benefit of mankind.

PARAPSYCHOLOGY IN TURKEY

Resat Bayer

I have been invited to this Conference to give a presentation regarding the history and development of scientific psychical research in Turkey and, more generally, in the Middle East. Although I know enough about the development of scientific psychical research in the Middle Eastern countries, I do not see myself entitled to speak here as a selected representative of all the countries of this section of the world. So, I will keep my survey within the bounds of the activities of my own country—Turkey.

As I am asked to give here the entire history of psychical research in Turkey from earliest days to the present time, I have to take a short glance over the history, and present some fabulous beliefs that may be considered psychical manifestations, but have certainly not been subjected to scientific research.

The Turks belong to the Turanian race which comprises the Manchus and Mongols of North China, the Finns and the Turks of Central Asia. The Turks lived in Central Asia periodically in many independent tribes and clans, and sometimes under feudal systems. Although Oguz is believed to have been the most powerful Khan of those distant times, he has a legendary personality rather than a real one. It is said that his mother, who was a princess, conceived him from a very bright light that descended from Heaven. This belief in his divinity was so deep that anyone after him who claimed the throne, in any Turkish state, had to be a descendant of Oguz Kahn. This rule prevailed from some thousands of years before Christ until the Turks had emigrated to Asia Minor, their present land. Even Osman Bey, who was just a warlord of the Seljukian Empire, had to prove, upon claiming the throne, that he was descended from Oguz Kahn. One night when he stayed as a guest of a certain Moslem Sheh, he had a dream. In this dream he saw a tree growing up from his own umbilicus and expanding to cover the whole world. This dream was interpreted by the Sheh to mean that descendants of Osman Bey would establish a very large empire that would influence the whole world.

The dream finally came true about the beginning of the seventeenth century, when Mohamet III ascended the throne.

During the rule of the Ottoman Empire (which took its name from Osman Bey), many emperors and sultans kept a band of astrologers in the palace. Some of the sultans were even inclined to decide all political and economic questions of the Empire according to the suggestions of those astrologers. In fact, about the end of the eighteenth century Mustafa III, noticing the wealth and power of Prussia, wrote to the king of that country asking him to send him three of his astrologers! As another example, there was the strong desire of Osman III, who lived about the end of the eighteenth century, to have a son who would become a very famous conqueror. He ordered his astrologers to tell him the best birth date and hour of this child so that he would become, without fail, a conqueror. After having made the necessary calculations, the astrologers suggested to the emperor the best time of conception for his purpose. After the necessary period had elapsed a boy was born but with a difference of two hours. The head astrologer, having noticed the error he made, at once changed the clock for fear of the emperor's rage. The newborn baby, who later became Selim III, developed into a good-natured man with great talents for music and poetry rather than the make-up of a conqueror. But he was raised in conformity with his father's desire; he, too, took himself to be a real conqueror, but those baseless beliefs brought him to a fatal end—he was assassinated.

I have kept myself so far within the bounds of a very short presentation about the inclination to psychic beliefs in Ottoman palace circles. If I dwell on the psychic beliefs among Turkish people and describe Dervish convents and cells where theosophy was greatly expanded and promoted while the main subject taught in universities was theology, I will not be able to keep my paper down to thirty minutes.

In summarizing we may say that in Turkey, as in many other countries, paranormal phenomena that seem to be inexplicable have occurred throughout the country for many centuries and have aroused curiosity in the population regarding the mystery of nature. Although it is not possible to state that curiosity has given way to scientific research, it is known that, especially at the beginning of the twentieth century, many private sittings have been held in home circles, with frequent endeavors to obtain messages from the world beyond through mediums, especially in cities such as Istanbul and others where there were many educated people.

Twenty years ago, in 1950, the eminent Dr. Bedri Ruhselman founded the first Turkish Metapsychical and Scientific Research Society in Istanbul, of which for many years I have been the General Secretary. This famous Turkish philosopher and Spiritualist is unfortunately unknown in Western countries because his many valuable works are in Turkish only.

I would like to emphasize here especially that, contrary to the practice of many other well-known Spiritualists of other, more civilized countries, Dr. Ruhselman never had any intention of explaining all the phenomena of Spiritualism, in his many works, within the framework of religious beliefs and institutions. I may say that Spiritualism in Turkey has never been kept within such a framework and thus it has found a way for free expansion. I believe then that Spiritualism in Turkey is far ahead and much more advanced than it is in many other countries. I have to add also that Turkey, not being restricted in this fashion, is ready and ripe for the parapsychological approach and progress.

Although Dr. Ruhselman was one of the most valuable codifiers of Spiritualism who elaborated a great deal on the works of the eminent Allan Kardec and brought many improvements to his famous book entitled *Le Livre des Esprits*, it is unfortunately impossible to present his endeavors as scientific activities, for they were all entirely based on messages apparently received from the world beyond with the help of various mediums.

We know that mediums may be honest people and that they may also be liars, charlatans and professionals with different aims, seeking different benefits, or innocent liars who give messages from their subconscious. We know also that Spiritualists who have acquired a reputation and fame only with the help of their controls, with whom they are in close cooperation, have avoided, so far, from fear, the use of methods that would distinguish real messages emanating from the world beyond from those futile prattlings and nonsense of their controls, though this would be easy to do.

In these circumstances Spiritualism which manifests its activities mostly in ordinary mediumship will never be acepted by universities and scientific research centers. Have we not to base our researches at least on something well known and studied to unveil the mystery of nature?

In this line of thought, and after many disappointments experienced in other countries and through exchange of letters with the world of Spiritualism, I have found it indispensable to steer our attention toward the scientific study of Spiritualism as a part of parapsychology and so I founded in 1963, in Istanbul, the first Turkish Society for Parapsychological Research. Since then I have, with the help of my colleagues, concentrated our endeavors on two phases of parapsychology: First phase—the experimentation in extrasensory perception with the use of Zener cards for telepathy, clairvoyance, precognition, and with dice for psychokinesis. For the latter we designed and made our own apparatus. Second phase—the study and investigation of spontaneous cases and various paranormal happenings.

After many experiments in extrasensory perception, we have noticed that the scores obtained by chance could never be eliminated from such experiments with the use of Zener cards and dice. Thus a conclusive result, the usual requirement of science, will never be reached and maintained.

Although some of our percipients were successful in obtaining even 18 hits with 25 cards, we were never sure enough about the influence of chance in the ESP experiments. Though, considering the calculation of probability, it seemed to us almost impossible to obtain such a high score by chance only, the result thus obtained was still far from being considered scientific proof. Thus, we found that we had to determine the degree of the influence of chance in those experiments. We wanted to know what scores could be obtained by chance only. So I made a simple apparatus just to be convinced that such high scores could not be obtained by chance. But, unfortunately the result obtained was very unexpected. The apparatus I made is just a simple cubical wooden box having sides about 15 cm. wide. Inside, it is lined with a thick cloth to muffle the noise of 25 white spherical marbles which are shaken in it. The box has two openings, with shutters, large enough to let the marbles in and out. A channel just large and long enough to hold all 25 marbles together on a straight line, is attached to the box near one opening. The marbles bear the same designs as Zener cards, made with black Chinese ink, i.e., five circles, five crosses, five squares, and so on.

The experimenter shuffles the Zener cards and puts them aside. Then, he places the 25 marbles in the box and after shaking it a while lets the marbles run out from the opening into the attached channel. Thus, the experiment is ended. The experimenter makes up the ESP record sheet with the call made with 25 marbles and the Zener cards that had been shuffled and put aside.

It is necessary to emphasize here that after many thousands of repeated experiments, such notably high scores as 16, 17, 18 out of 25 cards have been obtained. The important point in those experiments is that no extrasensory perception was involved and the scores were obtained only by pure chance, for there was no concentration, and no percipients, and the experimenter might sing or chatter with colleagues in the course of these manipulations.

In such circumstances, the vivid and very strong impressions which occur only in spontaneously manifested extrasensory perceptions such as telepathy, clairvoyance, precognition, etc., cannot be experimentally obtained and successfully studied regardless of what efforts may be made and however serious and sincere the observers and percipients are.

Regarding our psychokinetic studies, I have to say that, again to eliminate the influence of chance, I substituted for the experiments with dice a very sensitive scale put under a glass cover. In such an experiment we think it will be easier for the subject to alter the equilibrium of the scale rather than to obtain the scores required from the dice when they are allowed to fall from the opening of a revolving box which occurs in many different and very complex positions and conditions. On the other hand, when the equilibrium of the scale is thus altered, the observers will be categorically sure that the subject really exercised a psychokinetic faculty and they will never be under any suspicion about the influence of chance which is not in question in such experiments.

In the time available I cannot give you more details about other apparatus made by myself and by my colleagues and which may be used both in psychokinetic studies and in spiritism, replacing the incomprehensible mediums who have to be, sooner or later, gently and kindly excluded from the sittings. I seize this opportunity to declare here that machines are more reliable and deserve more faith than do their inventors, for we may take them apart to see whether they conceal some defects or falsifications, whereas the mediums will always be able to keep and hide their secrets.

Regarding the second phase of parapsychological studies, I have to emphasize the researches and investigations of various spontaneous paranormal happenings made so far in Turkey.

Without stopping to mention various spontaneous cases such as apparitions, vivid telepathic impressions, and clairvoyant phenomena which have occurred in my country, I would like to present here a phenomenon called "Idéoplasthie" which we have studied carefully.

The subject who has this faculty is a middle-aged woman. I give you here an example from her many sittings, basing my report on the proceedings signed by all the participants. I had about thirty similar white square cards of the same size, cut in a print house. They were 8 cm. long on each side. The subject was in her normal state. I gave her the cards one by one asking her to imagine herself seeing on these cards the picture of some object I was suggesting such as a hat, a ship, a car, a minaret, and so on, and also a written Turkish proverb. As she affirmed that she visualized on each card the object I suggested, I put on the back of the cards consecutive numbers from which we prepared a list presenting in front of each number the object suggested. After all cards passed one by one through the hands of the woman, I shuffled them very carefully and offered them again to her one by one asking her to give me the names of the objects she had already imagined and seen on those cards. She was 100% successful in giving the exact names of objects while the cards were still purely blank to all the observers. I have to emphasize here that when I returned the cards to her I was myself not then aware of what she had already visualized on them. It was only after she gave the name of each object that I examined the list to see whether she was correct or not. So, a telepathic transmission is not in question in that experiment. After the sitting was over I kept the cards and the list with me for about two weeks and I visited her again unexpectedly. Well, she was very successful and gave me all the names of the objects without the slightest hesitation or mistake.

Now, I would like to come to spontaneous cases suggestive of reincarnation which occur in abundance in my country. I will not linger on explanations about the general concepts among Spiritualists and among my parapsychologist colleagues in Turkey concerning reincarnation. We consider the subject quite differently and without the conceptions of metempsychosis and the law of karma.

When speaking about the investigations of spontaneous cases of reincarnation made so far in Turkey, I feel the sincere necessity to give here with great appreciation the name of my valuable and eminent friend, Professor Ian Stevenson of the University of Virginia. He has concentrated for many years on the subject of reincarnation, and the great task he has undertaken is really international. Through the many investigations he has carried out so far in many parts of the world, he has been able to register more than one thousand cases suggestive of reincarnation, ninety of which are in my country. I have been his research assistant and interpreter for Turkey for more than ten years.

Although the classics of Spiritualism, especially French classics, are full of cases of reincarnation—especially put forward by the famous "Colonel de Rochas" among others—they are not at present acceptable to scientifically-minded researchers and to skeptics, for it is quite impossible to turn back and undertake investigations about the authenticity of those cases since the subjects concerned and witnesses have long ago passed to the world beyond. But the cases we have now in hand are current cases whose subjects and witnesses are still alive. Those who will not be convinced after I relate some of those cases have only to come to Turkey and undertake personal investigations with subjects and witnesses at their disposal.

All these ninety cases we found in my country were located in the southern sections where people believe in reincarnation. They form a minority of Turkish compatriots of Arab origin who emigrated from Syria a century ago. I have often been asked why all those cases occur in the places where people have already a conception of reincarnation and why we do not meet such cases elsewhere. I think this question bears in itself the requisite reply: people who do not have any idea of reincarnation or have never heard about this concept would not pay any attention to the babbling of their children even though they chatter about a previous life giving some names and details. The parents would presumably consider these pretensions of the children as childish nonsense and thus the cases remain unknown. In the places where people have a conception of reincarnation or a belief in it the parents are at once alerted by the very first utterances of their children about previous lives.

In connection with these cases in southern sections of Turkey, another question has been put forward: Why do those alleged cases of reincarnation always have a connection with a life that ended with an act of murder, in conformity with the concept of the Arab minority in those cities? Really, if reincarnation is not a fancy but a reality as I do believe, it is not easy to consider that conception as being logical or having a sound explanation. Before I found the requisite reply, the very wise and very logical, but very simple, explanation was given by one of the witnesses we met during a visit to those sections with Professor Stevenson. This man said that everyone reincarnates, not only those who are killed, but those who are killed remember and those who die a natural death do not. Although this witness was not an educated man, his wise explanation was worthy enough to shed light upon the question. In fact it is easy to comprehend and to appreciate the very strong impression on the soul that murder would leave.

On the other hand, when we study many other cases of reincarnation so far reported and those which can be found in the classics of Spiritualism, we will of course notice that all reincarnates have brought from their previous lives at least some very important memories, if not a story of murder. For those who die a natural death, as their passing is normal and expected, especially in old age, they may not bring distinct memories to their next lives. But it might happen that they nevertheless bring to their present lives some misty and fugitive memories which may manifest in the "déjà vu" phenomenon.

Thus, most of the cases of reincarnation we met in those southern sections of Turkey had a previous life that ended with an act of murder. During our investigations they took off their garments to show us birthmarks which they claimed were at the very spots of knife stabs or bullets they had received on their previous bodies. When we consider that their previous bodies were long ago transformed to their original elements under the earth, it will not be easy to take those claims into consideration. But further studies I made on this point shed light upon this phenomenon.

It will be easier for those who have followed the publication of the Parapsychology Laboratory of Duke University in the United States, to appreciate the influence of mind or rather of spirit on matter. In that laboratory, among various and many experiments made to test extrasensory perception, it was established that some subjects had a psychokinetic faculty. In fact it has been determined that some subjects obtained the number of points desired on the faces of the dice when the dice were allowed to drop from a revolving box. Thus, we may say that mind or spirit may influence matter. Then, why not admit that the spirit might have a superior influence upon his own material body, especially when this spirit is totally concentrated on the fatal act of a stab which ended its corporeal life!

Let me give you an example of the influence of the spirit upon its own body. A patient who had been suffering from pain in his arm for a long time called on a physician. The latter, after having examined the patient, said to him that he could well free him from the pain by putting an active plaster on his arm but that he would then suffer from irritation for at least two weeks. This inconvenience having been accepted willingly by the patient, the physician, after having done what was necessary, asked him to come next day. The next day the patient came very happily for he had no pain in his arm. When the bandage was taken off, it was noticed that the arm was severely irritated as predicted by the physician. The most important fact of this example is that the physician had put on the arm a simple bandage wetted in pure water only.

After those explanations, I think that we have to accept that a spirit that has lost its corporeal body by an act of murder will be of course very much concerned with this unexpected event that has put an end to its life and, entirely concentrated on the murder, could unconsciously register on its new body, when it is in a stage of formation, all marks of the stabs its former body had received. It is absolutely necessary to emphasize here that those birthmarks happened to appear in the very spots where the bodies of the previous personalities had received bullets or knife stabs that had caused their death.

I would not, of course, want you to think that what I am saying is based on a simple supposition or theories. It is based on facts determined after long and very difficult investigations made at the hospitals where the previous personalities died or at the law courts where we obtained legal reports. We are fortunately well provided with documents to prove this reality.

PARAPSYCHOLOGY IN ISRAEL

H. C. BERENDT

It is a great privilege to report to this distinguished group about parapsychology in Israel, this tiny island in hostile surroundings. In former times, Israel with its Arab neighbors exerted an important and fruitful influence on the history of European thought and development in medicine, science and philosophy. This great human relationship and symbiosis has not yet been restored, so my report on the region has to be limited to Israel alone, its interest in parapsychology, the development and limitations of progress in the field, the psychological background for the present situation, and an evaluation of the modest contributions of Israel to parapsychological research.

I

When I wrote to J. B. Rhine in 1952 asking for material on ESP research and for some addresses of Israelis interested in the field, I promptly received introductory material, but much to his regret Dr. Rhine was unable to give me even one address of a research worker in Israel. It was only in 1958 that the first small group met in Jerusalem through the initiative of Mrs. Klausner of Tel Aviv. This small group, comprising as founder members Professor H. S. Bergman, Professor F. S. Rothschild, the late Professor Peri, Dr. Jacobson, and myself, found out very soon that their intentions and the object of their research were not identical with those of Mrs. Margot Klausner and her already existing Tel Aviv group, in which spiritualist tendencies and a broader acknowledgment of borderline fields are prevalent (i.e., astrology, belief in reincarnation, séances, ouija board, etc.).

In Jerusalem, the interest of some professionals and laymen grew steadily, and by 1964 the group consisted of about thirty members. Numerous guests joined them in the lectures of the then established Israel Parapsychology Society. At that time, especially in the course of my travels to Europe, the first contacts were made with international parapsychological research centers, including visits to Professor Tenhaeff (Utrecht), to the London SPR, and later to Professor Bender at the Freiburg Institute in Germany.

In the following year, Professor H. S. Bergman lectured here at Le Piol. He invited Mrs. Garrett to Israel and we were happy to have her with us in Jerusalem for the opening of the Parapsychology Foundation Library, a gift to us and a still growing undertaking, which is housed in the Medical Academy in Jerusalem.

During Mrs. Garrett's visit to Israel in 1965, plans were made allowing me to go on an extensive two-and-a-half month study trip to Europe and the U.S. where I had the good fortune to meet many of the most outstanding men in the field. This trip included my participation in the London and Le Piol Conferences of the Parapsychology Foundation in 1966. I returned home with numerous tape-recorded interviews and the results of a large number of psychometric experiments which had been performed during the trip. The results of my experiences will be published this fall in my second book in a German pocket edition by the Kohlhammer publishers.

My first book,* published in 1966, and now in its third edition, is still the only Hebrew introduction to parapsychology. Numerous lectures, radio talks, and a television program followed its publication.

The interest in parapsychology among Israelis was generally high, but it grew still more so after the Six-Day War and led to a certain split among the public, the greatest part of which was more strongly attracted to the field of the "occult" than to scientific parapsychological research.

The Tel Aviv group, now functioning under the almost identical name of Israel Society for Parapsychology, Tel Aviv, under the chairmanship of Mrs. Klausner, opened branches and extended its activities all over the country. I wish to quote verbatim from Mrs. Klausner's own summary:

The Society exists formally since April 1968. From that time until May 1971 we have organized and conducted 1,100 events, i.e., approximately one activity per day.

Lectures were given by the active members of the Society and sometimes by guest speakers from Israel and from abroad on various subjects such as: Parapsychology in general, Telepathy, Reincarnation, Dowsing, Spiritual Healing, Meditation, Yoga, Mediumship, Astrology, Chirology, Magic, Dreams, LSD, Precognition, Automatic Writing.

Over the radio, on TV, and in the press the subject also was of interest.

* *Parapsychology—the World Beyond our Five Senses* (in Hebrew). Jerusalem: Rubin Mass, 1966.

This was probably due to the mortal danger in which the country was plunged. In times like those, young and old start asking questions about eternity, spirit, and the hereafter, and their link to physical reality.

Regular courses and classes have been held in telepathy, astrology, and clairvoyance. With its foundation the Society began publishing a journal, *Mysterious Worlds.* Up to now twenty-two issues have been published, in which interesting results of research by our own members appeared, as for example "Reincarnation Cases amongst the Druses" by Margot Klausner which was reprinted in Germany in *Esotera,* and in the U.S.A. in the *A.R.E. Journal* in 1970. Mrs. Feingold's research in telepathy and Hans Zeuger's astrological political predictions were likewise published. We had the good fortune to introduce spiritual healing in Israel. Last autumn we inaugurated our parapsychology library; it comprises some 1,200 volumes. We received a generous donation of books from the Association for Research and Enlightenment, Virginia Beach. We do believe that our work is fruitful and that it has greatly helped in the development of parapsychological awareness in Israel.

There is no doubt that Mrs. Klausner's journal, by translating sections of international publications concerning parapsychological and related areas into Hebrew, provides the reader with some aspects of this challenging field.

The expectations of the public are as varied as is its psychological background. Those, for instance, who join our group in the hope of undergoing mystical experiences or to attend séances in subdued light leave the group quickly and are disappointed, and some of them now travel to Tel Aviv to take part in the meetings of that group. Others look for some substitute of religious renaissance or "Instant Zen." They, too, are not satisfied with the rather skeptical and scientific approach of our small group, which consists of physicians, psychiatrists, psychiatric social workers, students, and intelligent laymen.

II.

In this atmosphere of growing, general, non-specific interest, a surprising development took place. Suddenly a young man's name, Uri Geller, appeared prominently in the news (we received up to twenty newspaper clippings per week), which was full of reports about his unusual gift in the areas of telepathy and telekinesis. In literally hundreds of public performances he succeeded, in his charming and convincing way, in making a very wide public believe in his ability to utilize telepathy for obtaining numbers and names, for describing and drawing contents of ladies' handbags, moving from a distance the hands of wrist watches, crushing gold rings in other people's hands, etc.

There was only *one* thing which he apparently was unable to do, namely to comply with the repeated invitations (altogether eight—in writing, by telephone and personal contact) of our IPS in Jerusalem. At first he postponed appointments and later he refused to attend a meeting making various excuses, which made our group skeptical from the very beginning of his appearances.

It is not exaggerating to say that the country was divided into be-lievers and unbelievers, especially after Geller's successes before some groups of sophisticated intellectuals.

But the scientists have launched a frontal attack on Geller. His feats, they say, are tricks, deception, sleight-of-hand, fraud, optical illusions, presented with the air of showmanship. A group of psychologists and physicists staged their own demonstration of Geller's typical achievements and then revealed the hocus-pocus and trickery by which they were perpetrated. The exposure was most convincing, and a leading newspaper was led to publish an editorial on "The wane of Geller's glory" and "The decline of a pleasant national illusion."—C. ALPERT

It is astonishing how deeply rooted the controversy was in this tiny country, so that e.g., the film made of the exposure for TV, at which I was present, was subsequently cut off the program.

The same thing happened again, when, in the course of the only TV program on parapsychology, I complained that the film shown did not give an objective picture of scientific parapsychology by any means. The two opponents to parapsychology in this discussion, both lec-turers at the Hebrew University, were so violently biased against it that later on there came to my mind the words of a famous psychol-ogist who said that men of science can be as narrow-minded and stubborn as other human beings, but they just make better use of their intelligence—to formulate their bias.

This brings me to the unpleasant fact that *with very few exceptions,* parapsychology is almost taboo at the institutions of higher learning in Israel. And certainly the discovery and exposure of fraud has had a decidedly negative influence on those circles which should be in the forefront of the search for new fields of the human mind. All those already skeptical "men of science" were only too ready to abandon the field once charlatanism, hoax and delusion had been proved.

I found it necessary to go into detail because similar situations may be prevalent in other countries, too, and such experience should give parapsychologists new ideas on how to improve their approach to this ever-recurrent fight between scientific progress and the unwillingness to include parapsychology in the field of science at all.

There is one other problem, which may be general but is in some ways specific to Israel. Most of the members of our group are ready to come and listen, but only a very few are ready to *do* something, such as reporting on their own experiences or those of friends, giving summaries on books or current literature, taking part in Zener card tests, etc. The most important group should be one composed of young students, eager to discuss the ideas or facts of a changing world. But here we have to contend with one of our own problems: we have *no unrest* at our campuses! This is mainly due to the fact that the students have to work so hard for their examinations and often for their upkeep as well, that their spare time is strictly limited, and activities which have no direct bearing on the completion of their studies within the shortest possible time are almost eliminated. Another factor is the lack of encouragement by their teachers to look on parapsychology as a field of interest or of future importance. As a result, the observed initial readiness to explore this field dwindles rapidly to a very sporadic and irregular participation in lectures or courses on parapsychology.

Summarizing, you will probably find my analysis in this part of my paper rather gloomy and not very hopeful. Other countries possessing a greater manpower will certainly give better reports; but they may also have similar problems to face. Where should we discuss the facts, as they are, if not in this forum?

III.

You may now ask perhaps, if Israel has something to contribute to scientific parapsychology. I intend to tell you, in this part of my report, of some results that we have to our credit.

First of all I would like to recall to you the achievements of Professor H. S. Bergman, who is well known to the members of this forum and who was a devoted friend of Eileen Garrett's for many years. Now in his 87th year—and just translating Kant into Hebrew—he has been guide, guru, and wise old man to generations of younger scientists and philosophers. His direct and indirect contributions to parapsychology and the encouragement that he gives are real gifts to all those who come in contact with him.

I am also deeply indebted to Professor F. S. Rothschild who took part in the 1966 Le Piol Conference. His extremely wide knowledge of many fields of medicine and science on the one hand and of philosophy on the other enabled him to create his general theory of biosemiotics. Within the ambit of his work, parapsychology constitutes only one partial aspect of life, but what is important is that parapsychology is *included* within his theory as a link in his chain of evidence. In my opinion, any general theory of the development of life, of any *Weltbild*, which excludes paranormal phenomena, either as being unimportant or, even worse, as a swindle, has no right to be accepted as a really all-comprising world theory in the age we live in.

It is quite impossible to explain Rothschild's theory within the framework of this short report, and I want to include here only a few sentences selected from personal talks with him that may throw some light on his attitude to parapsychological problems.

It is my opinion that all the phenomena which relate to a knowledge, are communicated via our sign-systems within the person who communicates this knowledge.

I also believe that the common psychological power, which is inseparable from the earth, and which has formed these systems under a definite influence, can, as a potentiality of knowledge, establish an inter-relationship with everything that exists. When consciousness, being founded on this common psychological power, is in a state of stimulation, i.e., when its structure is excited, it can, by means of a system, establish communication with another, but similar, system. This is a fundamental principle; in other words, it can make statements which correspond to the meaning of the stimulation in the carrier of the second system. Thus we have before us a possibility of explaining paranormal, telepathic performances.

For clairvoyance, too, the seer draws from the connection in the common psychological power, which, as such, does not know anything, but which in the course of aeons, has created sign-systems in which psychical associations have found expression and the output of which is utilized by our consciousness. This knowledge is not based on a causal process in the material reality, but on the interpretation of a similarity-relation between signs. The whole history of our earth provides the basis for this relationship.

I am sure that before long Rothschild's theories, including those in the field of parapsychology, will make their impact on all those who are in search of a general theory or a deeply penetrating explanation of the paranormal processes in our lives.

I would also like to mention Professor H. Kreitler and his wife Dr. Shulamith Kreitler, both of Tel Aviv University, two of the very few on the academic staff who are the exceptions to the rule. Their specific

interest lies in finding experimental proof for the existence of psi phenomena and in the possible influence of these phenomena on psychology. Professor and Dr. Kreitler accepted the challenge of parapsychology and arrived at rather interesting conclusions as the result of a
detailed experiment the execution of which was made possible through
a grant from the Parapsychology Foundation. Allow me to give you
a summary of their methods and findings in the Kreitlers' own words:

The following four experiments were performed by Professor Hans Kreitler
and Dr. Shulamith Kreitler of the Department of Psychology, Tel Aviv University, with the help of a grant (made to the first investigator) by the Parapsychology Foundation, Inc., New York, in the years 1966-67.

The first three experiments were designed to investigate the possible effects
of ESP communications on the results of standard psychological experiments.
The first experiment dealt with the effect of ESP on the identification of
letters projected at subliminal speed and illumination. The second experiment dealt with the effect of ESP on the direction of perceived autokinetic
motion (i.e., of a stationary point of light in a dark room). The third experiment dealt with the effect of ESP on the occurrence of specific words and
themes in the stories subjects tell to TAT (Thematic Apperception Test)
cards.

In all these three experiments the subjects did not know that ESP communications were "sent" to them, the "senders" never met the subjects, and
both subjects and "senders" were naive in the sense that they were not particularly interested in parapsychology, were unselected, and did not get any
training for the experiments. The precautions undertaken against any
sensory contact between "senders" and subjects were highly complex and
included the spatial separation of "sender" and subject (they were in two
different soundproof rooms with another room between them), the decentral-
ization of information about the experiment among different people, strict
randomization of all stimuli and sequences, the use of experimenters who
were disbelievers in ESP, etc.

The results show that in every experiment there was a significant effect
due to the ESP communication. The effect was small, and evident only on
the group level, i.e., it was not due to any particular subject or "sender," or
to the ESP transmission of any particular message. Rather, the effect was
cumulative across subjects and messages. Further, the effect did not depend
on the sex of the subjects and/or the "senders," and was particularly pronounced with regard to responses with an initially low probability of oc-
curence.

The fourth experiment was designed to answer more specific questions. It
showed, first, that quantitatively the effect of ESP communications is similar
to that of subliminal stimuli; second, that on the average a sender instructed
merely "to think" about a message fares as well as a "sender" instructed "to
transmit" a message; and third, that the effect of ESP communication is

most pronounced when the messages of a "transmitting sender" are coupled with subliminal stimuli conveying a contrary message.

Two facts are remarkable concerning the Kreitlers' work: the first, that their rather revolutionary findings have not been published to date, neither in a parapsychological journal nor, of course, in psychological journals. That the latter would hesitate to publish a paper that casts a doubt upon long established methods and results of general experimental psychology, is somehow understandable. But I personally hope that interest will be widespread in parapsychological circles in a study which of course does not actually explain "the why and the how" of the phenomena, but which constitutes new evidence of their existence and even of their interference with so-called normal processes. And it is even one of the "repeatable experiments" which everyone is looking for.

Kreitler has left the field for the time being because, as he said, he was disturbed by the lack of a general theory that would allow him to follow the usual procedure in science, namely finding new facts, trying to include them in an expanding theory, proving these changes in the theory by new experiments, etc.

A further contribution, in this instance to the history of parapsychology, comes from Israel as a result of research: the exploration by Judge Bazak of parapsychological phenomena and their relation to Jewish history. Judge Bazak visited the U.S. in May, 1970 and lectured on his subject. Garrett Publications is publishing an English translation of his book, *Judaism and Psychical Phenomena*. Another publication, at present only in Hebrew, is Professor Zeitlin's book *The Other Side*, which delves deeply into the philosophical aspects of paranormal phenomena.

My own contributions to the field were published mainly in my first book and in a new one,* just in print, and short articles in the *Journal* of the SPR, in *Neue Wissenschaft*, in our own *Newsletter*, and in a paper presented at the 1968 Convention of the Parapsychological Association in Freiburg. Since the first book has been published only in Hebrew, and the second one has come out in German, I may perhaps be allowed to give short summaries of those of my findings which may be of interest to this group.

Lacking good and reliable paragnosts in Israel—a most serious problem and handicap—most of the experiments were made during my various stays in Europe. Being more interested in qualitative experi-

---

* *Parapsychology: Eine Einfuehrung.* Stuttgart: Kohlhammer Verlag, 1972.

ments than in quantitative, statistical, ones, I took some "emotionally loaded" material with me to London.

I was advised to see a Spiritualist medium who succeeded extremely well indeed, disclosing facts regarding the murder of a person, as well as many details which she claimed to have received from the spirit of the murdered woman. I myself tried later on to "translate" her findings theoretically from her spiritual approach. My analysis of her great ability and my explanations, which accepted the facts, but replaced the Spiritualist theory with an excellent telepathic contact with her sitter and his motives, were published in the *Journal* of the SPR, June, 1970.

My most successful experiments were performed with the German paragnost A. Orlop, whom I met a number of times on my visits to Europe. These experiments were of different kinds. Psychometric experiments showed good initial results. However, when we went into too many details, things became blurred.

One type of experiment with Orlop resulted in his drawings of locations not known to him and which had been mentioned only at the beginning of the experimental session. Two experiments were quite convincing successes. The outstanding fact in the first one was that he "saw" some earth excavations in front of the house and the slight slope of the street behind it, details which would not have been shown even on a big scale map of the region. Orlop's own theory of out-of-the-body excursions, for which there were some points in favor in the first experiment, failed when, in a second experiment, he produced a good parapsychological drawing of my house in Ashkalon and its surroundings and included an extended flagstone-covered area in front of the house. This area does not exist in reality, but my wife and I had discussed for weeks the idea of building it. Here again the telepathy theory seems to explain what could also have been an out-of-the-body experience. Actually, a third experiment in that direction failed. In this case, I myself had no knowledge whatsoever about the location of the home of a person from whom I had got the psychometric material. After the results of the experiment had been analyzed, no similarity between Orlop's drawing and the real location could be established. This, too, could point in the direction of telepathic contact or lack of it. The cases were published in detail in the journal *Neue Wissenschaft* and presented at the 1968 Convention of the Parapsychological Association in Freiburg.

Perhaps the most interesting experiment with Orlop was a long-distance chair-test experiment between Mannheim (Germany) and Jerusalem. Orlop chose one person among sixteen participants a fortnight before the experiment, and sent the recorded tape to our group before the evening on which the participants, in the chance order of their arrival, took out of a black bag one of a set of well-shuffled numbers. For seat No. 14, Orlop foresaw "A lady [correct], height 1m.70-1m.75 [actually 1m.72], age group 40-50 [actually 42]. Within the last half year, accident in own house injuring the knee by slipping on the steps [correct, except that—instead of the knee—it was the ankle]." Her profession: "Helping other people to spend their leisure time [she is an actress]." All these facts mentioned, and many more, were right *concerning her* and did not apply to the other participants. A graph plotted on the basis of the statistical evaluation of a questionnaire, based on Orlop's tape and answered by *all* participants, showed the position of seat No. 14 clearly separate from the clustered group of the fifteen other seats.

The detailed report with photographs attached for verification was accepted as a *separatum* at the ASPR Library.

Prior to my extensive trip abroad in 1966, the Israeli police agreed to provide me with some psychometric material from solved and unsolved cases in their files. I worked with a number of well-known paragnosts, but the outcome of this experiment was not very encouraging. One of the reasons may be that the material was already four years old in some cases, and had been handled by many persons. In spite of the generally negative results, which did not point to a direct usefulness of the parapsychological method, there were four points which struck the critical and matter-of-fact high-ranking police officers at the meeting at which the results were discussed:

1. A certain similarity between the main outlines of one case (the murder of a homosexual) and another murder case could be established. But the box containing the psychometric material showed the "wrong case-numbers," as if the material had been exchanged. (Actually, the small boxes of nine cases were put in one big box for the convenience of traveling, which may be one of the reasons for the mix-up and should be avoided in further experiments.)

2. In one case, the paragnost stated that other bones sent for examination with the skull did not belong to the body. The police investigator confirmed this fact and said that the examination at the forensic institute identified the other bones as the bones of a cow.

3. In another case, the paragnost, who had been told that a person's skull had been found, stated that he saw only the entry of a bullet but not the exit. Later investigations confirmed that the skull was incomplete and that the missing part possibly contained the bullet's exit hole.

4. The most striking fact, also verifiable on tape recorder, was the slow spelling out of a name, after which the paragnost asked me if that name meant anything to me. I said, "Yes, of course, he is my first cousin." "But I do not see a personal relationship!" Only then I suddenly remembered that the name of the police commander who was in charge of the whole experiment and who had handled all the boxes was the same as that of my cousin. Some facts given about the life of the police commander were astonishingly correct.

Although the results of this experiment were very few and none of the cases were seen correctly by the paragnosts, or could be solved through their comments, the assembled officers left the conference with a less negative attitude toward the possibility of eventual assistance by reliable paragnosts.

The question of reliability came up when I undertook an extensive inquiry, at the request of Professor Ian Stevenson, in a case of reincarnation alleged to have happened in Israel and reported in the magazine *Fate*. The *Fate* article said that King David had been reincarnated in an Israeli boy, the son of a dentist. My report, which was negative all through, gave the same results as another, completely independent examination of the matter. Both together were published later with an apology to the readers of *Fate*.

Negative results occur in our field and they are no less important in our search for truth than the successful cases. When I came to New York in 1966, I told Mrs. Garrett about a human tragedy: A missing son, *not* believed dead, concerning whom a famous paragnost had given me a number of hints and details (the adopted new name, the city and the factory where he worked as a medical orderly, and so on). As the paragnost was in Europe but the missing person had been located by him in the U.S.A., Mrs. Garrett kindly agreed to assist in the inquiry into the case by a private investigator in the city mentioned by the paragnost. This investigator succeeded in finding a man of the name given by the paragnost, working at the factory's small hospital as an orderly. Only when it was established beyond all doubt that the person in question was born in the U.S. to American parents —and not in Israel—did the failure become clear, leaving us with the vision of the paragnost—astonishing, but not directly connected with the psychometric material.

As only a small part of this material is available to the English reader, I took the liberty of extending this part of my paper.

IV.

What are the plans of our group for the immediate future?

1. A newly-conceived experiment of a chair test with Orlop which could permit an "uncontaminated" statistical evaluation.

2. A long-distance Zener card experiment with the parapsychology working group of Basle.

3. An introductory course to scientific parapsychology.

4. A detailed examination of reported cases of reincarnation amongst the Israeli Druses (in cooperation with Professor Stevenson).

5. An inquiry, in cooperation with the Department of Social Studies of the Hebrew University, into different sects in Israel, including Spiritualists as well as anthroposophical and theosophical groups.

6. A statistical survey of the attitudes to parapsychology amongst students at the Hebrew University and the University of Tel Aviv (subdivided into students of natural sciences and humanities). This study may provide an analysis which in turn may give hints toward a new approach to the inclusion of parapsychology as a field of study for the coming generation at our universities.

V.

This brings me directly to the next point, namely: How can we or should we change the attitude of the general public, specially that of scientists, from their indifference and their cynical denial or bias against parapsychology to a more positive, acknowledging and even cooperative attitude?

Let me remind you that I am actually speaking of Israel, but I feel certain that similar suggestions may be of assistance regarding other countries.

1. There is no doubt that internationally acknowledged personalities (so-called VIPs) always have a much greater authority and impact on local news media and on the attendance of listeners at meetings than local researchers. We saw that very clearly when Dr. Ehrenwald and later on Douglas Johnson visited Jerusalem. We therefore will welcome most warmly and heartily all the visitors who come to the "Holy City" and to Israel. Our limited means do not permit us to pay travel expenses but we can invite visitors to live in private homes during their stay. It would give us the greatest pleasure to be the guides of our guests and to show them some inside aspects of Israel (away from the beaten track).

Please accept this as an invitation to all participants and other friends and researchers in the field!

2. It seems to me of the utmost importance that our institutions of higher learning (the universities in general, the psychological departments in particular, the Technion and the Weizmann Institute) should be bombarded with scientific material on research in parapsychology. I wish to come back to my suggestion that the material should be reprinted and widely distributed, a method which brought about the acceptance of the Parapsychological Association as a member of the American Association for the Advancement of Science, this most important event in the history of parapsychology in the last few years. The expenses for such reprinting and distribution may be high, but I am sure that the result will justify the cost.

3. When—or should I say if?—our endeavor in opening "the doors of perception of the psychologists" should bear fruit, various research projects could be suggested to the students, with competitions for prizes (a motivation not to be neglected especially in our country).

4. The mass printing of concise pamphlets written specially for high school and/or university students, but comprehensible also to interested laymen, could be of great help. Such pamphlets containing general information on the introductory issues and concerned later on with more specific areas in the field, such as giving definitions, examples, and suggestions for further reading or contacts, could slowly grow into a collection of basic information for interested novices and could be collected in loose-leaf binders.

5. The assurance of continued financial assistance would certainly allow our small group to do some long-range planning and enable, e.g., the translation of the above-mentioned or other important material into Hebrew and its distribution here.

VI.

Although we may all agree on the importance of attracting young people to our field, nobody should close his eyes to the unpleasant fact that to go full time into parapsychology is an almost unattainable goal except for a very few, a goal which should actually be decided upon only in later years for reasons mentioned below.

It needs much courage to go into a field when even one of its famous explorers, Dr. West, has some serious doubts about the very existence of psi phenomena, which he expressed in the *Parapsychology Review* of March-April, 1971. I do not share his attitude. But I agree with him that paranormal phenomena "are not unlike other delicate psychological phenomena, such as creative inspiration." This indicates that our interest and our inquiry should at least be evenly distributed between those qualitative experiences which we either can collect or sometimes evoke, and the purely quantitative methods. We may have to include here a fact which is somewhat analogous to one well known in modern physics, namely that by concentrating on and observing *one* aspect of the problem, i.e., the statistical aspect, we may inhibit another, that of inspiration or psi-production.

It is here that I want, in conclusion, to make some personal remarks about the field in general and my own attitude to its problems.

There is no doubt that a young, intelligent student may start to study parapsychology as a special branch of psychology, that he may succeed in experimental work and, under wise guidance, arrive at new, perhaps important results and statistical or psychological evaluations. But having been in the field now for approximately twenty years— starting relatively late—I have come to the conclusion that there is almost no field of science in which the interrelationship with other sciences is greater than in parapsychology. One cannot probe the depths of the problems without studying physics or biology as well; one should know something about depth psychology and ethnology; one must understand basic physiology; normal sensory perception; the origin of language; and the history of philosophy and religion. One should start studying these subjects at an early age if one wants to understand paranormal processes. And one should make at least one of the above-mentioned fields (and they do *not* comprise all of them) the subject of special study, or one's profession (to make a living), and have a good working knowledge of the others.

Such knowledge, together with openmindedness, positive criticism, and the ability to grasp impressions which may transcend the aspects of pure scientific approach, may be the most important precondition to research in parapsychology.

In a lecture at the Schweizer Parapsychologische Gesellschaft in Zurich, I spoke about "Natural Science and Parapsychology" as parallel fields of human exploration. I tried to explain there that it is not unlikely—and the comments of a number of men of science themselves point in the same direction—that we can expect explanations for paranormal processes and a general theory of parapsychology only if we are ready to shift from research *within* the natural sciences to a level where a "meta-science" allows us a new conception of both fields, that of the physical world and that of the mind and values, under a higher common determinating aspect.

This new perspective was expressed by Geoffrey F. Chew, a nuclear physicist from Berkeley, California who concluded a paper about "the Bootstrap, a Scientific Idea" (concerned with problems of atomic sub-particles) with the words: "Our current struggle with the Hadron Bootstrap may thus be only a foretaste of a completely new form of human intellectual endeavor, one that will lie outside physics, but will not even be describable as 'scientific.' "

It is to this "new form of human endeavor," that parapsychology may contribute most and it is here where I see the greatest importance of parapsychology in the future.

PARAPSYCHOLOGY IN GERMANY

HANS BENDER

In the year 1889 a young German philosopher and psychologist, Max Dessoir, invented the word "parapsychology." Using the Greek prefix *para*=beside, he tried to designate by this term psychological and physical phenomena which happen or seem to happen outside of familiar events. The new name for the "unclassified residuum of our experience"—as William James characterized the exciting realm of the "occult"—needed about forty years to become internationally accepted and to triumph over "psychical research." A landmark of this triumph was a book by a fellow student of Max Dessoir's, the zoologist and philosopher Hans Driesch. As a professor of philosophy at Leipzig University he published in 1932 the first methodology of our field of research under the title *Parapsychologie, die Wissenschaft von den "okkulten" Erscheinungen* (Parapsychology, Science of the "Occult" Phenomena). This was a revolutionary event in a country of which F. C. S. Schiller, the English psychical researcher, said with some malice in a review of the fifth edition of Dessoir's well known book *Vom Jenseits der Seele* (Beyond the Psyche), in 1921: "His general attitude is that of a very critical psychical researcher . . . and even this demands a deal of courage in Germany, where authoritarianism and a priori dogmatism have always been at home, and the mental atmosphere seems still to be very similar to that prevailing in England forty years ago" (*Proceedings Society for Psychical Research 32* [1922]: 146). In the same volume of the *Proceedings*, F. C. S. Schiller reviews a work of Dr. V. Schrenck-Notzing: *Physikalische Phänomene des Mediumismus, Studien zur Erforschung der Telekinetischen Vorgänge* (Physical Phenomena of Mediumship; Studies on the Investigation of Telekinetic Events). The author, a Munich physician, was the outstanding pioneer of physical mediumship. He began by taking part in sittings with Eusapia Palladino in 1894, worked with the Polish medium Stanislawa Tomczyk among many others, and got his best results with the brothers Rudi and Willy Schneider from Braunau, Austria. His work, which included the investigation of poltergeist phenomena and hypnotism, was much contested but, under the bombardment of his critics, he continuously improved the conditions and finally reached results which could cope with any reasonable skepticism. His poltergeist investigations now seem justified by recent developments in this long taboo field, which could, perhaps, even impress some very unyielding psychical researchers who believe in the curious subsoil water theory of Dr. Lambert's. Munich was a favorable place for parapsychology. Another pioneer lived there from 1921: Dr. R. Tischner, also a physician, whose qualitative studies on telepathy and clairvoyance have great merit. His controversy with the psychologist Dr. R. Baerwald, author of the book *Die intellektuellen Phänomene* (Mental Phenomena, 1925), proved to be well founded: Baerwald, head of the so-called school of telepathy, only accepted telepathy as compatible with the physical laws of nature and rejected the possibility of clairvoyance, a bias which has been thoroughly refuted by the later findings of experimental parapsychology, and which Tishner has always unveiled as a pseudoyphysical prejudice. As part of the parapsychological scene in the twenties, two university professors should not be forgotten: the psychologist August Messer of Giessen University, and the many-sided philosopher T. K. Oesterreich, of Tübingen, whose publications dealt with the philosophical impact of parapsychological phenomena and on the dissociation of personality and the phenomenology of possession. Germany did not have an organization which could be compared with the British and American Societies for Psychical Research. A journal, the *Zeitschrift für Parapsychologie,* edited by Dr. Sünner and financed by Dr. v. Schrenck-Notzing followed the old journal *Psychische Studien* in 1926, and ceased publication in 1934. A year later, an important work struck the balance of the pro and con of what was still called "occultism" at that time. *Der Okkultismus; Täuschungen und Tatsachen* (Occultism; Delusions and Facts) by the Swiss born author Mrs. Fanny Moser who later—she died in 1953—would become a generous donor to the Freiburg Institute for Border Areas of Psychology.

In the foreword of his revolutionary methodology, Hans Driesch bitterly complained of the lack of interest of the German universities. "This insupportable situation," he wrote, "has to be characterized with clear-cut words. No doubt that universities should adopt a critical attitude toward new topics; but they are by no means pure institutions of preservation allowed to behave as if all which can be regarded as 'essential' is already known and should only be elaborated in detail." The breakthrough took place at Bonn University where Erich Rothacker, head of the Psychological Institute, encouraged experimental work on motor automatisms and clairvoyance. I was the experimenter and had the privilege of submitting to the Faculty of Philosophy the first German thesis on a parapsychological topic which yielded positive results (*Psychische Automatismen*, Bonn, 1933). A second contribution to the problem of extrasenory perception followed shortly after and was published in the conservative *Zeitschrift für Psychologie* in 1935.

Just before I finished my paper, Dr. Gerda Walther—still one of the best informed parapsychologists, specialist of mystical experience and physical mediumship—sent me a recently published book by a young American author: J. B. Rhine's *Extrasensory Perception*. This was most encouraging and strengthened my wish definitely to introduce parapsychology into a German university in an institutionalized form. But I had first to finish my studies of medicine and to obtain a chair in psychology. It was only after World War II that the realization of this plan could be followed up in my native town, Freiburg im Breisgau. It began with the erection of a somewhat miraculously financed Institute for Border Areas of Psychology and Mental Hygiene which opened its doors in 1950. The establishment of a chair for Border Areas of Psychology at Freiburg University and the affiliation of the Institute followed in 1954.

In 1966 the chair was extended to cover general psychology as well as border areas of psychology (parapsychology), and a Department for the Border Areas was established at the Psychological Institute of Freiburg University. This development shows the progressive and now total integration of parapsychology into the academic framework. Parapsychology is regarded as part of psychology and not as an independent discipline working in a sort of "ivory tower."

With these and the following remarks I repeat the survey on the Freiburg Institute which I gave to the 11th Convention of the Parapsychological Association held at Freiburg University in September, 1968. Teaching and research cover the entire field of parapsychology: history, methods, findings, hypotheses, problems, and, more and more, the interdisciplinary relations of our field to comparative psychology, folklore, ethnology, theology, medicine, and physics. Social psychology and mental hygiene are involved in studies of beliefs in alleged exceptional capacities such as unorthodox healing or scientifically unaccepted practices of "divination," including, for example, chiromancy and astrology. All these topics are dealt with in the frame of normal and depth psychology as well as psychopathology. Much activity is devoted to the struggle against superstition. For this work in the domain of mental hygiene we chose the slogan "positive critic of superstition," which means that we seek to induce enlightenment based on unprejudiced scientific research. In this context we are involved in information about the practical use of psi capacities, which deals with advice for legal proceedings, and with mental disorders which stem from pathological reactions to genuine or delusionary occult experiences.

The Freiburg Institute has a monopoly in the Federal Republic of Germany. We should prefer it to be different, but there seems to be little chance that other departments of parapsychology will be formed in a foreseeable future. The dynamic initiative of an enthusiastic researcher could perhaps create a new center. Psychology as an academic institution has not yet developed the feeling of scientific responsibility with regard to the importance of psi for the understanding of human and perhaps animal behavior. Psychologists seem more imprisoned in the ivory tower of defined or undefined prejudices than, for example, physicists. Physicists are more flexible, more used to radical changes in the basic principles of their science; they are more likely to foster new aspects of nature and even of the psyche as a means of detecting a hidden world.

With regard to the monopoly of the Institute, its staff is much too small for the continuously increasing tasks. Two assistants are paid by the University; one assistant and a secretary are remunerated by the Moser Foundation. Students collaborate in a most effective way. The funds which are permanently at our disposal are so small that we would be limited to a very small scope of research possibilities if we did not get support elsewhere from time to time. We are much obliged to the Parapsychology Foundation which has helped us generously in critical situations. The Deutsche Forschungsgemeinschaft (German Association for Scientific Research), a government subsidized official institution, gave us a three years' grant for studies in extrasensory perception and psychokinesis and invited me to deliver a paper on "New Developments in Poltergeist Research"—an event which was widely and favorably discussed in the German mass media under the title "Poltergeists have become fit for society." It should be added that the German word "Spuk" is hardly less shocking than "poltergeist." It will take some time to replace it with the inoffensive expression RSPK—recurrent spontaneous psychokinesis. The Volkswagen Foundation enabled us to reorganize and complete our 6,000-volume library (which includes the Schrenck-Notzing and F. Moser collections of literature). After this reorganization the care of the library will probably be taken over by the Deutsche Forschungsgemeinschaft. The library will then become a circulating library for Western Germany, a "Schwerpunktsbibliothek," a center library.

These achievements are partly due to a very good collaboration with the mass media. Newspapers, magazines, broadcasting and television have been in contact with the Freiburg Institute since its establishment and strive to give objective reports on our field. This had a strong influence on public opinion and helped to point out the necessity for an academic center.

In its invitation to this conference, Parapsychology Foundation asked each participant to present an account of his own research and experiments in the area of his major interest within the overall context of the history and development of parapsychology in his geographic locale. I tried to sketch the overall context but I feel it is incomplete without mentioning the most effective help the Freiburg Institute is constantly getting from sympathizing scientists such as the physicists Dr. Karger and Dr. Zicha (Munich), especially in poltergeist investigations, or from Professor Petzold (University of Marburg), a theoretical physicist, who advises us in problems of psi and physics which are beyond our competence. What I said a little ironically about the unyielding attitude of psychologists, is not generally true. There are most encouraging exceptions, and I feel deeply obliged to an increasing number of colleagues such as Professor Dyker (Marburg), Professor Undeutsch (Cologne), and Professor Wallek (Mayence), who fully realize the importance of psi research and give every possible help in its academic integration.

I will now give a short survey of the research work of the Freiburg Institute recently completed or in progress:

1) Attitudes in regard to psi

K. H. Nissen presented a thesis on "Ideology (*Weltanschauung*) and attitude toward parapsychology. An inquiry on German students of psychology."

A representative inquiry into attitudes of Catholic and Protestant theologians toward occultism, spiritualism and parapsychology is in progress, conducted by two psychologists, G. Hammers and U. Rosin.

2) Spontaneous phenomena

E. Hanefeld continues his analysis and classification of spontaneous phenomena which he first presented at the 11th P.A. Convention at Freiburg University.

Miss Ute Pleimes collected and factor-analyzed reports on psi in animals. I will later summarize her papers "Psi in Animals?" recently published in the *Zeitschrift für Parapsychologie und Grenzgebiete der Psychologie 13* (1971), Nos. 2 and 4.

3) Work with sensitives

The "observation in expectancy" of possible paranormal dreams with the actress Mrs. Christine Mylius is continuing. Since 1954 she had been sending to the Freiburg Institute dream reports that are recorded in our files as study material for possible precognitive coincidences with future situations. (See "The Gotenhafen Case of Correspondence between Dreams and Future Events: A Study of Motivation," *International Journal of Neuropsychiatry 2* (1966): 398. When this article was written, we had about 1,300 dreams; we have now more than 2,000 and the coincidences continue in a striking way. I will tell you later of a recent observation with this dreamer which might throw a light on the concept of a psi field. A new seat experiment with the Dutch sensitive Gerard Croiset, with students of Freiburg University, statistically evaluated by the method which U. Timm described in our Journal (*8* [1965]: 78) proved to be significant.

4) Quantitative experimental work

Ch. Wiesinger presented a thesis on "ESP experiments in the social field of the classroom." He found highly significant coincidences between the call sequences of classmates (which he analyzed according to the sociogram), but only chance results in relation to the agent.

J. Mischo undertook a broad scale experimental investigation on basic problems of statistical evaluation and conditions of psi performance to which I will return later.

5) Psychokinesis

New poltergeist cases have been thoroughly investigated by the Freiburg Institute: a reconstruction of probable RSPK-events on the coastal boat *Hannelore S.* and a case in the little Bavarian village of Pursruck where raps could be video-tape recorded in the ambiance of two 11- and 13-year-old sisters.

Experiments with the alleged "voices from the dead," which Friedrich Jürgenson claims to receive on tape, were continued with positive results in regard to the physically unexplainable origin of some of the voices. I think this extraordinary phenomenon is worthwhile commenting on later. Quantitative experiments on the problem of a possible relation between frustration and PK are being conducted with groups of students.

Let us now have a closer look at some of the topics. First, let us consider psi in animals. The inquiry of Miss U. Pleimes was focused on the subject of unexplainable behavior of animals before catastrophes but was not limited to this pattern. With the cooperation of the mass media the Institute got about 500 reports of unusual animal behavior. Many had to do with probable telepathy and psi-trailing, but half of the material concerned animal premonitory behavior. On the basis of the first analysis, a questionnaire was constructed containing 94 items and sent to 190 correspondents. One hundred forty were returned and evaluated. Characteristic patterns became evident. The similarities concerned mostly the type of event, for example "behavior before bombing raids." The data were computer-evaluated, the frequency was determined, correlations examined and a factor analysis performed. Among the dimensions which became evident was a factor dealing with the contact (proximity and intensity) of the animal with other animals. Others comprised the non-directivity of animal premonitory behavior, the relation of the animal to its master, the degree and type of the danger, etc. Strict selection criteria reduced the obviously paranormal cases to 25; further 25 cases involved a concomitant paranormal factor. The other cases were partly phenomena mixed with sensory clues or they seemed not to be reliable enough to be accepted. The determining influence of affective fixations on contact persons could be verified. This study of anecdotal material should be continued by experimental research, but this is a problem of the capacity of the Institute for new programs.

To the topic "work with sensitives" I add a recent experiment with Mrs. Mylius that had an unforeseen issue: I tried with her the technique of "ordering dreams" that had proved to be successful in former normal dream work of the Institute. I asked her to open an envelope before sleeping and to meditate for a while on the phrase that she would find enclosed. It ran: "My lottery ticket wins the first prize." The next morning Mrs. Mylius, who spent a couple of days in Freiburg, reported her dream that she said had unfortunately nothing to do with the dream suggestion: "A street leading through a valley in the outskirts of Freiburg. Some villas. I had formerly been in one of them. A musician I know is living there. I recognize the house and ring the bell. A flaxen-haired young man wearing dark horn-rimmed spectacles answers when I ask for my acquaintance: 'No, he is not here' and adds, 'He does not exist or it is not his house.' I am strangely bewildered by this contradiction and feel that something is wrong." The following evening, Mrs. Mylius met an actress whom she had known when she lived in Freiburg some ten years ago. A collaborator of the Institute—an amateur actor who had proved to be a catalyst for paranormal events—had told her the day before that this actress had a young friend but his name was not given. Mrs. Mylius's colleague was accompanied by this friend: a flaxen-haired young man with dark-rimmed spectacles. It came out that he was the son of the musician Mrs. Mylius was trying to visit in her dream and that he lived in his father's house after the father's death some years ago. The key word "dream" made the young man tell an extraordinary dream that he also had the night before. He had bought a lottery ticket and won 15,000 marks; enough to emigrate to Brazil where he wanted to escape from the police who were searching for him.

This entanglement of coincidences needs no comment. It seems to indicate the formation of a psi field in which my collaborator may have been instrumental. I find observations of this kind—if they are well documented—highly elucidating for an understanding of how psi works in life situations. I remember in this context a remark of C. G. Jung's in the preface to Fanny Moser's book *Spuk* (1950). With regard to psi phenomena and their dependence on special conditions of the unconscious, he said, "The individual nature of the more complex phenomena of this kind does not allow a statistical approach. In this respect we are therefore totally left to the well observed and verified particular case."

All collaborators of the Freiburg Institute are engaged in both qualitative and quantitative research. Dr. John Mischo, who published with me the "Gotenhafen case," is now doing quantitative work. With a group of graduates he is actually re-checking 100,000 calls of significant and not significant trials of the Institute in regard to problems of evaluation stemming from shuffling habits, call habits, preferential targets, etc. Computer programs were developed for cross-checking the experimental data in every possible form of permutation.

In new multivariate ESP experiments Dr. Mischo is investigating the correlation of the results with attitudes to psi, different dimensions of personality and the social relations of the subjects. He is trying to determine the psychological impact of the stimuli (Zener cards and emotionally loaded pictures) by means of the semantic differential of ERTEL (dimensions "excitation," "valency" and "potency"). For these experiments he uses the automatic ESP testing machine, Psi Recorder '70, which has been developed and built for the Freiburg Institute by courtesy of the Institut für Experimentelle Nachrichtentechnik of the Technical University of Darmstadt. A random signal generator produces the targets and the subjects put in their call statements at consoles in separate rooms. Trials and hits are automatically counted and recorded on punched tape which can be processed directly by a digital computer or printed out on a teletype. The series of cards and calls is submitted to computer controls for many factors, among others the randomness of the target series and the occurrence of preferential targets in the call series. The latter are submitted to an evaluation of the empirical chance expectancy, which proves to be sometimes considerably different from the theoretical values. Positive results in GESP-situations allowed for a factor analysis on the basis of an attitude scale, a personality inventory, the social contact between agent and percipient and the challenge of the stimuli.

Let me close with an example of PK qualitative work with sensitives. I will try to sketch briefly some aspects of our investigation into alleged spiritual voices on tape. Quite a number of people actually claim to receive voices from "discarnate agencies." A Latvian born author, Konstantin Raudive, just published an English translation of a German book on his experiments under the title *Breakthrough: An Amazing Experiment in Electronic Communication with the Dead* (1971). The first report on this new method stemmed from Friedrich Jürgenson, a 67-year-old painter of Baltic origin who has been living in Sweden since 1943. His publication *Voice Radio with the Beyond* was translated into several languages. An occasional observation of unexplainable voices on a tape record he had made was the beginning of an extensive, rather solitary experimental work that is still going on. He proceeds in two ways. After the recording of a normal conversation on tape by means of a microphone, the tape is sometimes found to include voices of unknown origin which appear between normal words, are superimposed on them, or come out in artificial pauses. The other way is to plug the recorder to a radio set and to record when an appropriate position on the waveband without actual transmissions is found. The voices are mostly very low, often merely whispering, and it needs a long training, Jürgenson and his followers point out, to fully understand what they are communicating. They talk in different languages, often in a mixture, but always in those known to the experimenter. In most of the voices Jürgenson recognizes dead friends of his. He lives in a permanent communication with them and has the missionary idea of persuading mankind of the experimentally proved life after death. The impossibility of proving these claims I will not discuss here, but will restrict myself to the problem of checking if there are unexplainable voices or not.

First exploratory experiences in 1965 seemed to be encouraging. Thus, the physicist Dr. Karger, a student and I had a short tape recorded talk with Jürgenson. He told us that when transcribing a tape with voices for the Freiburg Institute, he found new voices on the copy and consulted a radio expert who was unable to explain the phenomenon. On replay of our tapes—we used two recorders—we heard in this context a voice rapidly saying in German "Von Wo" (wherefrom). Three normal explanations had to be excluded:

1. We simply project these words onto the background noise of the tape. They are not objective acoustical events. Years later we were enabled to cope with this hypothesis. A laboratory of the German Post in Berlin procured for us visible speech-diagrams which allow one to recognize vowels and voiced consonants by characteristic fields of energy. "Von Wo" proved to be an objective acoustical event. The first counter-hypothesis was excluded for this case, but was later found to explain quite a lot of other experiences.

2. Someone among the sitters was uncontrolled and had uttered these words. This counter-hypothesis could not be excluded.

3. As under certain conditions a tape recorder may function as a radio set, the word could be a fragment of a broadcast. This explanation seemed to be highly improbable as the words fitted into the context of the normal conversation and seemed to comment on actual statements.

New experiments could be performed only in May 1970 and July 1971. Jürgenson invited our team to his old country house, Nysund, near Mölnbo, Sweden, some forty miles from Stockholm. We used directed microphones, an oscillograph, and a video-recorder. An electronic engineer who accompanied us supervised the recorders for radio reception. I will mention two examples which seemed to defy the three counter-hypotheses.

Before one of our sittings, Jürgenson demonstrated a very emotional voice which he attributed to "Lena," a Russian girl, one of his dead friends. I was impressed, thought of similarly expressive voices, and remembered in this context the voice of a young collaborator, Brigitte Rasmus. In the following experiment I started a conversation with remarks on the impressive voice of Lena. I had to fight against an attack of coughing and had difficulties pronouncing the word "emotion." On replay, a voice was heard at that spot, whispering "Rasmus." I was the only one present who knew this name. The visible speech-diagram shows that the word is objective and furthermore the analysis of the Berlin specialist, Jochem Sotscheck, makes sure that I cannot have whispered it. My interpretation is that Jürgenson got the name from me by telepathy and transmitted it to the tape—a psychokinetic effect as bewildering as the psychophotography of Ted Serios. In another sitting, we concluded the experiment with a pause of one minute and carefully controlled ourselves not to move our lips. We observed the oscillograph which showed deflections twenty-two seconds before the end. On replay we heard a voice whispering in English, "Stop as you like." What followed was hardly understandable but could be checked later. Then, we heard, "One paus(e)." This last word was pronounced in German. A paranormal origin of this phrase is also highly probable.

Our recent experiments began with a surprise. We had difficulties in finding our way and arrived at Nysund late during the night. One of our team, Gisela B., complained of a terrible toothache while we were driving through endless woods. Jürgenson, waiting for us, had tried a radio experiment. He got voices. One said in German—and he showed it to us the very minute of our arrival: "Sie kommen bald. Zahnarzt. Zahnarzt." ("They will arrive soon. Dentist. Dentist.") I cannot enter here into details of our experimental design but will only demonstrate one result to you, tiny but perfect: There was no woman in the house when we had the sitting in question. A voice was heard on the brand new Sony cassette tape, wedged in a phrase. It said "Peng" and resembled closely the voice of our assistant Gisela who at that time was in Stockholm to get her aching tooth treated by Mrs. Jürgenson, who is a dentist. "Peng" is a sort of German interjection and is used when some striking event happens.

We are actually preparing new experiments with a view to finding out which part of the recording system the supposed PK influence is acting upon.

Striking the balance of the actual situation of parapsychology in Germany, I think we can be hopeful for the future development of our more and more accepted field of research. An ever growing interest of the younger generation in psi is most encouraging. It seems to be part of its most exigent desire for an extension of consciousness.

PARAPSYCHOLOGY IN EASTERN EUROPE

MILAN RYZL

I am afraid my paper will destroy a myth which I involuntarily helped to create: that parapsychology in Eastern Europe is far ahead of similar research elsewhere in the world.

Allow me to start by recalling my role in building up this myth. Until 1967, I lived in Czechoslovakia. During my visits to the USSR and other East European countries, I was fortunate enough to meet nearly all the important parapsychologists in these counrites.

In the 1960s interest in parapsychology in Eastern Europe grew rapidly, and the situation of East European parapsychologists had several promising features, such as government interest, emphasis on practical application, and innovative research ventures.

In reports published in the West [1-9] I tried to convey an idea of these highly promising features, which really existed and to some degree still exist. But many readers apparently understood them as testimony that some spectacular breakthrough was achieved in Eastern Europe, which definitely did not happen. This wrong impression was strengthened by the widely read book *Psychic Discoveries Behind the Iron Curtain,* [10] which has dramatized and exaggerated the results of East European parapsychological investigations. It has become a kind of popular fashion to glorify these East European researches on the basis of incomplete reports available, and overlook the fact that the majority of these glorified researches were inadequate with respect to scientific method.

After my defection from Czechoslovakia, my East European friends severed all contacts with me, and I could learn about their work only indirectly, through the incomplete testimony of Western visitors who went to meet these East European parapsychologists, but whose communication with them was usually greatly impeded by the language barrier. What I learned through this testimony seemed to indicate that, after the climax in 1967, parapsychology in Eastern Europe began to decline.

I could understand the difficulties these visitors had, since I experienced them years ago myself, in spite of the fact that I had the best possible opportunity to learn what my colleagues in the USSR were doing. I could interview them in their own language, without the inconvenience of interpreters. Or, to put it better, I did not interview them at all; rather, we usually chatted with each other as close friends. Moreover, I had been living for decades in a communist country, and I could understand their problems.

Yet I found it often difficult to reach an authoritative judgment about their work. Now and again, I held the opinion that I was meeting people who belonged to two extreme groups: Some of them were very open, eager to discuss their past experiments and most fantastic future projects, while others were unusually reserved, hesitant to tell anything about their work, and seemed determined to obtain as much information as possible from their visitor while telling as little as possible about themselves.

The talkativeness of the first group made one suspicious. These people must have made tremendous progress—or are they only boasting, hiding the fact that their progress has actually not been that great? This dilemma was confirmed by the impression gained from the members of the other group: Either they are working on secret, classified projects sponsored by their governments—perhaps military—or is their reticence concealing the embarrassing fact that they have nothing of significance to report?

The situation was what Winston Churchill once characterized as a "riddle wrapped in an enigma." To make things worse, East European parapsychologists (perhaps even more than their Western counterparts, and probably for similar reasons) are split into several competing factions, and there are some individuals who prefer to work alone and not to have much in common with the rest. A recent visitor to the USSR [11] characterized it poignantly: "Dr. X doesn't speak to Dr. Y, Dr. Y doesn't speak to Dr. Z, Dr. Z won't speak to anybody. Much work is 'secret,' so secret we are not even sure it exists."

Comparatively recently my East European colleagues began to correspond with me again, and this made it possible for me to look somewhat more closely into their problems anew. Because of my defection, however, I cannot visit them now. Therefore, I am giving this review deprived of the benefit of close insight into their work, for which free conversation and on-the-spot observation are invaluable.

Carefully judging my recollection of personal visits, combined with new impressions from published reports and personal correspondence, I have the feeling that the truth about their work is somewhere in between the two extremes—though I still find it hard to say where precisely.

To my knowledege, there is no full-time parapsychologist in Eastern Europe who would be paid by some governmental institution for his work in parapsychology, except, perhaps, for one single person whose present status is obscure. However, there are several people who are pursuing research on problems relevant to parapsychology at universities or other respectable scientific institutions. These persons are either working full-time on problems only remotely related to parapsychology (though possibly of considerable potential significance), or are working on problems more closely associated with parapsychology, using the equipment of their institutions, but as a hobby, after their full-time engagement in some more orthodox field.

Though there presently seems to be no apparent direct government support of parapsychology in Eastern Europe, this situation amounts, in East European conditions, to some limited governmental support. The researchers are allowed to work, on their own initiative, on problems relevant to parapsychology, using scientific instrumentation that belongs to the State.

Generally, East European parapsychologists have continued their investigations at great personal sacrifice, and with means that are far below the support available for similar research in the West. They have achieved some impressive experimental results, but there is definitely no breakthrough that would outclass the work of their Western colleagues. The importance of their work seems to lie more in suggested novel methods of research than in real accomplishments. Unfortunately, there seems to be also much dilettante amateurism and ostentatious exaggeration of results—but I would not claim that Western parapsychology is absolutely free of these defects either.

Historically, the development of East European parapsychology was influenced by the ideological and political situation. The prevalent materialistic ideology suppressed mysticism, supernaturalism, and speculations on religious implications. Instead, it led the investigators to emphasize a down-to-earth, pragmatic approach. There was no occult background of palmists, professional psychics, fortunetellers and astrologers to influence the general public, which began to view psi phenomena without mysterious undertones, soberly, merely as new, not-yet-explained natural phenomena which natural science will explain in due time.

Aside from these positive factors, however, the general climate was hardly favorable for the development of parapsychology. In the Stalin era and in early post-Stalin years, parapsychological research had to proceed underground, since all activities not expressly sponsored by the communist government were dangerously suspicious.

I can show the climate of political oppression which obstructed research with one anecdote from my own experience. In 1953, I managed, with some difficulty, to send out a brief historical survey of parapsychology in Czechoslovakia which was published in the Swiss magazine *Neue Wissenschaft*.[12] After some time, I wondered why I had not received a copy of the magazine containing my article. The Swiss editor explained that the first copy of the magazine he had sent me got lost. He sent me another copy by registered mail. This second copy, which could not get simply lost, was returned to him with the note "Not permitted in Czechoslovakia." I could not even get a copy of my own paper at that time!

After a few years, however, the situation changed. I began negotiations with Czech scientific institutions trying to establish a parapsychological research laboratory in Prague, and informatory articles in Czech newspapers and magazines followed in increasing numbers, especially in conjunction with the parallel publications of L. L. Vasiliev in the USSR. The sudden advance of East European parapsychology in the 1960s was a surprise not only for Western observers, but also for those of us who lived through it and helped to implement it.

Vasiliev's well known work was also done underground at first, but the last ten or twelve years have seen the gradual acceptance of parapsychology in communist countries. The progress of Vasiliev's work is so characteristic and illuminates so well the conditions under which parapsychology developed there, that it deserves to be dealt with in more detail.

In his effort to stimulate the Russian public's interest in parapsychology, Vasiliev proceeded gradually, with noteworthy prudence. After having probed the general opinion with a number of articles in popular magazines, he published a book, *Mysterious Phenomena of the Human Psyche* (1959),[13] in which he fought against superstitions and gave a natural explanation for many seemingly mysterious phenomena, such as sleep, dreams, hypnosis, and possession. In this book he devoted one chapter to a description of some telepathic experiments. Significantly, he confined himself mostly to the description of experiments by Russian authors. Under the heading "Does the Brain Radio Exist?" he said, carefully, in effect, this: There are observations which seem to indicate that telepathy occurs; many investigators are of the opinion that—if it occurs—it may be explained in terms of some kind of electromagnetic radiation; of course, this cannot be in contradiction to dialectical materialism.

When this book was favorably accepted, he brought out another popular one, *Long-Distance Suggestion* (1962).[14] In it he quoted numerous evidential experiments testifying to the existence of telepathy. Without saying so explicitly, he left the reader convinced that telepathy does indeed occur. Moreover, he quoted with emphasis numerous arguments, including the description of his own experiments, to testify that telepathy cannot be explained in terms of the electromagnetic field.

These bolder claims were again accepted without excessive opposition. Consequently, the second, enlarged edition of his *Mysterious Phenomena of the Human Psyche* was published in 1963. He expanded the chapter on brain radio by including the description of numerous Western experiments, and he added two more chapters on the topic of parapsychology: "What do We Know about ESP?" where he favorably discussed the possibility of clairvoyance (deliberately neglected in his earlier publications), and "The Possibility of Transmitting Muscular Force at a Distance" (note the careful wording!) with a description of numerous PK experiments, including E. Osty's sittings with the medium Rudi Schneider.

Vasiliev's early work in parapsychology was little known outside of the USSR. I learned about him as late as 1959 through a German physician, M. Jun, who corresponded with Vasiliev and whom I met when he visited Prague for a medical conference, which had nothing to do with parapsychology. But once Vasiliev's first book was published (followed in 1962 by his countryman B.B. Kazhinsky's *Biological Radiocommunication*),[15] it became widely known that isolated researchers have been working on problems of parapsychology in the USSR, right through the communist era.

After 1960, when Vasiliev officially began his researches on telepathy at Leningrad University (some say he was committed to work on some classified government project) further development was rapid. Numerous research groups—big and small, of varying qualties and endurance—were mushrooming in different cities of the USSR, thanks in great part to the organizational initiative of E. K. Naumov.

An important episode in Russian ESP research was the exploration of finger-reading (skin-optic sensitivity) following the discovery of Rosa Kuleshova in 1962. She was able to distinguish colors or even printed text by what appeared to be the visual sensitivity of her fingertips. The investigation of her ability in scientific laboratories in Moscow [16] proved that she really had this talent—at least at one period of her life (later she lost it). Some scientists maintained that finger-reading might be a kind of anomalous visual sensitivity of the skin, which would be a physiological, not a parapsychological phenomenon. However, there are reasons (such as its occasional presence also in darkness) to believe that at least some cases of finger-reading are instances of ESP.

Later, interest of Russian parapsychologists was directed especially to experiments in telepathy (such as those of I. M. Kogan [17, 18] who is a specialist in radiocommunication), mainly with the object of determining its practical application in telecommunication.

In their exploration of telepathy, Russian parapsychologists have paid little attention to the activity of the percipient (who "reads" mental states, or thoughts, of other persons). Rather, they have emphasized the activity of the sender. This can be recognized in their terminology: they prefer to speak about "mental suggestion" rather than telepathy.

Vasiliev's early experiments [19] dealt primarily with a sender's mental influence on the behavior of another person. He studied the transmission of telepathic signals, such as to "fall backwards," with emphasis on telepathic hypnosis. Some of his subjects were successful in receiving a hypnotist's telepathic orders to fall into a hypnotic trance. Later investigators continued this line of research into the possibilities of telepathically influencing the behavior of other people. For example, Bulgarian psychiatrist G. Lozanov telepathically transmitted signals for the subject to press down one of two telegraphic keys.

The year 1967 saw a climax of governmental interest in parapsychology in Eastern Europe. For me, personally, the consequences of this interest were paradoxical. For many years I had fought for official recognition and government support of parapsychology in Czechoslovakia. In 1967, this support was really forthcoming, and parallel support was apparent in some other Communist countries. This support, however, was associated with conditions that were unacceptable to me, and which compelled me rather to leave my native country.

In 1968, a marked decline in Russian parapsychology became apparent. It was due mainly to two factors: One of them was an unsuccessful long-distance telepathic experiment between Moscow and Kerch (about 1,800 miles) organized by one of the leading Soviet newspapers, the *Literary Gazette*.[20] The experiment was carefully organized and broadly publicized. Well known Russian sensitives, such as K. Nikolaev and Y. Kamensky participated in it, but it failed. The committee, when evaluating the results, nevertheless recommended that research continue, but it was evident that some of the former claims of Russian parapsychologists were exaggerated.

Another fiasco was that of the International Parapsychological Conference in Moscow in June, 1968. After long efforts, and after having overcome great difficulties, Russian parapsychologists organized a big conference to which delegates from numerous foreign countries were invited. After several postponements, the conference, which was originally supposed to last one full week, was suddenly condensed to one single day of presenting papers and addresses, which was followed by a showing of films on Russian experiments. The disfavor of Soviet officialdom at that time was manifested by a strongly critical article in the leading newspaper *Pravda* right on the day of the conference. The article attacked the well-known, but controversial Russian subject, N. Kulagina-Mikhailova, who years ago exhibited finger-reading, and who later was well known for her alleged ability to move various small objects telekinetically. The article blatantly accused Mikhailova, who was to be the central figure of the conference, of cheating. Probably as a result of this criticism the host of the conference (House of Friendship with Foreign Nations) reversed its former hospitality, and the film showing was transferred, thanks to the assistance of some Czech parapsychologists, to the Embassy of (the then liberal) Czechoslovakia.

These two unfortunate events definitely diminished the publicity parapsychological activties had enjoyed in Eastern Europe until that time.

Some recent reports about East European parapsychology (especially Ostrander and Schroeder's popular book) [21] have presented a number of alleged discoveries by East European parapsychologists such as biological radiations, Kirlian photography and various physical effects. I deliberately have not included them in this review, because I have serious doubts about the validity of some of these claims, and, of the others, I do not think that they belong in the area of parapsychology at all.

If I were to describe briefly the present situation of parapsychology in Eastern Europe, after the setback in 1968-1970, I would characterize it as "a cautious Renaissance."

My impression is that parapsychologists in the East and in the West —in spite of the different political and ideological systems they are living under—have markedly similar problems. This should not be surprising, since science does not recognize political boundaries. Both have their special characteristics, but neither is significantly ahead of the other. And neither has so far succeeded in fully convincing scientific colleagues in other fields of the value of parapsychology. Eastern parapsychologists may be in a more difficult situation (less financial means, political restrictions), but they may have more endurance and more dedicated enthusiasm.

I personally strongly endorse some research tactics which were primarily emphasized on the East European parapsychological scene and which seem to prevail there:

(1) Effort to bring parapsychological abilities under regular laboratory control, preferably by training new subjects.

(2) Emphasis on the practical application of research findings.

(3) Interdisciplinary approach to problems of parapsychology, involving cooperation of scientists from many different fields.

(4) Application of new research techniques involving the use of more sophisticated instrumentation.

These goals which seemed to signify a more imaginative approach by East European parapsychologists, were soon adopted also by Western parapsychology, and former differences were soon wiped out. On the contrary, Western parapsychologists have probably found it easier to equip their laboratories with modern instrumentation than did their East European counterparts.

In my opinion, one important asset of East European parapsychology is the attitude of the general public. Compared with the Western public, the Communist public accepts parapsychology more rationally and seriously, as a new science, perhaps underdeveloped, but nevertheless a field which is bound to grow and bring forth more knowledge and practical values in the future. Not only college students, not only intellectuals, but also the lay public are reading books and articles on parapsychology—not so much for the thrill of the unknown, not from the eagerness to hear anecdotes about some supernatural mysteries, but in a serious effort to learn more about the not-yet-discovered forces in nature.

This public interest is really impressive. There is for example the book *Telepathy and Clairvoyance* [22] which was recently published in Czechoslovakia. This volume is a collection of short articles written by leading parapsychologists from all over the world, such as J. B. Rhine, L. L. Vasiliev, G. Murphy, H. Bender, and W. H. C. Tenhaeff. It is not always easy reading. The style is difficult to understand, and several chapters involve complex mathematics, tables, and graphs. Yet this book was published in nearly 30,000 copies—in a small country like Czechoslovakia. Translated into American conditions, it is as if the publisher, in the first printing, counted on a rapid sale of much more than half-a-million [!] hardcover copies.

After the recent setback, however, the government attitude to parapsychology in the USSR seems far from favorable. This can perhaps best be seen by the fact that a recent authoritative publication on parapsychology in the USSR was not a book by some Russian advocate of parapsychology, but a translation of C. E. M. Hansel's critical book.[28] In the postscript to this book, the influential Russian critic of parapsychology, A. I. Kitaygorodsky, says among other things: "Why was it necessary to translate the book by Hansel? It would seem that [in parapsychology] we have to do only with nonsense which does not deserve any attention, that we dispute with an insignificant group of misled individuals who do not influence society. Unfortunately, this is not the fact. Hansel's book has exposed in detail all the fabrications and frauds which have been presented in some of our books and offered as sensational discoveries of a progressive science. . . . In my opinion, [Hansel's] book has only one defect—it is too objective. In my opinion, the topic deserved more temper, it needs anger and wrath, embitterment and surprise, alarm and concern, wit and sarcasm. This is not what Hansel's book is like."

Individuals who are involved in East European parapsychology (again, not unlike those in the West) are of different kinds. Some of them are interested mostly in publicity. They are merely journalists and propagandists who do no significant research of their own. Others are engaged in serious experimental research, but we do not learn about their work, since they are not interested in premature publicity. My personal impression is that in recent reports on East European parapsychology the publicity achieved by an investigator is in inverse proportion to the quality and solidity of his work.

The propagandists are responsible for some of the discredit that East European parapsychology suffered in 1968–1970. They took advantage of a somewhat more liberal attitude toward publishing in Eastern Europe, and made known observations that were not solid pieces of scientific research. Not only did they discredit the field in their own countries, but in their contacts with Western parapsychologists and journalists gave a wrong impression of their work and situation.

Allow me to conclude my review by listing a few centers that, in my opinion, offer the greatest promise for East European parapsychology. The list may be incomplete, but these are the centers that seem to be involved in the best type of research, that which is meticulous, solid and promising. The high scholarly standard of these centers—though they are working more or less on the margin of parapsychology—promises more respect for the study of psi phenomena, regardless of whether they avow direct adherence to parapsychology or not.

Brief descriptions of the activity of these centers will explain why I characterized their parapsychological relevance as "a cautious Renaissance." We shall see that, so far as solid pieces of research are concerned, there is no more the former broad scope of pioneering ventures, no more a Vasiliev's purposeful pushing through of the whole thematic range of parapsychology. The more spectacular ventures, which are most publicized, are more science fiction than solid pieces of scholarly study. The relevant scientific work proceeds in a few restricted areas only, and all effort is made to remain safely within the limits of scientific orthodoxy. Research in parapsychology is on the defensive in Eastern Europe now, but the best scientists keep the door open for future progress.

1. Laboratory of Physiological Cybernetics, University of Leningrad (Director: Professor P. I. Gulyaev). Gulyaev and a group of his colleagues [24-28] discovered that all living bodies are surrounded by a faint electrostatic field (called an "electrical aura"). They were able to detect this field with a specially sensitive piece of apparatus constructed by V. I. Zabotin. This field undergoes changes in the course of time. For instance, muscular contractions, even as small as the ideomotor movements accompanying a mere imagination of a movement, give rise to changes in it which can be detected.

These changes in the "electrical aura" represent signals which carry certain information. They could be, first, the basis of some process of information transfer among animals, probably atavistic in nature—such as communication between some fish, or some insects, and second, they could have also a technical significance. There is, for instance, a theoretical possibility that the changes in the aura, initiated by man's mental activity, for example those accompanying the thought of some movement, could be used to exert a distant control over some apparatus.

This electrostatic field also changes with alterations in the location and electrical properties of objects in the surrounding space. Since the body may also be sensitive to changes in this surrounding field, there appears to be a possibility of perceiving surrounding objects through this new type of "electric sensitivity," which really exists in some fish species. There is also the possibility that a record of the "electrical aura" of the body or of some individual organs could be used for diagnostic purposes.

Gulyaev's researches also provide some foundation for the revived Russian interest in dowsing, stimulated especially by the activity of the geologist N. N. Sochevanov. The possible explanation is that the aura interacts with geophysical fields.

2. Bioinformation Unit in the A. S. Popov Scientific-Technical Society for Radiotechnics, Electronics, and Communication in Moscow

(Chairman: Professor I. M. Kogan). Kogan approaches the problem of telepathy from the point of view of his specialty in radiocommunication. In his theoretical contributions [29-30] he was trying to show that telepathy can be based on electromagnetic signals. Experimentally, he has been studying the velocity of information transmission in telepathy, as measured in bits per unit of time. He claims that with increasing distance the velocity of information transmission decreases.

A recent report of Kogan's co-workers [31] indicates that they have probably achieved a considerable degree of control over ESP in their subjects. Also, their work gives a corroborative testimony that ESP can be developed. They used a modification of Ryzl's method of training subjects in ESP.[32] They trained their subjects in visual imagery to prepare them for an experiment in which they attempted to transmit one-digit numbers telepathically (with a chance hit probability of $p = .1$). During the experiment the sender visualized a white screen on which the transmitted number was projected. The receiver visualized a blank screen and waited until a clear image of some number appeared on that screen. Though he was allowed to name all numbers which appeared on his imagined screen, only those of his images were counted which were clear and distinct. In 135 trials they recorded a surprisingly high number of 105 hits and only 30 errors.

3. Pedagogical Institute in Sverdlovsk (Professor A. S. Novomeysky with a group of co-workers in Sverdlovsk and adjacent Nizhny Tagil). For nearly a decade these scientists have been meticulously investigating finger-reading. They have worked without any significant publicity so far, publishing their results in local scientific media with limited circulation. Their work, however, deserves serious attention.[33-37] Essentially, they claim that man has the ability to distinguish colors through opaque screens by the sensitivity of the skin of his hands. The explanation offered is that the skin is sensitive to characteristic electrostatic fields around colored objects.

In former experiments with the skin-optic sense, the subjects were asked to name the colors. In the newer development of the technique (which gives more objective results) the experimenter asks the subject to move his hand toward the colored surface until he feels a "barrier," a subjective feeling of some influence of the target on the outstretched hand. Each color is characterized by a specific distance to its "barrier."

In addition to the above three centers I am tempted to add one more area of investigation in Eastern Europe where we may expect some development that may be of value for parapsychology. This is the Institute of Suggestology, Sofia, Bulgaria (Director: Dr. G. Lozanov). This center is only of potential importance for parapsychology. G. Lozanov was engaged in some investigation of ESP in the past (for example, he studied the famous Bulgarian clairvoyant Vanga Dimitrova). Now he seems to be fully occupied with researches of a non-parapsychological character. He is investigating suggestion, especially from the point of view of its possible role in stimulating the learning process. However, because of his lasting interest in hypnosis and in ESP, it is possible that he will choose to investigate ESP at some future time again, provided favorable conditions prevail.

Finally, I wish to comment on the widely publicized psychokinetic claims of Mrs. Kulagina-Mikhailova, a young woman who allegedly is able to move light objects in daylight by the mere power of her concentration. A few American visitors have seen her successfully demonstrate her feat—though under informal conditions only.[38] I regret I had no oportunity to witness her performance myself, and cannot base my opinion on direct personal experience.

REFERENCES

1. RYZL, M.: "Research on Telepathy in Soviet Russia," *J. Parapsychol.* 25 (1961): 75–85.
2. ———: "A Brief Report of a Journey to the USSR," *Parapsychol. Bull.* (1961), No. 59: 1–3.
3. ———: Review of B. B. Kazhinsky's *Biologicheskaya Radiosvyaz* (Biological Radio), *J. Parapsychol.* 26 (1962): 221–226.
4. ———: Review of L. L. Vasiliev's *Vnushenie na rasstoyanii* (Long Distance Suggestion), *J. Parapsychol.* 27 (1963): 50–55.
5. ———: "Report on a Second Visit to the USSR," *Parapsychol. Bull.* (1964), No. 69: 2–4.
6. ———: Review of L. L. Vasiliev's *Tainstvennye yavleniya chelovecheskoy psichiki* (Mysterious Phenomena of the Human Psyche), *J. Parapsychol.* 28 (1964): 56–59.
7. ———: "Pioneer of Soviet Science: L. L. Vasiliev" (Obituary), *J. Parapsychol.* 30 (1966): 114–117.
8. ———: "Parapsychology in Communist Countries of Europe," *Int. J. Parapsychol.* 10 (1968): 263–276.
9. ———: "ESP in Eastern Europe and Russia," *Psychic*, June-July 1969, pp. 14–18; August-September 1969, pp. 40–46.
10. OSTRANDER, S. and SCHROEDER, L.: *Psychic Discoveries Behind the Iron Curtain* (Englewood Cliffs, N.J.: Prentice-Hall, 1970).
11. MILLER, S.: Letter to the author.
12. RYZL, M.: "Parapsychologische Forschung in der Tschechoslowakei" (Parapsychological Research in Czechoslovakia), *Neue Wissenschaft* (1953), No. 3: 362–367.
13. VASILIEV, L. L.: *Tainstvennye yavleniya chelovecheskoy psichiki* (Mysterious Phenomena of the Human Psyche). (Moscow: Publishing House of Political Literature, 1959; 2nd. ed., 1963).
14. ———: *Vnushenie na rasstoyanii* (Long-Distance Suggestion). (Moscow: Publishing House of Political Literature, 1962).
15. KAZHINSKY, B. B.: *Biologicheskaya Radiosvyaz* (Biological radiocommunication). (Kiev: Publishing House of the Ukrainian Academy of Sciences, 1962).

16. BONGARD, M. M. and SMIRNOV, N. S.: "O 'kozhnom zrenii' R. Kuleshovoy" (On the "Dermal Vision" of R. Kuleshova), *Biofizika* (1965), No. 1: 148–154.
17. KOGAN, I. M.: "Telepatiya, gipotezy i nablyudeniya" (Telepathy, hypotheses and observations), *Radiotekhnika* (1967), No. 1: 95–99.
18. ———: "Informatsionny analiz eksperimentov telepaticheskoy svyazi" (Information analysis of telepathic experiments), *Radiotekhnika* (1968), No. 3: 89–92.
19. VASILIEV, L. L.: *Eksperimentalnye issledovaniya myslennogo vnusheniya* (Experimental research on mental suggestion). (Leningrad University, 1962).
20. *Literaturnaya Gazeta:* (Long-distance experiment organized by this publication). "Effect telepatyi ne obnaruzhen" (Telepathic phenomenon not detected), published June 5, 1968, p. 12.
21. OSTRANDER, S. and SCHROEDER, L.: *Op. cit.,* ref. 9.
22. REJDAK, Z. (ed.): *Telepatie a Jasnovidnost* (Telepathy and Clairvoyance). (Prague: Svoboda, 1970).
23. HANSEL, C. E. M.: *ESP; A Scientific Evaluation* (New York: Charles Scribner's, 1966. Trans. *Parapsikhologiya* (Parapsychology) (Moscow: Mir, 1970).
24. GULYAEV, P. I., Zabotin, V. I. and Shlippenbakh, N. Y.: "Elektroauragramma nerva, myshcy i serdca lyagushki, serdca i muskulatury cheloveka" (Electroaurogram of the nerve, muscle and heart of the frog, and of the heart and muscles of man), *Doklady Akademii Nauk USSR* 180 (1968): 1504–1506.
25. ———: "Elektroauragrammy cheloveka i zhivotnykh" (Electroaurograms of man and animals), *Nervnaya Sistema* (1968), No. 9: 159–76.
26. ———: "Registraciya elektromagnitnykh poley voznikayushchikh pri dvizhenii nasekomykh, ptic i zverey" (Registration of electromagnetic fields appearing with the movements of insects, birds and animals), *Nervnaya Sistema* (1969), No. 10: 177–83.
27. GULYAEV, P. I., ZABOTIN, V. I. and others: "Electroauragrammy nasekoymykh v Svobodnom polete" (Electroauragrams of insects in free flight), *Doklady Akademii Nauk USSR* 191 (1970): 699–701.
28. ———: "Eksperimentalnyi analiz informacionnogo soderzhaniya auralnogo elektricheskogo polya cheloveka" (Experimental analysis of the information content of the aural electric field in man), *Nervnaya Sistema* 11 (1970): 145–149.
29. KOGAN, I. M.: *Op. cit.,* ref. 17
30. ———: *Op. cit.,* ref. 18
31 FIDELMAN, V. E., GULEVSKY, V. V. and others: "Metodika i rezultaty eksperimentalnoy proverki vozmozhnosti telepaticheskoy svyazi" (Method and results of experimental verification of the possibility of telepathic communication), *Radioteknika* (1970), No. 7: 109–110.
32. RYZL, M.: "A Method of Training in ESP, *Int. J. Parapsychol.* 8 (1966): 501–532.
33. NOVOMESKY, A. S.: "O prirode kozhno-opticheskogo chuvstva u cheloveka" (On the nature of the skin-optic in man), *Voprosy Psikhologii* (1963), No. 5. Trans. in *Int. J. Parapsychol.* 7 (1965): 341–367.
34. ———: "Rol kozhno-opticheskogo chuvstva v poznanii" (The role of the skin-optic sense in perceiving), *Voprosy Filosofii* (1963), No. 7: 131–139.
35. ——— (ed.): *Materialy issledovaniya kozhno-opticheskoy chuvstvitelnosti* (Materials on research of the skin-optic sense). (Chelyabinsk, USSR: Pedagogical Institute, 1965).
36. ——— (ed.): *Problemy kozhno-opticheskoy chuvstvitelnosti* (Problems of the skin-optic sense). (Sverdlovsk, USSR: Pedagogical Institute, 1965).
37. ——— (ed.): *Voprosy kompleksnogo issledovaniya kozhno-opticheskoy chuvstvitelnosti* (Questions of complex research on the skin-optic sense). Sverdlovsk, USSR: Pedagogical Institute, 1968).
38. ULLMAN, M.: Interview in *Psychic*, May-June 1971, pp. 5–7.

HISTORY AND DEVELOPMENT OF PARAPSYCHOLOGY IN SOUTH AFRICA

Marius F. Valkhoff

In November 1954 a few members of the British and of the Dutch Society for Psychical Research and people interested in American parapsychology met at Mrs. V. Carleton Jones's Parktown residence in Johannesburg and founded the Study Group for Psychical Research. The group met monthly and aroused such an interest that it was decided to develop it into a South-African Society for Psychical Research with a constitution corresponding more or less to that of the British SPR. The inaugural public meeting took place in the Chelsea Hotel on June 28, 1955 with Professor Arthur Bleksley delivering a lecture on "The Quantitative Method in Parapsychology" which he followed with a collective ESP experiment. In this way we made history in South-African science, because this had never happened before.

It may be stimulating to note that the latest collective ESP experiment took place in the main Geology amphitheater of the University of the Witwatersrand (Johannesburg) on August 11, 1970. It was devised by our present chairman Dr. D. C. Pienaar, and conducted by him with our Research Officer Dr. J. C. Poynton and a number of other collaborators. It attracted such a crowd that we had to refuse entrance to very many latecomers. Due to the absence overseas of Professor Bleksley, the experiment was organized by the above-mentioned people on behalf of the South-African Institute for Parapsychological Research (SAIPR, established in 1969), of which he is the Director.

From its inception, the South-African SPR has always been open to all races and, for this reason, we never applied for a Government subsidy, which we probably would have obtained, but that would have tied our hands and forced us to observe racial discrimination.

South Africa with its multiracial population offers a great potential for psychical research. We have Africans, Indians, and the "Coloureds" (approximately two million descendants of white settlers and Hottentot and slave girls). We have some classical studies dealing with paranormal phenomena among them, such as Dr. B. J. F. Laubscher's *Sex,*

Custom and Psychopathology among the Xhosa (London, 1937), written when he was a physician in the Transkei, and Afrikaans poet I. D. du Plessis's books on the beliefs of the Cape Malays, such as *Poltergeists of the South* (Cape Town, 1966).

Since 1937, very little has been published from a parapsychological point of view about psi among the Africans, by far the largest population group in the Southern African racial setup (eighteen million in the Republic of South Africa alone). Therefore it is particularly pleasing that we now have with us as colleague and friend Dr. John C. Poynton who specializes in this type of research among the Zulus, our main Bantu tribe.

However, we did investigate cases reported to us. In the early 1960s, in collaboration with a few journalists, I investigated a poltergeist case in a Bantu location near Germiston, and I had a witchdoctor and herbalist, called Joshua, in my own yard for nearly a year. He and I became friendly and I will tell you something about his working methods. In 1957, my University had already accepted an M.A. thesis entitled "The Study of Ukuthwasa" by L. Mqotsi. One might freely translate "Ukuthwasa" as "phenomena announcing paranormal aptitude among youngsters and young men and women." On March 7, 1960, we presented a lecture by the African psychologist Nimrod Mkele on "Divination and Diviners among Africans"; it was published in our fourth yearbook. But I do not want to cut the grass from under the feet of my old friend John. So I will move on to experiments with the white population.

Now, when I left Holland and came to South Africa in 1951, I was soon struck by the unique opportunities for research into paranormal phenomena, as compared with my native country. One might at first ascribe the high incidence of phenomena in South Africa to the wide variety of racial and cultural groups. But when I read Dr. Laubscher's book *Where Mystery Dwells* (Cape Town, 1963) in order to write the preface, I noticed that most of the cases he presented had occurred in Afrikaner (or Boer) families. I would agree here with the famous South-African anthropologist Dr. M. D. W. Jeffreys that the Hottentot and halfcast Hottentot nurses are responsible for this. They were very prone to belief in the supernatural and very near to the paranormal and, for more than two centuries, have brought up the Afrikaner children. To this day, they are still found amongst South-West African white families. They have been absorbed by the so-called "Coloureds" and they still regularly—and secretly—pass the color-bar into the white population, usually the Afrikaans-speaking section.

This observation should not prevent us from noting the large number of Spiritualistic circles and churches in the big (mainly) English-speaking towns, Johannesburg, Cape Town, and Durban, which also offer a great variety of paranormally gifted people. Last year I took part in the investigation of two remarkable bona fide mediums, Mrs. Gertrude Harding and Miss Sheila Wahl.

At the (Johannesburg) National Institute for Personnel Research, Dr. A. Mundy Castle not only initiated mescaline and LSD experiments with volunteers, but also started research into EEGs of spiritualistic mediums. These mediums were tested and selected by us on their bona fide, and this is to my mind the reason why this research, continued by Mr. Gordon Nelson, Mundy Castle's successor, has proved successful (see *Parapsychologica IV:* "Preliminary Study of Encephalograms of Mediums" by G. Nelson).

In the late 1950s we started a series of ESP experiments in Professor Bleksley's laboratory, with Mrs. Mary Heideman, Mrs. L. O. McKerchar and Miss Viviane Valkhoff as principal agents. We carried on for some two years with members and other interested people volunteering for it. We concentrated on a particular phenomenon: there was often more agreement between recipients, especially if closely related, than between agent (sender) and recipient (receiver), even when most of their guesses were wrong. After recording the results, we called it cross-connection. Recently Professor Bleksley has taken up the old file again, studied the rate of success of the various agents, and discovered significant differences.

A Marius Valkhoff Medallion was created for meritorious work in the field of psychical research. It was presented for the first time in 1960, to Dr. Eugene Marsh who had been the first to write an extensive doctoral thesis on a long-distance psi experiment between students of Rhodes University (Grahamstown) and an agent in Cape Town, who was completely unknown to them. Marsh's work gave rise to a long controversy with the Johannesburg Rationalist Society, which finally had to resort to the disreputable "fraud" hypothesis. This thesis on a parapsychological subject was followed by a number of others on similar themes.

Also in the 1960s, Professor Bleksley was awarded the Eighth McDougall Award for his most significant so-called "clock experiment" with a Dutch immigrant, Mr. W. van Vuurde, who could wake himself up at set times, unknown to him, indicated on a clock 900 miles away. ("An Experiment on Long-Distance ESP during Sleep," *Journal of Parapsychology*, 27, 1, 1963). This piece of research by Professor Bleksley was a landmark in the history of parapsychology in South Africa.

Another milestone was reached when the Society was invited by the

South-African Psychological Association to take part in a Symposium on Parapsychology at their September 1966 Congress. Four of our members were chosen to present papers on this great occasion.

In the late 1960s the Students Art and Science Councils of the University of the Witwatersrand invited Bleksley, Poynton and myself to organize a symposium on, and an experiment in ESP in collaboration with them. About the same time, the University Library Committee gratefully accepted a grant from the Parapsychology Foundation to set up a section on Parapsychology in the Witwatersrand University Library. This section had up to then been accommodated in the Alfred Hoernlé Collection; the late professor of philosophy had been the first to show a marked interest in this subject (he was a member of the British SPR) and to introduce it to the University.

These two events (the Students Symposium and the acceptance of a Parapsychology Book section) show both a change of opinion in favor of parapsychology and the close relationship with professors, lecturers and students of the University of the Witwatersrand. Several have been members of the Society or even Committee members (I will just add here the name of a faithful supporter, Professor L. A. Hurst, Head of the Department of Psychiatry, who was also our vice-chairman and chairman for two years).

Now most of us South-African parapsychologists—not only the University teachers—had full-time occupations and also social commitments. Every time our Society is mentioned in the press we receive fan mail relating to presumptive cases of paranormal occurrences, some of which we would like to follow up. We had to run our Society as well as devise experiments, answer letters and accept invitations to spiritualistic séances, or to meet people who think themselves psychics.

Fortunately this difficult situation was alleviated by the appointment of Dr. John Poynton (in 1964), and later on, of Dr. D. C. Pienaar, as Research Officers. Finally, in 1969, the South-African Institute for Parapsychological Research (SAIPR) was established under the kind auspices of the Parapsychology Foundation and the Directorship of Professor Bleksley, and it ought to bring relief to this difficult situation of a Society whose role should be mainly informative.

To wind up this aperçu, which may be easily elaborated on, I cannot do better than to make mine the concluding words of Mrs. Phyllis Scarnell Lean, one of our Johannesburg "first ladies" and our competent Honorary Secretary in 1969 and 1970 (see report in *Parapsychologica IV*):

"It is not for a reporter, preparing a news sheet, to say what should be the next move. Mine is a de post facto job, but on a personal note,

I have enjoyed making many new friends and have found the effort of this new approach to the unexplained laws of nature and the powers latent in man to have been very worthwhile. One thing is certain, the conduct of the affairs of these twin societies, the SPR and the SAIPR, requires, as does any other business, money, efficiency and enthusiasm."

PARAPSYCHOLOGY IN SOUTH AFRICA

J. C. POYNTON

South Africa has a relatively small and extremely heterogeneous population spread over a wide geographical area. This gives the country peculiar difficulties and opportunities, and this paper, if it is to present a reasonably accurate picture of parapsychology in South Africa, will have to pay more attention to the difficulties and opportunities than to the definite achievements to date.

RESEARCH ON THE BANTU

This is nowhere more obvious than in the case of parapsychology research on the Bantu, or African Negroes. In all the tribes and nations of the Bantu in South Africa, belief in the efficacy of witchcraft and the action of ancestral spirits is very strong, even in urban populations. This provides an obvious field for research, and much excellent work has indeed been done. But I should turn to the difficulties immediately by emphasizing a distinction that I think should be made between what may be called the anthropological-sociological level of research and the truly parapsychological level of research.

I would include in anthropological-sociological research the study of beliefs, customs, materials and techniques associated with the practice of witchcraft and ancestor-worship, and also the sociological and psychological implications of these supernatural beliefs and practices. This level of research also includes the comparative study of these beliefs and practices in different tribes, and attempts to trace their common sources.

The parapsychological level, on the other hand, I consider to be concerned with the question of whether there is in the practice of witchcraft and ancestor-worship a demonstrable operation of psi. Parapsychological research would thus investigate, for example, what score a professional diviner could obtain above a clearly-determined chance level of scoring, or what type of experience and manifestations (if any) help to maintain a belief in the action of ancestral spirits.

To date, research into Bantu witchcraft and ancestor-worship has been almost entirely at the anthropological-sociological level. On the one side there has been a tremendous amount of research into customs, techniques and materials used in supernatural practices, and on the other side there has been research of a more sociological nature, well summarized in the following extract from an inaugural lecture delivered in 1954 by P. Mayer, Professor of Social Anthropology at Rhodes University, Grahamstown:

"Social Anthropology, then, is concerned with finding out what is the basic reality underlying witchcraft ideas. When I say reality I do not mean physical fact. Even the most optimistic fieldworker does not expect to see anyone flying on those well-known broomsticks. The kind of reality we are searching for is social and psychological."

This excerpt reveals an attitude held by probably the large majority of those working at the anthropological-sociological level, namely a disbelief or lack of interest in evidence for the operation of psi. To give a more recent example, in a lengthy symposium published in 1969 under the title *Spirit Mediumship and Society in Africa,* there is—despite the suggestiveness of the title—practically no information of a strictly parapsychological nature.

It is for this reason that I think it is necessary to recognize a distinction between anthropological-sociological and parapsychological levels of research, and also to recognize that although a great amount of investigation has been made into supernatural practices at the anthropological-sociological level, almost nothing of this research can be included under the heading of parapsychology.

This is not to deny that the anthropological level of research is relevant to parapsychological research. On the contrary, it would be hopeless for anyone to launch into a parapsychological study of the Bantu without many years' grounding in Bantu customs and the approach of the Bantu to the supernatural. Their approach and customs are very different indeed from what one is used to in Western European civilization. And here indeed lies one major reason why almost no truly parapsychological literature on the Bantu exists: the field of research demands a rare combination of both anthropological *and* parapsychological knowledge, understanding and talent. The other major reason for a lack of parapsychological literature is that those who possess this combination are involved in so many other affairs—including the matter of earning a living—that they simply have not sufficient time to write adequately in this enormously difficult field.

However, I am glad to be able to report that two distinguished authors are at present writing up their extensive observations on psychic phenomena amongst the Bantu. One author is a psychiatrist, Dr.

B. J. F. Laubscher, who has made a study of the Xhosa of the Eastern Cape Province. The other author is an educationalist and Zulu historian, Mr. C. T. Binns, who has been working with the Zulus of Natal. I would have liked to report that parapsychological studies were also being taken up by Bantu investigators themselves, but so far contributions by Bantu writers are essentially at the anthropological-sociological level of research, and are influenced by contemporary prejudice against any serious study of the supernatural.

As regards my own work in this field, I have been trying to circulate an out-of-the-body questionnaire amongst the Zulus. This questionnaire, which I shall discuss later, met with success amongst the white population of South Africa, and I translated it into Zulu with the intention of carrying out a comparative study amongst the Zulus. So far I have obtained a very poor response, but I believe this is due to difficulties that could be called anthropological rather than to a lack of actual parapsychological material. There is indeed much preliminary evidence that OOB experience is known to Zulus.

I think it would be out of place in this paper to discuss the great difficulties involved in this type of research, since they involve intricacies of local custom and procedure that are of psychological and anthropological rather than parapsychological interest. I have, however, attempted to get some idea of the frequency of occurrence of this experience amongst Bantu subjects by conducting a survey amongst first-year Bantu medical students at the University of Natal. Only four out of sixty-seven students reported having this experience, giving a percentage of about six. This is low compared with percentages of nineten and thirty-four obtained by Celia Green from students in the U.K. This matter is still being investigated.

JOHANNESBURG AND PRETORIA

I would like to turn now to parapsychological studies amongst the white population of South Africa. Most of the achievements in this field have some connection, direct or indirect, with the South African Society for Psychical Research, founded in Johannesburg in 1954. As the principal founder of the Society, Professor Marius Valkhoff, is here in person to tell us about it, I need only say that, since his retirement from South Africa last year, the Society has been continuing in its Johannesburg center. A study group for psychical research is in the process of forming in Pretoria, including amongst its members staff from the two universities located there. A study group has also recently been formed in Natal.

DURBAN

I would like to spend a little time discussing the state of affairs in Natal, because the difficulties and opportunities encountered there to a large extent summarize the situation in the rest of the country, even in Johannesburg. A freely-constituted group of some fifteen people has been meeting at irregular intervals in Durban to attend talks or demonstrations concerning various aspects of psychical research. Amongst the group are senior members of the two local universities, medical and other professional people. It is acknowledged by most of the group that there would be a strong public response to the formation of a branch of the South African Society for Psychical Research in Durban, and that an opening meeting addressed by someone like Professor Arthur Bleksley would go far toward filling the Durban City Hall.

One may well ask, why not start a branch? The answer, I think, gives a good picture of the general situation in South Africa today. Firstly, it is doubtful if the majority of people turning up would be satisfied for long if the Society kept firmly to a strictly scientific approach. The Durban area has a large number of people who support spiritualist circles, yoga schools, flying saucer groups, healing centers and occult societies, and the attentions of most of these people are not particularly helpful to any scientific and scholarly approach to the subject. The tremendous increase in shelving set aside for "psychic" and "occult" books in local bookshops is witness to this enthusiasm.

The second point is that those who at present form the psychical research group realize that, even amongst themselves, too few have done enough solid research into psychic matters to provide a sufficient number and variety of speakers. And so the scientific approach is as little able to meet the present requirements as is popular enthusiasm.

I would not say that popular interest and enthusiasm *necessarily* involve a lowering of scientific standards. But, as in any popular movement, this is always likely to happen simply because of a lack of acquaintance with rigorous procedure. Generally speaking, those who support the various "psychic" circles and groups show a genuine desire to apply scientific standards to their explorations. They fail more through lack of training than through lack of proper intention—although it is certainly true that metaphysical and broadly religious issues are always likely to be pulled in and cause slanted thinking. But it is only fair to say that those of us who have a scientific or academic training do little better in the long run, because we feel paralyzed by heuristic problems. There is a growing feeling in South Africa that a completely new approach to psychical research is needed, and that the whole field and its basic concepts are due for a thorough reassessment.

CAPE TOWN

I would now like to touch on the activities in the third main center in South Africa, namely Cape Town. Professor J. H. M. Whiteman, of the University of Cape Town, has perhaps been given a better parapsychological platform at the University of the Witwatersrand, Johannesburg, under the auspices of the S.P.R. However, last year he gave a series of nine lectures centered around mysticism at the University of Cape Town's Public Summer School. The lectures contain much of parapsychological interest, and are due to be published. It cannot be said that his most recent book, the *Philosophy of Space and Time,* has as yet gained much ground in South Africa, but this is hardly surprising in view of the vastness and difficulty of the ground it covers. However, it seems likely that Whiteman's views will contribute greatly to the impending reassessment and redefinition within the field of psychical research.

Speaking for myself, I find that his *Philosophy of Space and Time* provides the essential conceptual framework for my treatment of out-of-the-body experience. In a later section of this paper dealing with OOB research, I shall try to illustrate this briefly.

The overall situation in Cape Town seems to be very similar to the situation in Durban, but I should mention the Cape Town Psychic Club and Library, which was founded in 1939. This group has a current membership of 187, and a collection of some 2,000 books. Its interests and activities are centered around Spiritualism in a broad sense, which includes the practice of clairvoyance and psychic healing.

SPIRITUALISM

Spiritualism has a wide following in South Africa, despite strenuous opposition from several churches. As a movement, it is consolidated in the Spiritualist Union of Southern Africa, centered in Johannesburg. According to a newsletter published by the Union this year, in South Africa and Rhodesia there are thirty-one associated churches holding services open to the public, with a known following of approximately twelve thousand people. These belong almost entirely to the white population, but a Bantu Independent Healers' Association is registered with the Union.

In passing I might make the observation that Spiritualism seems the obvious form in which Christianity can be carried across to the Bantu, since the Bantu are, through their own religion of ancestor-worship, in one sense practicing Spiritualists already. But practically all Christian missions are in fact totally opposed to Spiritualism.

CURRENT RESEARCH IN JOHANNESBURG AND PRETORIA

Professor A. E. H. Bleksley, Director of the South African Institute for Parapsychological Research, Johannesburg, is working on a final report of his "clock-waking" experiments. Recent work includes an attempt to identify psychological factors that make for successful ESP scoring, but so far no clear correlation between these factors and ESP scoring has emerged. Professor Bleksley has also introduced card-guessing tests into clock-waking experiments on his subject, Mr. W. van Vuurde, and he found that success in card guessing was accompanied by a fall in the success rate of waking according to clock settings.

A mass ESP experiment was held at the University of the Witwatersrand under the auspices of the S.A.I.P.R. last year. The results of this experiment have been worked out by Dr. D. C. Pienaar, but have not yet been published. The aim of the experiment was to study variations in ESP scoring, using three different agents and an audience of some 240 percipients. Zener cards were used. Two sessions were held. In the first session an effort was made to depress scoring by not introducing the agents to the percipients, and by keeping them out of sight throughout the session. Negative scoring was obtained with each of the agents. Before the second session, a lecture on ESP was given, and each agent was then personally introduced to the audience before each test run. In this second session there was significantly positive scoring with two agents, while the third produced a more negative score. The results suggested that by enhancing interest there was an enhancement of ESP scoring, in the sense that the scores shifted significantly further away from chance expectation.

This year Dr. Pienaar was awarded the degree of Ph.D. by the University of South Africa, Pretoria, for a thesis entitled *Studies in ESP: an Investigation of Distortion in ESP Phenomena*. This study was aided by a grant from the Parapsychology Foundation. A particularly interesting feature of this project is the use of a clock card technique. The percipient has to "guess" the position of an hour hand on a printed clock face, a technique which allows evaluation not only of full hits but also degrees of near hits. Significant results were obtained with two percipients. With one percipient the score was significant at a displacement of three hours from the correct position, while the other percipient produced a highly significant score directly on the target.

Tests with Zener cards and color cards were also run. The percipient who was most successful in the clock card tests was also successful with Zener and color cards. This percipient was first spotted through his success in guessing the distribution of cards in the game of bridge. It is interesting that his ESP performance fell after the implications of the test results were discussed with him. He liked to think of his success at bridge and ESP tests as being sheer "luck." ESP and all that it implied did not entirely fit into his picture of life, and he became worried when the full implications of his test results were pointed out to him.

Dr. Pienaar also studied factors in the relationship between percipient and agent, and found that ESP scoring was influenced by three factors: "sheep-goat" and "friends-strangers" differences, and other agent-centered or percipient-centered factors. These various factors show the importance of the type of interpersonal "field" or "climate" established between agent and percipient in laboratory tests.

This year the University of South Africa also awarded the degree of M.A. to Mr. C. Plug for a thesis entitled *A Study of the Psychological Variables Underlying the Relationship Between ESP and Extraversion.* In this project a five-choice screen was given to percipients, which involved picking one of five positions in which the target might appear. No significant results were obtained, but a further exploration of the five-choice screen seems worthwhile.

Research into radiesthesia is being conducted by several members of the South African Society for Psychical Research, notably by Dr. E. Alan Price, who has commenced a study of medical diagnoses made by a successful radiesthesic practitioner. Radiesthesia has been neglected as a field for ESP research, despite the fact that it appears to produce highly reliable results. Figures are not available, but I know of at least twelve full-time radiesthesic diagnosticians in South Africa, all with large practices. Homeopathy is the preferred type of treatment with these practitioners, and some also use radiesthesic "broadcasting" with apparent success. The pendulum and forms of the de la Warr "box" are the instruments used.

Dr. G. K. Nelson of the National Institute for Personnel Research, Johannesburg, is continuing his EEG studies on mediums and other sensitives as material becomes available.

Before leaving the Johannesburg-Pretoria scene, I should mention that plans are being considered for a national conference next year to review parapsychological research in South Africa. This will probably be held in Johannesburg under the auspices of the South African Society for Psychical Research and the Institute for Parapsychological Research.

OUT-OF-THE-BODY RESEARCH

Professor Whiteman has made a signal contribution to the study of OOB experience, a contribution that has been based very largely on his own personal experience. I have approached this field of research as an outside observer, greatly helped by many discussions with Professor Whiteman. I have also received great financial help from the Parapsychology Foundation.

My work is based on a questionnaire of 15 items. This questionnaire is arranged to allow comparisons with a longer questionnaire that is being circulated in America by Dr. C. T. Tart. My questionnaire was initially published in the most widely circulated newspaper in South Africa, the *Sunday Times*. A Zulu translation of this questionnaire was subsequently published twice in the principal Zulu newspaper, *Ilanga lase Natal,* and copies have also been circulated privately amongst the white, Bantu and Indian communities. To date only 122 usable replies have been received, practically all from whites.

Regarding prior physical and mental conditions investigated by the questionnaire, the majority of experiences (76%) occurred during a state of physical relaxation, and when feeling "just normal" mentally (55% of the experiences). A great variety of conditions is shown, including cases ranging from physical activity to coma, and depressed to excited mental states; but as the majority of experiences occurred during a normal physical and mental state, the survey gives no indication that any commonly-occurring stress situation, physical or mental, is potentially useful in increasing the frequency of OOB experiences.

Sixty-five per cent of the experiences occurred without any previous knowledge of OOB experiences having been reported by other people. The accounts clearly stem from raw experience, and the absence of established doctrinal or traditional preconceptions makes consistencies in the patterning of the reports all the more significant. All the main features described in the literature were independently confirmed by those subjects who stated that they had not heard or read of this type of experience prior to having had it.

Seventy-six per cent of the experiences involved "some body or form that you could distinctly see or feel," and in 62.5% of the cases, the forms were reported to be similar to the physical body. In 81% of the experiences, the physical body was reported to have been seen from some position away from it—a state of affairs that convinced many of the subjects that the experience was not a dream. The surroundings were classified as being "normal physical" in 83.5% of the cases.

These results show that, in the majority of cases, OOB experience was very much like physical experience in character. Indeed, several of the experiences were reported to present information about the physical world which was later shown to be correct. Twenty-seven per cent of the cases appeared to give external confirmation of the reality of the experience in this sense, at least in principle, but the question of what is meant by the "reality" of an experience is in fact extremely complex, and much attention is given to this and related problems in the report I am preparing.

"REALITY," MONISM AND DUALISM

What is one to understand by the statement that an experience is "real"? In conventional thinking, an experience is understood to be "objectively real" if it has its basis in physical perception. If it lacks a physical perceptual basis, then it is taken to be subjective or imaginary in some way. But this conventional viewpoint imposes serious limitations on psychical research—indeed, OOB experience becomes subjective or imaginary virtually by definition. Therefore it has to be looked into very closely.

This conventional view, that an experience is "objectively real" only if it has its basis in physical perception, is supposed to be truly empirical (if one takes the essence of empiricism to be that all knowledge has its basis in what is perceived, as opposed to having a basis in speculation or in "innate ideas"). But the conventional view is in fact a distorted form of empiricism that is stunted by a hidden presupposition, the presupposition being that all "objective observation" has its basis in physical sensation only. No allowance is made for the possibility that valid perception can have its basis in some form of *nonphysical* sensation. This physicalistic presupposition distorts true empiricism into the notion that all knowledge has its basis in what is *physically* perceived, and only physically. From this it is easy to argue that psychical research (whose declared field of study is objective nonphysical perception and events) is not a truly empirical or "scientific" field of study.

This damaging physicalistic presupposition can be traced back to naïve ideas about perception. We easily understand that any effective perceiving device acts in part as a screen as well as a receiver, screening out an immense amount of potential data so that only one particular type of reception becomes possible. This screening process is familiar to us in radio tuning, for example. But it rarely occurs to us that our physical sense organs, together with their many extensions provided by modern technology, might also be screening out an enormous amount of potential information that could otherwise be handled by us. Because this possibility does not normally occur to us, we tend to assume that there is in fact *no* information beyond what our physical sense organs and their modern physical extensions are "set" to.

As a result, we posit "objective reality" solely as a three-space-one-time-dimension field that is registered by our physical senses, and which, animal-like, we conceive as the "natural" or physical world, the basis for all our "natural" experience. Having established this, we then automatically tend to disregard the possibility of registering events in other and perhaps more complex space-time fields. In fact, the very idea of such a possibility is commonly felt to be not merely "unreal" but a threat to mental security. It is for this reason that the "supernatural" is a decidedly taboo subject in conventional science.

This animal-like habit has an obvious physical utility, and so its entrenchment during the course of biological evolution can easily be understood. Yet such a habit, which has become congealed in the physicalistic presupposition, cannot sensibly be held to determine an absolute and final standard of "reality." Neither can it be taken for granted that organisms seen to be evolving in a physical system will be absolutely unaffected by conditions which at least to some extent are not referable to that particular system. Whiteman has introduced the term "autonomously objective non-physical experience" to cover orderly experience which open-minded inspection does indeed show to be irreducible to the three-space-one-time physical field, and this class of experience needs to be recognized in addition to the conventionally recognized classes of "objective physical" and "subjective or imaginary" experience.

That the term "objective" is appropriately applied to such non-physical experience is indicated by the possibility of confirmation or corroboration, in a situation allowing detached observation with full powers of reflection and rational judgment. For this is what the term implies in normal physical usage. Such observation shows that the non-physical events have a rational coherence, or conformity with recognizable "laws," which gives an "autonomous" quality to the experience.

Moreover, as Professor Whiteman has said, "The experience is concerned with *things* manifested to all [non-physical] senses and in [non-physical] space and time, as are physical things, and with the same impression of a substance ('reality') behind, prior to, or unifying the appearances." It is therefore possible to speak of non-physical things as well as non-physical perception as being objectively real, recognizing

that the type, range or setting of the perceiving system determines the
type of thing perceived.

The matter of "setting" is very complex, involving the state of the
object and the percipient, and to reach some understanding of the
"realities" of OOB experience, it is necessary to come to grips with
these complexities. Considering first the state of the object, Whiteman
in his *Philosophy of Space and Time* maintains that an object is not
simply its *appearance* to an observer in the physical world; it belongs
"to a substructural or potential universe transcending the physical
universe," so that fundamentally there is the *potentiality* for the object to appear (or become actualized) to an observer who is in either
a physical or a non-physical state.

Now in considering the "realities" of OOB experience, it must be
borne in mind that the actualization of this potentiality will proceed
differently according to the state of the observer. Professor Whiteman
says:

". . . for the actualization of any object to any subject an elaborate
process of selection between the space-time fields of given object, in-
termediate objects and subject, must occur, with an integration or
synthesis, the final result of which is an actualization for the subject
according to the total circumstances on each occasion of the observation."

It follows that if the object enters into some OOB "occasion of observation," differences from a physical manifestation are bound to
occur, since different (entirely non-physical) "processes of selection"
and "integration" are taking place. Therefore it would be naïve to
insist that what is observed in an OOB experience must necessarily be
an exact copy of the physical world if the experience is to be considered veridical. In the early stages of research, a close agreement
with physical experience may be reassuring because of the strength
of the presupposition that an experience is "real" only if it conforms
to physical experience. But the possibility must be kept to the fore
that a deviation from physical experience can have objective causes,
these causes being connected with the process of actualization in states
other than physical.

The ordinary person who is fixated on the physical world will tend
to perceive physical-like surroundings during an OOB experience, because his "processes of selection," being physically conditioned, will
incline toward a physical-like actualization. It will then be quite
natural for him to take this manifestation to be a true physical one.
But the results of my survey incline me to follow Whiteman in believ-
ing that this is a mistaken view. The physical environment, including

the actual physical body, cannot be perceived by the non-physical sense organs. It is not the physical body and other physical objects that are being perceived (or actualized), but rather non-physical copies of them extended in the actualized spatial field of the observer while in the OOB state. To put it somewhat crudely but suggestively, the scene is being actualized at a "level" that is not physical, although the "level" is sufficiently "close" to that of physical manifestation to be mistaken for it.

This matter of levels of experience seems an extremely important factor in considering the reality of OOB experience. The available evidence suggests that there is not one single level or grade of non-physical experience. Rather there is a possibility of individual consciousness manifesting in a hierarchy of levels of experience, and the physical level of experience can indeed be included as the lowest in this hierarchy. Consequently the classification of experience merely into "physical" and "non-physical" must be regarded as an over-simplification.

The grading of experience appears to be strongly related to the degree of physical disengagement. But since no language exists for adequately describing levels at which physical disengagement is strongly developed, current research understandably prefers to keep to the physical-like end of the scale. Indeed, an investigator who tends to consider an experience real only if it copies physical experience would be inclined to disregard the more mystical cases of OOB experience.

But this procedure seems to be seriously limiting. My reason for saying this can take as its starting point the current mind-body controversy, well summarized in the book *The Mind-Brain Identity Theory,* edited by C. V. Borst. The view put forward by Identity Theory is that "mind" and "matter" do not really stand for anything that is different. The commonsense alternative to this view is *Interactionism,* a type of dualism which is generally adopted in psychical research. It is believed that "mind" and "matter" stand for categories that are different, and that there is a real and direct interaction between the two. Its modern form is expressed as "non-Cartesian dualism" (e.g., Smythies, 1967), in which "mind-brain theory" is discussed in terms of different but interacting space (or space-time) fields.

Now the ordinary, physical-like level of OOB experience could be taken to support the idea of some form of dualism. But one can question whether a dualistic "ghost in the machine" conception is of much value in providing a clear understanding of our nature. Indeed, behind the modern Identity Theory there is evidently the realization that dualism ultimately can never provide the basis for a completely intelligible picture of our nature. But because of the prevailing physicalistic bias of contemporary thought, Identity Theory attempts to get beyond dualism by adopting a *physical* monism, and consequently ends in immense philosophical difficulties.

A study of the more mystical (i.e., less physical) type of OOB experience offers a way out of this impasse. For, according to authors such as Whiteman, at higher levels of experience the integration between mind and body (or form) is so complete that the term "duality" hardly applies. The extreme self-evidence or intelligibility that is stated to characterize these levels is indeed attributable to the "one-ness" of potentiality and actualization, of inmost disposition and form. In contrast, in a state of duality, actualized features might be *significant* regarding inner potentiality, but never immediately and completely *intelligible*.

A tendency to disregard the more mystical cases of OOB experience merely keeps research at the level of dualism and inhibits any open-minded study of levels of experience where intelligible non-duality is—according to worldwide meditative or mystical testimony—attainable. Therefore, although in the initial stages of research it might be reassuring to concentrate on physical-like cases, it seems highly desirable to keep in mind the need for a more comprehensive picture of consciousness and its various levels of manifestation.

The recognition of a hierarchy of levels of experience and reality * seems to provide the comprehensiveness that is required, and takes the whole matter beyond the current identity-duality controversy. According to the hierarchical view, an essential "body-mind" identity may be recognized at the highest level of intelligibility, while at lower levels tending toward physical experience there is the development of an increasingly marked body-mind duality (among other kinds of particularization). Finally, at the physical level, lack of intelligibility is such that reality can even appear to be limited to that one level alone, thereby giving rise to a highly paradoxical physical monism. This is the proverbial seeing through a glass darkly, a condition that the study of OOB experience at all its levels can help to set right.

By way of summary, I would like to run through the questions raised in the invitation to participants of this conference.

1. What scientific disciplines are involved in psychical research? In South Africa, work is still very largely exploratory and observational. Standard disciplines, such as psychology and statistics, are naturally involved; and the only specialized technique to be employed so far

---

* See for example Whiteman, *Philosophy of Space and Time*, pp. 365–366, 411–412.

is EEG examination, used by Dr. G. K. Nelson in his study of mediums.

2. Are the various psychical societies, groups or individuals in your area orientated toward the scientific approach, or do they lean to occultism, Spiritualism and related fields? I do not think there is a clear alternative here. I do not believe that a leaning toward occultism and Spiritualism necessarily involves a waiving of scientific standards. In fact, I would say that an interest in serious occultism and Spiritualism might, in the present state of heuristic uncertainty, provide benefits in suggesting ideas for new approaches. But taken generally, apart from the South African S.P.R. and its offspring, the Institute for Parapsychological Research, the tremendous array of groups, circles and societies lean strongly toward occultism, Spiritualism and related fields. The conditions under which a branch of the S.A.S.P.R. is forming in Durban are cited in this paper as an example of the general situation.

3. Is there a marked increase of genuine interest and research in parapsychological studies among students and other young people? There appears to be a marked increase of interest throughout the whole population, and I do not have the impression that this is especially well marked among younger people. I shall take this matter further in the next question.

4. Would you say that the acceptance of parapsychology in American science applies equally in your part of the world? The fact that the 1966 Congress of the South African Psychological Association held a symposium on parapsychology shows that the subject is now being taken seriously. To my mind, student interest in this field is not as significant and immediately important as a marked increase in genuine sympathy and interest among scientists and other academics in the 30- to 45-year range. Many of these, already in senior positions, openly express the need for a fair hearing of scientific research into psychic matters, whereas more than ten years ago I think that very few people in such positions would have cared or dared to express any considered opinion at all.

Speaking of my own experience, I have to say that I was forced into nationwide publicity when I launched my out-of-the-body survey nearly four years ago, and I have no evidence that my standing as a scientist has been affected as a result. Nor have I suffered any unpleasant personal encounters. Yet I believe that ten or more years ago the story would have been very different. It seems that the case for parapsychological research is no longer likely to be questioned in South Africa. What is needed now is the manpower and funds to work this fantastically rich field.

I am most grateful to members of the committee of the South African Society for Psychical Research in Johannesburg for reading and discussing a draft of this paper. Similar help and advice were also given by Professor J. H. M. Whiteman and Mr. J. J. Scheepers of Cape Town, and Mrs. Phyllis Lean, Mr. L. H. van Loon and Dr. A. R. Robertson of Durban.

BIBLIOGRAPHY

BEATTIE, J., AND MIDDLETON, J.: *Spirit Mediumship and Society in Africa* (London: Routledge & Kegan Paul, 1969).
BLEKSLEY, A. E. H.: "An Experiment on Long-distance ESP during Sleep," *J. Parapsycholol.* 27 (1963): 1–15.
GREEN, C.: *Out-of-the-Body Experiences* (Oxford: Institute of Psychophysical Research, 1968).
MAYER, P.: *Witches* (Grahamstown, South Africa: Rhodes University, 1954).
NELSON, G. K.: "Preliminary Study of Electroencephalograms of Mediums," *Parapsychologica* 4 (1970): 30–36.
SMYTHIES, J. R.: *Science and ESP* (London: Routledge & Kegan Paul, 1967).
VILAKAZI, A.: *Zulu Transformations* (Pietermaritzburg, South Africa: University of Natal Press, 1965).
WHITEMAN, J. H. M.: *The Mystical Life* (London: Faber & Faber, 1961).
———: "Parapsychology and Mystical Experience," *Parapsychologica* 2 (1967): 5–15.
WHITEMAN, MICHAEL: *Philosophy of Space and Time* (London: George Allen & Unwin; New York: Humanities Press; 1967).

THE NORDIC COUNTRIES OF EUROPE

Jarl Fahler

One of the most interesting questions in parapsychology is: What scientific disciplines are involved in psychical research? Most people interested in the subject, and with enough experience both in parapsychology and science in general, would answer, "Many." It is also quite possible that developments in a variety of scientific disciplines may open the door to further, perhaps even rapid progress in parapsychology.

As far as I understand, parapsychology is more or less concerned with the inexplicable and the unknown. So is also the thinking man since his earliest philosophical searches. Parapsychology deals with the study of certain phenomena that do not fit the pattern of prevalent knowledge, or do not quite correspond to the laws of nature as viewed by present-day science.

But what do we actually know? Almost everything is unknown and it might well be that we are using the wrong methods of research. We do not even know, or to be more precise, understand the instrument for the search, the human mind.

There are such great scientific capacities in man, and yet so much anarchy. This imbalance is a cause of havoc in the world. The intellectuals, who have played with so many theories and ideas, have certainly not found the way out of the greatest difficulties. Not even the most expanded science has helped. It is quite obvious throughout our world of neurotic conflicts and compulsions, and aching misery, that no religion, no law, no social morality, not even all the science of the day have been able to bring about sanity and harmony. Is not the explanation for all this—in the widest meaning—that we do not understand the human mind? Our own mind and, perhaps, at the same time, the mind of man?

The mind, with its extraordinary capacities for scientific discoveries and their implementation, is still so narrow, so petty, And parapsychology has, for sure, very much to do with the mind. Man does not, with all his science, understand the world he is living in. The reali-

ties, or the reality parapsychology is investigating—it may be called
ESP, telepathy, clairvoyance, precognition, psychokinesis and so on—
will probably become, by necessity, more and more a very important
science.

The interest of psychical researchers has led to investigations of
spontaneous phenomena or seemingly paranormal events that occur
outside the laboratory or outside any designed or planned setting, as
well as of laboratory experiments. This activity has in turn led to researches of significance to psychology, psychiatry, physics, physiology,
medicine, pharmacology (psychopharmacology) and religion.

The position of parapsychology is the direct result of its heritage.
It must deal with phenomena that, because of their unusual character, have traditionally aroused a high degree of emotionalism. One
readily observes that in many civilizations both past and present, phenomena carrying magical connotations continue to create reactions
that range from superstitious total acceptance to some sort of defensive total disbelief. But we also know from the whole history of man
that many dreams of the magical have been translated into techno-
logical inventions and practical applications.

Parapsychology already offers a challenge to many other scientific
disciplines because it so often calls for the services of their most advanced insights and means of exploration. For instance, the fields of
parapsychology and psychology always tend to interact upon each
other. A good deal of work by people in parapsychology has had psychological significance. At the same time, much of the psychical research in recent years has been undertaken by psychologists. (The
same can, at least to some extent, be said about the relations between
parapsychology and physiology and parapsychology and psychiatry.)

One of the first discoveries was that phenomena called telepathy,
clairvoyance, and so on, were connected with a process that was, more
or less, unconscious. It was also noted that unconscious processes do
not necessarily operate according to the logic of the conscious ones.
A problem many investigators have encountered is that the logical expectations of the conscious reasoning may not be those of the unconscious.

Parapsychological research certainly does not exist in some sort of a
vacuum, isolated from other human research. Like any other organized activity, it is a response to needs, individual or social. These
needs have in many old cultures connected parapsychology with what
we call "pharmacology." A process of seeking has been going on all
the time. It is certainly not anything new in the behavior of man.
Man has long tried to get a clearer understanding of the world he is

living in. He has had a feeling that his clarity is dimmed—but does not understand how—and when clarity is dimmed, one's own perception is dull. Then life is rather shallow, meaningless and mediocre. Therefore, man has probably tried for thousands of years to get help from all sorts of herbs and mushrooms.

People often believe that, under the influence of such substances as fly-agaric or mescaline, they have had psychical experiences of great value. It has been thought that the knowledge of the senses and the usual processes of thinking hides another, higher knowledge, from us. This higher knowledge has usually been experienced as timeless and spaceless. Also, parapsychology has recently included, by necessity I feel, studies of altered states of consciousness, often with the help of hypnosis or such chemical compounds as LSD-25, mescaline, and psilocybin. Future discoveries in the field of pharmacology may result in the development of drugs more suitable for effecting changes in the mind favorable to parapsychological experimentation. For one reason or other, man is now turning to the "golden drug" that will bring about sanity and harmony, drugs that promise a psychedelic expansion of the mind, great visions and intensity.

Physiological studies in the field of parapsychology may be viewed as part of the effort linking physical and psychological phenomena. The traditions on which physiological studies in parapsychology are based, are part of man's desire to influence the physical events of the world around him. Man has tried to accomplish this with religio-psychological action such as prayer, incantation and all sorts of magic. Scientific work in this area, at least in the West, began only a little more than a century ago. Among the phenomena arousing interest have been such physical manifestations as alleged apparitions, levitations, and poltergeist phenomena, as well as some form of healing. Much experimentation has been carried out in such different but related fields as psychophysiology, electroencephalography, psychopharmacology, and endocrinology.

So many of us have for so long been used to thinking that psychic phenomena are nonphysical. Why must there be some kind of duality? It is not at all necessary to view psi phenomena or the psi-factor as a response to a nonphysical world. Why could not psi be an aspect of the physical world? Many experiences may not at all contradict the world picture of science, as has been thought, but, on the contrary, may support it.

Whether apparently acausal physical phenomena are analogous to parapsychological phenomena of a certain type may be revealed in the future with the help of more research. There are, however, very

many experiences of mystics, yogis, and others, that appear to support
the modern world picture of the physical sciences. A lot of people
have experienced the disappearance of the borders between the self
and the environment and have found that "inner" and "outer" space
are basically synonymous.

These experiences must be taken seriously. The world is evidently
a whole in spite of its many aspects. The aspects are only the results
of our own reactions to what is called "the world." We are, of course,
a part of the world; we do not stand outside looking at it. And notably in the area where psychology and physics appear to meet, parapsychology may have much to offer.

In the future—so it appears to me—explorations of the self will be
more and more interdisciplinary and will bring together parapyschol-
ogists, psychophysiologists, physicists, psychologists, biologists, anthro-
pologists, investigators of religious beliefs and also searchers from other
professions. After all, has this not happened already? It seems to me
quite correct to call parapsychology the "Science of Man," the science
of integration of all sciences, and, of course, the science of the integration of the mind of man.

There are many psychical societies in the Nordic countries of Europe. Some of them are very definitely oriented toward the scientific
approach. But it is not always so easy for the members of the Board
of a society to keep it that way. The spiritualistic press may fight the
Board's policy with help from such members as want to believe in
their spirits and are seeking comfort, not truth. In the Nordic countries the spiritualists have their own societies, but many of the spiritualists are also members of the psychical societies. In the Scandinavian
countries and Finland, I would say, there is a determination to
strengthen the ties between parapsychological researchers and centers
of education. There is a deep mystical tradition, but also concrete
academic accomplishments. Because many of the members of these
psychical societies have also been outstanding researchers in the fields
of philosophy, medicine, biology, electronics, and so on, it can be
said that the societies and scholars in various sciences have long
worked hand in hand.

I will try to give a brief overall survey of the developments in the
Nordic countries—according to my present knowledge. I will begin
with Sweden.

In Stockholm, we have the 25-year-old Sällskapet för Parapsykol-
ogisk Forskning (Society for Parapsychological Research). As long as
I remember it has been a society with very high standards. It has also
been rather active and stands definitely on a scientific ground. A few

years ago the Society went through a process of reorganization involving changes in the members of the Board. The well-known physician Gösta Rodhe was the former president and Mrs. Eva Hellström, a clairvoyant, respected for many years for her energetic activity on behalf of the Society, was the secretary. Some of the members of the Society also published papers which, in my opinion, were of good quality.

Under the new Board, with Dr. Rolf Evjegård (president) and Eric Uggla (secretary), the Swedish Society for Parapsychological Research seems to be very active. Many of the meetings have been of high standard with prominent lecturers from several fields. A group in the Society has carried out experiments in psychometry at the initiative of former secretary Eva Hellström. Eric Uggla, the new secretary, continued the experiments in psychometry and also carried out a series of experiments in precognition. The results obtained in precognition are promising. There were also some experiments in hypnosis. A book about the spontaneous psychical experiences of Eva Hellström, written by Rolf Evjegård, is under way and will probably soon be published in English.

There is very marked increase of interest in parapsychology in general, notably among students and other young people. The conservative scientists in Sweden have not changed their opinions; they are as much against parapsychology as ever. The positive interest among the students, however, shows promise for the future. At this time there is no parapsychological chair to be expected at any Swedish university.

In Ludvika (Sweden) Haakon Forwald, who has for many years been active in parapsychology, continues his well-known psychokinetic experiments. The details of the experiments will be published later, probably in an American journal.

For some years Martin Johnson, perhaps the most active person in parapsychology at this time, has carried out research in Lund; also Nils Olof Jacobson has continued his experiments. Articles about Jacobson's research were published in the *Journal* of the American Society for Psychical Research (January 1969). The Swedish Society for Parapsychological Research possesses a good library. It is now located at the University where it is more easily accessible to students and other interested people.

In Denmark, Aage Slomann was well known for his parapsychological interests and activities. A graduate chemical engineer, Slomann worked in the United States, France and Denmark. At the time of his retirement from the Board of Directors at the Colgate-Palmolive Company in Denmark, he took up full-time parapsychology. He was the president of the Danish Society for Psychical Research and his activities included the establishment of a good library for the Society. This took him many years. He was a tireless lecturer, in Scandinavia as well as in Finland and many other European countries.

Aage Slomann's wideranging interest in psychical research is illustrated by articles in *Psykisk Forum* and other Danish publications, as well as in the Journals of the American Society for Psychical Research and of the London Society for Psychical Research. At the time of his death at the age of 79, in November 1970, he was still active and at work on several articles in the field of psychical research for an encyclopedia. His death was a great loss for psychical research in Denmark, and at this moment it is difficult to say who will take over his work.

Professor Thorstein Wereide was for many years the leading figure in Norwegian psychical research. When he retired, the well-known psychologist, Professor Harald Schjelderup accepted the Presidency of the Norwegian Society for Psychical Research. Schjelderup is the author of *Det Skulte Menneske: Udbevisste og Ukjente Krefter i Sjelslivet* (The Unknown Man: Unconscious and Unknown Elements of Man), a book that has attracted wide and lasting attention in all Nordic countries. It does not, however, deal with the more modern experiments and accomplishments in the field of parapsychology.

The general atmosphere for psychical research in Finland is good. There are, of course, a lot of people who cannot understand that their own picture of the universe might be incomplete or at least imperfect, or that there might be forces at work they have not experienced or do not understand.

Some found these views reinforced by Gösta Lindholm's thesis on ESP, in the Psychology Department at the University of Helsingfors ("Fehlerquellen der sog. ASW-Versuhe," Helsingfors, 1967). Lindholm's concluding statement is: "The ESP researches performed heretofore do not fulfill the requirements set for empirical, psychological experiments. The test procedures in which the sources of error can be exposed in detail are so deficient that from the point of view of science nothing can be said about the phenomena intended to be measured."

Lindholm repeated his statement many times over the radio and on television, and many persons without much knowledge of the field of parapsychology have been influenced by it. But Lindholm's material is so weak, his approach so strongly dogmatic, and his refusal to listen to other people in public discussions so obvious, that intelligent people do not seem to take him seriously. There has been very strong criticism, not only of his thesis, but also of his inflexible attitude and his refusal to seek proper information.

The lack of funds is the only obstacle to time-consuming experimental projects requiring proper technical equipment. This is a pity, because what really is needed is the kind of investigation that goes on uninterrupted from year to year. But it is a fact that there are no funds for parapsychological research at the moment. It is apparently easier for organizations concerned with spiritism, flying saucers and other such beliefs to obtain funds.

As is the case, for instance in Sweden, the conservative scientists in Finland have certainly not changed their negative attitude; they are as much against parapsychology as before. But there are some young scientists, a great many students, and some of Finland's most outstanding older scientists who not only have an open mind in general but also a genuine interest in psi phenomena and parapsychological research. To mention a few scientists: Sven Segerstråle, professor in biology who devoted many pages to parapsychology in his books *Det Underbara Livet* (The Wonderful Life) and *Elämän Arvoitus* (The Mystery of Life), the latter published in 1968; both are biology textbooks used all over the country; Sven Krohn, professor of philosophy at Turun Yliopisto and former president of Parapsykologinen Tutkimusseura; Professor Väinö Auer, internationally known geologist; and Professor Uuno Saarnio, philosopher and mathematician.

A great number of the younger physicians in Finland have a genuine interest in parapsychology. One proof of this is that both my books *Parapsykologia* and *Hypnoosi* got exceptionally positive and lengthy appreciation in reviews printed in the medical journals. Some of the well-known older physicians have publicly revealed their positive interest in psychical research. Also, during recent years, I have been approached by some university students for help with their projects in parapsychology and related subjects.

I feel it safe to state that the increase of genuine interest and research in parapsychological studies among students and other young people is quite remarkable, although language barriers often are a hindrance in obtaining proper information about international research. The students, of course, understand three to five languages, but people without higher education are rather isolated in this respect (the only textbooks in Finnish in the field are my own: *Parapsykologia*, second edition, 1969, and *Hypnoosi*, second edition, 1968. *Hypnoosi*, although a large textbook on hypnosis and the first ever written in the field in Finland, contains much material directly concerned with parapsychology in its relation to hypnosis.

The Society for Psychical Research in Finland is the oldest parapsychological society in the country. It was established in 1907, under the name "Sällskapet för Psykisk Forskning i Finland—Suomen Psyykkinen Tutkimusseura." For more than thirty years it was the only society of its kind in Finland. Some of Finland's most outstanding men in science, education and medicine have been its presidents. Many worthwhile experiments were conducted and well-known sensitives in Finland and from other countries were invited to Helsingfors. As early as 1910, a book was published by the then president of the Society, Professor Arvid Grotenfelt, on experiments in psychometry with the well-known English medium, Mr. Peters.

Between the two World Wars, the Society was very active. Numerous experiments were conducted with mediums and other sensitives, as well as long-distance experiments in telepathy. Many books on the paranormal were published by Dr. Uno Stadius, the president at that time. One of the books *Ur själslivets Gåtfulla Värld* (The Mystical World of the Mind), published in 1933, should also be of the greatest interest to persons not understanding Swedish.

I was president of the SPR in Finland for many years. It was a period of great activity, with study groups in meditation, hypnosis, yoga, telepathy, and psychometry. Sensitives and lecturers from other countries were invited to Helsingfors, among them the well-known Swedish clairvoyant and psychometrist Lilly Åkerblom; Dr. John Björkhem, from Sweden; Aage Slomann from Denmark; and some mediums from Denmark and England. I attempted to investigate cases of poltergeists, precognitive dreams and many others. I also published numerous articles on parapsychology and related topics in many papers and magazines. My textbook *Parapsykologia* was written to bridge the gap and give some information about the more modern parapsychological activities. Later on, many more books were published that should interest people with a deeper feeling for the mysterious world we are a part of.

My parapsychological researches at the time I was secretary or president of the SPR in Finland as well as later on, have included experiments with ESP and PK (psychokinesis) at a distance and close at hand; studies of the psychological aspects of ESP in hypnotized subjects; mediumistic predictions under hypnosis with the use of pharmacological substances; and precognitive factors in relation to introspective awareness. I also engaged in a survey of spontaneous cases of psi phenomena in Finland and investigated states of awareness in hypnosis with the aid of mescaline, LSD-25 and psilocybin. Some of the experiments have been published in Swedish, Finnish and English.

The articles in English have for the most part been in the *Journal of Parapsychology*, the *Journal* of the ASPR, and *Tomorrow;* one about ESP in Finland appeared in the *Parapsychology Review*, May-June 1970.

The present president of the Society for Psychical Research in Finland is Stefan Tallqvist, engineer and a specialist in advanced radio-electronics. Under his presidentship, many good lectures have been heard at the meetings of the Society. ESP experiments of an exploratory nature are being conducted; one such series with random numbers and an automatic correlator, invented and constructed by Stefan Tallqvist, is in process; others are being planned.

As the Society's official language is Swedish, although many lecturers have given their talks in Finnish when their knowledge of Swedish is insufficient, it has fewer members than the other parapsychological society in Helsingfors, Parapsykologinen Tutkimusseura, whose official language is Finnish. The relations between the two societies are very good (the former president of the Swedish-speaking Society is also a member of the Board of the Finnish-speaking organization). The Society for Psychical Research in Finland is oriented toward the scientific approach.

In 1938, the Society for Psychical Research, which at that time was bilingual, established the Parapsykologinen Tutkimusseura, with Pentti Vuorenjuuri, engineer by profession, as president, and Orvo Raippamaa (who is also a member of the Board of the Institute of Parapsychology in Finland), as secretary.

Parapsykologinen Tutkimusseura is very active. It has about 400 members, and at the monthly meetings held from September 1970 to May 1971, the attendance numbered between 150 and 200. Qualified lecturers have delivered talks (Sven Krohn, Sven Segerstrale, Uuno Saarnio), but there have also been lecturers on such subjects as flying saucers and astrology.

Some years ago, the majority of the members of Parapsykologinen Tutkimusseura were old. Now, most of the members are young or middle-aged. Many of them are students. Study groups discussing various topics meet two or three times a month. Parapsykologinen Tutkimusseura is, according to its charter, oriented toward the scientific approach. The Society shares the library established and maintained by the Society for Psychical Research.

In 1965, the Institute of Parapsychology in Finland was established in Helsingfors, and I have been its director since that time. It was established to supplement the work of other organizations and to coordinate research activities. According to its charter, the Institute was set up to encourage the study of the "deepest layers of the mind," specifically the "origin and nature of parapsychological phenomena, to make available the results of such research and to establish and maintain international contacts and communications in the field."

Most of the work of the Institute has been in the area of public information, to satisfy the great need that exists all over the country. That has, indeed, taken a lot of my time. I have also tried to encourage young people to conduct experiments on a scientific basis, and to acquaint themselves with modern work in parapsychology. I am glad to observe some success in this important task, and it seems to me that we can look forward to some interesting results.

In this connection, one more thing is worth mentioning. I am also president of the Society for Hypnosis in Finland. We have a large scale educational program, both for therapeutic and experimental purposes. The Board of this society has decided to include parapsychology in its educational program. And, indeed, many of the members (physicians, dentists, psychologists, teachers, nurses and persons in other professions related to the field of hypnosis) are interested in parapsychology.

There is still one parapsychological society to be mentioned: Tampereen Parapsykologinen Tutkimusseura, in Tammerfors (Finland). This Society, under the presidentship of the architect Gunnar Strömmer, has directed its efforts toward public information about psychical research and related topics. Gunnar Strömmer has also taken part in mediumistic investigations, and has investigated a poltergeist case. It seems to me that this Society leans much toward spiritualism.

What may then, at the end of this short survey, be said about parapsychology in Scandinavia and Finland at the present time? First, that there is a real interest in parapsychology, and because parapsychology touches so many scientific disciplines, it attracts many representatives from those disciplines. Second, the students are more than ever interested in psychical research, but the academic acceptance of parapsychology in the form of one or more possible chairs in Nordic universities is not to be expected.

HISTORY OF PSYCHICAL RESEARCH IN SWITZERLAND

Theo Locher

This report consists of three parts. The first part deals with the activities of ten Swiss researchers; the second part reviews the development of Swiss parapsychological societies; and the third part, at the request of the President of the Parapsychology Foundation, Mrs. Coly, is a survey of courses in parapsychology at Swiss high schools.

1. TEN SWISS RESEARCHERS

In publishing my "Short Reports on Swiss Parapsychologists" in *Orientierungsblätter*, my aim was to keep alive the memory of eminent scientists. We owe this to our pioneers!

Maximilian Perty

A professor at the University of Berne, Maximilian Perty, as early as 1856, dared to publish his studies on the supernormal. Among his books are *Reality of Magic Forces and Influences of Man, Spiritualism and its Disciples, The Visible and the Invisible World.* In his two-volume *The Mystic Apparitions of Human Nature* he included spontaneous cases down the ages. Professor Perty was familiar with all forms of occult phenomena and his goal was to get nearer to the secret of life and soul. In his younger years, he was convinced that all facts can be explained without the acceptance of the survival of personality after death. Later, he changed his mind.

One must admit his courage and perserverance in his struggle to prove the existence of paranormal phenomena years before the foundation of the Society for Psychical Research in London. We are astonished to find in his books such modern concepts as: "In the original condition of the human soul, space and time, near and far, past and future are not separated."

Theodore Flournoy

Dr. Flournoy, a psychologist and philosopher, born in 1854, was a professor at the University of Geneva. He was especially interested in mediumship and somnambulism. Under controlled conditions he observed Eusapia Palladino's mediumship in her successful séances in Paris. In 1911, he published the results of a questionnaire of the Spiritual Society of Geneva, combined with his own researches, in his book *Esprits et Médiums; Mélange de métapsychique et de psychologie.*

For five years he worked with Hélène Smith, the famous medium who produced the "language of the Martians," an artificial script and language of her subconscious mind, as we have to assume. Speaking and writing fluently while in trance, in this grammatically well-built language, without prior training is a demanding performance. As an Indian princess, in her trance, she displayed detailed knowledge about life in India in former times. Professor Flournoy, however, refused to accept the spiritistic explanation for all these phenomena. His best known book is *Des Indes à la planète Mars.*

Georg Sulzer

A High Judge of the Canton of Zurich, Georg Sulzer, who died in 1929, specialized in mediumship. He published numerous works on trance states, séances, the significance of psychical research to religion, etc. Sulzer postulated a world of fine matter, invisible to most of us, where many different entities are living. He exerted a great influence on the young engineer Karl E. Müller of Zurich, of which we will speak later.

Carl Gustave Jung

C. G. Jung, born in 1875, must be considered the most important psychologist of the subconscious. His experiments in 1899-1900 with a young medium resulted in his doctoral thesis "On the Psychology and Pathology of the So-Called Occult." He was a professor at the University of Zurich and at the Federal Polytechnical University in Zurich. His association test brought him the doctor honoris causa of a university of the United States. Some of his theories, such as on Synchronicity and on Archetypes, showed us new ways to understand extrasensory perception.

The paranormal events in Jung's life were published by Aniela Jaffé in 1961, after his death, in the book *Erinnerungen, Träume, Gedanken.* With Professor Eugen Bleuler and Dr. von Schrenck-Notzing he conducted experiments in psychokinesis and materialization with the famous trance-medium Rudi Schneider. Later, with Professors Bleuler and Bernoulli, he obtained other paraphysical manifestations with a Zurich medium. In the C. G. Jung Institut in Zurich, about 1500 spontaneous cases, gathered by a Swiss newspaper, were examined and compiled in a book published by Aniela Jaffé.

Mrs. Fanny Hoppe-Moser

A researcher in biology, Mrs. Moser got interested in psychical research after witnessing a violent and long-lasting table levitation in 1914 in Berlin. Her two-volume *Okkultismus—Täuschungen und Tatsachen* (Occultism—Deceptions and Facts) was published in 1935. Emphasizing the animistic point of view, the work comprises nearly all psychical and physical types and it remains to this day a valuable reference book because of its extensive index of names and subjects. In 1950 Mrs. Moser published in her book *Spuk* the 27 best verified haunting cases of her great collection.

Guido Huber

Guido Huber was a high-school teacher in Davos, and founder of a private school. He died in 1953 after a hard life devoted to the study of survival. His rich personal experiences in the supernormal and in altered states of consciousness, combined with his fundamental studies of related literature, led him to the conviction that a narrow connection exists between our world and the world beyond. In his book *Akaca* (the mystic space), he offers the third explanation for paraphenomena, the world-consciousness, which is touchable and which is beyond space and time. Dr. Peter Ringger edited two of his works posthumously. One is *Life After Death* which contains numerous cases of varied paranormal phenomena with evaluations of actual theories. The other, *Extrasensory Gifts* deals mainly with paraphysical events.

Karl E. Müller

Karl Müller was born in the States in 1893. He took part in trance séances when still a young boy. As president of the Geistige Loge Zürich he held a responsible position. He spoke many languages, lectured extensively abroad and participated in the congresses of the International Spiritualist Federation. He was president of the Federation from 1958 to 1963. By his careful development of a gifted medium, he succeeded in producing telekinesis, direct voice and materialization in his apartment in Zurich. A number of infrared photos of these physical phenomena were the successful result of his experiments.

His main interest was in reincarnation. He left unfinished a work on this subject when he died in 1969. Many publications in different languages, mainly on spiritualism and exteriorization, made this kind and humorous researcher known in many countries.

Gebhard Frei

Dr. Frei (1905-1967) was a priest and a professor of philosophy and comparative religion at the Theological Seminary of Schöneck-Beckenried. His more than 400 publications touch upon many different sciences. An important contributor to the parapsychological journal *Neue Wissenschaft*, he wrote articles on magic, problems of fluid dynamics, meditation in Christianity and Yoga, etc. In his work *Rätsel der Seele*, he gave us an extremely valuable bibliography of the literature on the psychology of the subconscious, listing the parapsychological works of about 420 authors.

Up to his death in 1967, he was the president of Imago Mundi, an international group of Catholic philosophers and parapsychologists which issues irregularly a publication of the same name.

Peter Ringger

Dr. Ringger founded in Zurich, in 1951, the first scientific Society in Switzerland, the Schweizer Parapsychologische Gesellschaft. The previous year, he had started publication of the periodical *Neue Wissenschaft,* and for eight years, remained its editor. Thanks to Dr. Ringger's numerous international contacts with many well-known researchers, the *Neue Wissenschaft* was supplied with a great many articles of importance, and reputed scholars, Swiss and foreign, lectured at the Schweizer Parapsychologische Gesellschaft.

Dr. Ringger's principal works are *Parapsychology, The Problem of Obsession* and *The Creed of Parapsychology.* In a very objective way, he treats the problem of Animism-Spiritism.

Friedrich A. Volmar

Friedrich Volmar was awarded the second prize for 1970 by our Swiss Association for Parapsychology for his book *Berner Spuk.* For years, Volmar devoted himself to the study of the literature on and the investigation of haunting cases.

We know that this list of Swiss parapsychologists is by no means complete, and we hope that at a later date, a competent collaborator of our Association will work out biographies of all Swiss parapsychologists worthy of mention. However, these ten briefs of Swiss researchers show that our small country did add a valuable contribution to the investigation of the paranormal and of the "other side."

2. SWISS SOCIETIES

In our larger towns in Switzerland, we have many spiritualistic groups, working in private. Other groups are more public-oriented. Geistige Loge Zürich organizes public conferences with trance subjects. Many small organizations, groups, religious circles, often with grandiloquent names, pursue studies in paranormal phenomena, but not in a scientific way.

There are some bookstores in Zürich, Berne, and other large towns, specializing in esoteric, occult and parapsychological literature.

For a long time there were scientific spiritualistic organizations in Lausanne and Geneva, especially in the time of Dr. Raoul Montandon, who was also a very active parapsychologist and published several books on physical phenomena.

Schweizer Parapsychologische Gesellschaft Zürich (SPG)

In 1951 Dr. Peter Ringger of Zurich founded the periodical *Neue Wissenschaft,* as already mentioned. In 1952 in this periodical he made an appeal to his readers for the foundation of a Society, and that same year, the Schweizer Parapsychologische Gesellschaft was established by 40 members with Dr. Ringger as its president. He was greatly helped in his administrative duties by H. E. Hammerschlag of Berne, and other members.

The chief interests of the Society were the investigation of haunting cases and trance mediumship. To further the cause of parapsychology, Dr. Ringger sacrificed his health and his money. In 1958, his illness forced him to leave the presidency to Dr. Hans Naegeli-Osjord, who has been the president until now. Among Dr. Ringger's publications are *A Self-Witnessed Haunting Case, Parapsychology Today,* and *Psychopathology of Man Seen by Psychiatry and Parapsychology.* From time to time, Dr. Naegeli also lectures in other towns and countries. Vice-president of the Society is Dr. Hans Wyss, who published in his own publishing house several books on border areas of psychology, written by him and others.

The SPG organizes a large lecture program every year, but only in the town of Zurich. Unfortunately, there is little note of this in the press. Most of the administrative work rests on the shoulders of Mrs. von Muralt, the leader of the Arbeitsgemeinschaft. Although there are working-groups for different subjects, no results of experiments were published. The SPG owns a precious library of 500 books. Last year, it resumed the publication of its own small periodical, the *Parapress*.

Our Swiss Association for Parapsychology

The newspaper *Schweizer Beobachter* published in 1954 numerous cases of paranormal phenomena gathered by our people. This was the beginning of my intensive study of the scientific literature of parapsychology. In 1966, after attending two courses at popular high schools, a group founded a local society for psychical research, the Vereinigung für Parapsychologie, where Professor Dr. C. A. Meier from Zurich gave a lecture. The aim of our Society is:

a) The diffusion of information on paranormal phenomena and possible explanations of the phenomena.

b) Mutual exchange of experiences.

c) Examination of cases and research.

d) Collaboration with Swiss and foreign societies.

As President, I was greatly helped by Ernst Studer of Nidau, a retired teacher well-versed in parapsychology.

Also in 1966, I began to publish our *Bulletin für Parapsychologie,* which appears twice a year. It contains news of research abroad, new spontaneous cases and their explanation, as well as reports on the activity of our Society. Every lecture organized by us in Berne, Bienne, Solothurn, or other towns is summarized in the Bulletin. The Bulletin also gives a short course on the various types of phenomena. Many of my collaborators, especially pupils from my school, help with the mailing of the Bulletin and of other publications.

This summer, our first issue of the *Orientierungsblätter* (information sheets) was published. This information is for members only. It concerns present problems or gives surveys of the work of former researchers or mediums.

Our activity consists of public lectures, discussions, information to the press through advertisement, announcements of lectures and reports of them, interviews, mailing of the Bulletin, of the information sheets, of our bibliography, of separata of articles in newspapers and of our "green sheets," which give brief outlines of various phenomena. We also send samples of our Bulletin to thousands of clergymen, psychologists, and psychiatrists.

In addition to this, we established high school courses in nine towns, which aroused great interest in the public.

In the last years, our administrative duties increased so much that we are thankful for the help of all our collaborators in Zurich and other towns. As our activity spread over German-speaking parts of the country, in 1969 we changed the name of the Society to Schweizerische Vereinigung für Parapsychologie.

Regarding our research work, we conducted experiments in levitation with pupils as subjects, under a great variation of conditions in thirteen sessions. The results were evaluated with a view to deriving natural laws. Eight factors were found to be significantly influencing this still unknown "levitation power." Dr. Schiebeler of Germany, a physicist, has now repeated these experiments in a much more scientific manner with technical instruments.

Treatment by a healer was studied in more than twenty cases of illness: verification showed that, as a whole, the healer's influence was effective, although we don't know what sort of influence it is (this healing effect was discussed in an issue of our Bulletin).

Investigation of the famous haunting case of Thun gave me an opportunity to gather observations from the neighbors of this house (about ten). The full report was published in Swiss newspapers. It is the same case that was verified by Professor Bender, by Mr. and Mrs. Paul Andres and by Mr. Friedrich A. Volmar.

A student organized a survey, by means of a questionnaire, of the attitude of two selected groups, in rural and in urban areas, toward twelve paranormal phenomena. She presented the statistical results in colored graphs, a copy of which is in the hands of the Foundation.

We tested many people, especially people with paranormal gifts, with our new test-recorder under different conditions. This fully electronic recorder registers the scores of clairvoyance tests in the past, present and future in the same series. To date, we have to admit that no results of any significance have been obtained. Our experimenters were people educated for different professions and we hope we can later enlist their cooperation in our research program.

More than twenty voices on tapes were systematically analyzed and results entered on special sheets by twelve reliable people. One of our scientific assistants is now working out the statistics of the results, i.e., an evaluation of the vowels, the consonants, and syllables.

A medical student is now experimenting on the influence on plants of water treated by a famous Swiss healer.

Last summer, I had the opportunity to study the phenomena produced at Camp Silver Belle in Ephrata, Pennsylvania. My comments on the numerous physical manifestations I witnessed were published in our Bulletin of May 2 and June 1. Every one of us heard the voice of his "Master," who was always a famous personality of history. Every one "saw" a number of his dead relations, who neither understood nor spoke their mother tongue. The most astonishing fact for me was that nearly everyone in our European group—we were 49—remains convinced that those direct voices, full materializations, etc., were genuine.

Since 1968 our Swiss Association for Parapsychology, on the occasion of its General Assembly in the University of Berne, has given out prizes for scientific work in levitation experiments; clairvoyance evoked by suggestion; research on voice tapes; new precognition tests with Duke University students; influence of water treated by the laying on of hands on the growth of beans; compilation of explanations of paranormal phenomena since Immanuel Kant; Dr. Gerda Walther's life work in parapsychology; and investigation of cases of haunting in the cantons of Berne and Valais.

The 1971 prizes were given for the following work: Experiments in radiesthesia and its useful application; extremely successful card tests in France; and contribution to research on the haunting case of Rosenheim. Prizes were also given to the late famous trance medium Willy Schneider of Braunau and to the constructor of our test-recorder, Gerhard Badertscher.

This prize-giving was well received, and our Association intends to continue it. As the number of researchers in Switzerland is still very modest, the majority of the prizes went to researchers from Germany, Austria, France and the United States.

During the first two years of the foundation of our Association, we were very careful in our selection of subjects for public lectures, public high school courses and notices in the press, so that parapsychology and our Society were never attacked in the public. We have always made the most of every possibility to make parapsychology better known. We are happy to say that thanks to our efforts the science of parapsychology and our Association have a good reputation and parapsychology is now known to a great part of our lay people as well as in academic circles. Many of our members are college students, but we do not have enough students who could enter psychical research in coming years. However, our young people show definite interest, as evidenced by their attendance at our lectures and popular high school courses.

From time to time, I teach classes at the High School of Economics of Bienne and I lecture to other groups. Although our Association displays a very satisfactory activity at present, I feel that too much depends on me and on my health. Therefore, I am looking for a young scientist as chief collaborator.

Parapsychological Association Basle (PAB)

After a lecture given at the Basler Psychologische Arbeitsgemeinschaft in the summer of 1967, Professor Bender suggested the formation of a parapsychological group in Basle. He and his assistants were willing to come to Basle for lectures and discussions. Mr. Güldenstein, at that time secretary to the Basler Psychologische Arbeitsgemeinschaft, gathered a number of interested persons. A university extension class which I gave at Basle in the autumn of the same year helped to increase the number of those interested. Due to the very friendly co-operation of the SPG of Zurich, the SVPP of Bienne, and Professor Bender's Freiburg Institut für Grenzgebiete, the Parapsychologische Arbeitsgruppe Basel was always able to get good lecturers. By the autumn of 1968, the PAB became independent—with about 40 members. The constantly growing interest is best shown by the fact that the number of members is expected to have increased to approximately 100 by the autumn of 1971. An average of ten lectures yearly were given (a few of them were open to the public). Apart from these lectures, the members had the opportunity of discussing special problems in small groups and to carry out experiments.

Mr. Matthias Güldenstein from Riehen, near Basle, is a most active and enthusiastic teacher. He is a clever organizer, who from time to time edits a *Mitteilungsblatt* (a newsletter). He is also the organizer of the first Swiss Conference for Practical Parapsychology, which will take place in September of this year.

One of the experiments mentioned above seems worth describing: A subject, obviously extremely well suited for this type of experiment, was hypnotized by Dr. Konrad Wolff in the presence of several other members. Mr. Güldenstein, acting as sender, sat in a separate room. He was equipped with earphones and was listening to vocal music from a magnetic tape. He was trying to transmit his impressions to the subject, known for his affinity to music. At the same time he was also endeavoring to express his impressions by drawing on a sheet of paper. The subject's statements given under hypnosis were taken down in writing. A later comparison of these statements with Mr. Güldenstein's drawings and the "target music" showed such a high degree of thematic and formal similarity that participants in the experiment termed it a great success. This experiment however, can only be regarded as a very encouraging pilot test, as, so far, no objective evaluation of it has been made by outside judges. It is, however, our intention to repeat this and similar experiments on a larger scale and with the greatest possible objective evaluation.

3. POPULAR HIGH SCHOOL COURSES

A popular high school in Switzerland provides academic adult education on a higher level. Such courses are taught in every larger town or district.

From 1965 up to 1971, I gave courses three to six evenings in nine popular high schools. The aims of my courses are to:
—provide objective information about paranormal phenomena and proof that they can be explained by the psychology of the subconscious;
—give a better understanding of the nature of man and his world;
—spread the knowledge of parapsychology to reach the greater part of our population and to bring about public acceptance;
—win new members and subscribers.

How to develop a course

Members and subscribers to our Bulletin are informed in advance of the dates and subjects of the course. We try to publish an article in the local press prior to the course as well as advertise it. We ask a local bookstore to display books on parapsychology with a note about the course. As much as possible, we draw attention to its educational side. Through personal contact with editors of newspapers, we sometimes manage to have an article published giving the subject of every lecture before or at the end of the course.

As for the lectures organized by our Association, we send out invitations to a number of local personalities and have invitations displayed on the doors or windows of many local shops. We try to cooperate with Societies in different fields and to get rooms in well-known lecture rooms. The dates of our courses and lectures are often published in periodicals other than our own.

All this has so far demanded a great deal of administrative work. Thoroughness and faithful perserverance are necessary.

Subjects dealt with in these courses

At first the danger of public attacks was great. Therefore, in my first courses, I confined myself to the subjects of telepathy, clairvoyance, precognition and veridical dreams. I used Professor Rhine's card tests and spontaneous cases from the scientific literature as a basis, and never mentioned such terms as haunting, telekinesis, or spiritualism.

In the beginning, I always had to explain what parapsychology is and what phenomena are part of this young science. I used to demonstrate this with two concentric circles: in the inner circle I wrote down such phenomena as are accepted by the strict parapsychologists; between the two circles I wrote those phenomena called occult, esoteric, superstitious or supernatural in a religious sense.

I often emphasize that the events and gifts called parapsychological have been proved to exist for quite some time, that many laboratories are experimenting in ESP, that there is a rich scientific literature with hundreds of cases and many periodicals, and that all these phenomena and gifts can be explained. Speaking on Carl Gustav Jung's contributions to parapsychology, I had to expound the thesis of synchronicity in a comprehensible way.

One evening, I gave a survey of the devolpment from occultism to parapsychology, mentioning the foundation of the Society for Psychical Research in London and the work of some famous pioneers. Methods of experimentation were presented with examples, and I showed that some phenomena are independent of space and time.

The following subjects were given in later sessions: psychometry, automatic speaking and writing, the acoustical and visual double, transposition of human senses, paranormal events in the life of C. G. Jung, tests with illustrations, Zener cards and dice, tests under hypnosis, psychokinesis, poltergeists, healers and their methods. Last winter, at three popular high schools, I dealt with the following themes: famous people with extrasensory gifts, such as Harry Edwards, Gerard Croiset, Abbe Mermet, Kurt Trampler and Therese Neumann; gifts that can be tested and those that are helpful to humanity; medical healing and its different methods and experiments with our test-recorder.

I now want to make some suggestions on how to organize such a course. If you wish your listeners and the public to accept the facts, you have to emphasize the scientific character of the quantitative experiments in laboratories such as those of Professors Rhine or Bender. People believe in results, when these are obtained at universities and published by professors. It is of importance that our Association gives lectures at the University of Berne and that we can always refer to courses and lectures that were held there. New instances of our own relationship with the University help people to accept the "impossible." During lectures, I often show books of esteemed researchers. The best way to convince a critical audience of the existence of ESP is to speak in the terminology of natural science and its methods, giving exact details and hinting at the mathematical background. Every explanation, interpretation, definition has also to be scientifically correct from the point of view of the psychologist. It is really not easy to follow all these requirements and at the same time be comprehensible to all listeners as we must never forget that most of them do not hold academic degrees. Examples and a perceptive manner help to make our subject understandable to everybody: the commercial employee, the primary school teacher, the housewife and the artisan. Both the workman and the medical doctor should profit from our course. We often have to repeat a thing in different words, to clarify, to make ourselves understood through the use of illustrations. The academic among the listeners has to realize the exactitude, the thoroughness and the systematical construction of this introduction to a limited group of paranormal phenomena. We must formulate our sentences in such a way that no inexactitude, no error nor false interpretation can be found.

To make our courses more attractive, we often make use of the blackboard and speak freely from our prepared text. It is only in the discussion following a lecture that I speak in our Swiss dialect. Lectures are always held in High German in order to stress the scientific approach.

The progress of one evening

When people enter the auditorium, they either find the main subjects of the lecture outlined on the blackboards or they get the "green sheets" explaining these particular subjects. About halfway in my lecture, I stop and for a few minutes speak of our periodical and of the aims and activity of our Association. Interested people can fill out a coupon for subscription to the Bulletin or to membership.

At the end of my lecture, I or a member of the popular high school would open the discussion. We invite the audience to relate well-remembered spontaneous cases of their own. It often occurs that one of these cases helps to corroborate the given theory. Naturally, there are also muddle-headed thinkers who take the floor for too long a time and try to impress the audience with their weird ideas. Then I stop the discussion and declare the session closed, adding that all interested persons can meet in a neighboring cafeteria to continue our discussion. These conversations in the restaurant are often very useful and create personal contacts. In a short while I often collect a few new interesting cases to verify later on.

After the course

I frequently receive letters and phone calls telling me of paranormal gifts and events. People send me articles from newspapers and draw my attention to healers, clairvoyants or haunted houses.

I usually publish a summarized report of the subjects dealt with in the course in the next issue of our Bulletin. We lose no opportunity to inform people about parapsychology in private and in public.

Special experiences in these courses

There is a fair number of listeners who really follow our courses to obtain objective information on parapsychology. Many of them will maintain this interest. A great part of the listeners themselves or their relatives have experienced paranormal events. Few of them have paranormal faculties. Still fewer are material for scientific research. As to new collaborators, we find them in most cases during discussion after the course. I found many helpers in my own relationships; others came forth after having read our Bulletin or an article in a newspaper.

It is not surprising that in every course there are credulous, mystically-minded people who hope to find a new religion or a confirmation of their sometimes very confused beliefs. More surprising is that they are convinced that I have spoken about their personal beliefs. They find in my words only what they hope and want to hear. They don't understand any of the scientific approach. But my course is nevertheless useful to them; they leave in a happy state of mind and to them the speaker is a fellow on the combat team.

These popular high school courses contributed most to the public's acceptance of parapsychology in Switzerland and its increased interest. As to scientific collaborators, there are educated people keen on experimental and other scientific work. As for myself, I am sorry to say that I have hardly any time for research, as I am fully occupied with the organization of our research program. Besides the management of our Association and the publication of the two periodicals, I am employed as a teacher of mathematics and geography in Bienne. In addition, my work in school problems and in practical psychology demands time. Therefore, I am eager to find young scientific helpers who later can take over some of the courses and lectures.

Let me express in conclusion that we are convinced of the effectiveness of our work and know that it will endure. We remain optimists!

PARAPSYCHOLOGY IN ARGENTINA

J. Ricardo Musso

When the Parapsychology Foundation asked us to write a report about both our work in parapsychology, and the development of parapsychology in our geographical area for this Conference, we felt it was a great responsibility. And we felt so because the request forced us—in a way—to undertake an evaluation and interpretation of other Argentine investigators' work. This was not easy to do, because the methodology we propose for parapsychological studies has not been accepted by other Argentine investigators. They are not present at this Conference and thus will not be able to explain their own points of view on the subject.

To outline the process through which parapsychology as a discipline achieved university status in Argentina, somehow means to tell about the struggles that took place between different methodological tendencies. We say "methodological" tendencies, not "ideological." Though the ideology on which certain hypotheses are based sometimes can influence the methodology with which such hypotheses are justified, when the scientist has to evaluate that justification, methodology, not ideology, is relevant to him and in the Declaration of Principles of the Argentine Institute of Parapsychology we stated our purpose as follows: to subject every hypothesis to a strict scientific examination, so that only those that have withstood the most stringent tests remain.

This methodological principle always prevailed in our own investigations, as well as in our attitude toward others' work and in our classes of parapsychology at the Rosario University (formerly University of the Litoral). We think that this, together with our careful selection of foreign works on the subject (which were translated into Spanish and put out by important publishers in our country), contributed to the fact that parapsychology achieved acceptance and respect on the university campus. But we have not always been understood by other workers in the vineyard. Spiritualists, who for several decades have been actively interested in promoting their own spiritualistic ideas through parapsychology, called our attitude "material-istic" and tried to impede its spread among those who studied the subject. This methodology was also rejected by other colleagues who were not spiritualists, but who carried on their research along a non-critical, qualitative line (the one "metapsychists" applied to those "consulting sessions" with mediums, psychometrists and clairvoyants that prevailed in parapsychology up to the thirties). Our attitude, in-stead, was the one we observed in modern parapsychologists. It led us to investigate with a quantitative methodology and critical caution, attributes that characterize modern work in parapsychology. For our colleagues, though, this methodology was "quantitativist" and too restrictive. They prefer the qualitative methodology we have already referred to. Perhaps they did not realize that, though their methodo-logy was valuable at certain steps of the investigation, it also had its clear limits. It was useful only for the initial steps, those taken to ex-plore the ground and to bring forth ideas for the formation of hy-potheses. But when it was a matter not of formulating hypotheses but of verifying them scientifically, the only methodology which could satisfy strictly scientific requirements was the one we used.

But it is no wonder that scientific methodology in psychology was resisted in our country. In fact, psychology itself had to face resistance. Today it is known that there is no possible science without scientific raw data, and that scientific raw data are empirical (i.e., relative to an observable fact) and have been obtained under such conditions that they can be interpreted without any ambiguity (or at least with a very small margin of ambiguity). It is also known that with raw sci-entific data there must be good control of "strange variables," for if these variables were not controlled, it would be possible to give data a different interpretation from that proposed in the hypothesis and which it is intended to confirm or deny. Finally, it is also known that only one technique, statistical experimental design, can control strange variables when, because they are elusive or unknown, these cannot be controlled through manipulation as is usual in physical experi-ments. Without statistical methodology many branches of modern sci-ence could not have achieved their present development. It is par-ticularly necessary in psychology, as many of its objects of study are not observable and cannot be controlled by manipulation. Without statistical methodology it would have been impossible in parapsychol-ogy to verify scientifically certain hypotheses, such as ESP or PK, which had become plausible through metapsychists' investigations, but had not attained scientific confirmation. In the fifties, when we became interested in statistical techniques because we realized how important they were in parapsychology, they were almost unknown among our psychologists. In our country, investigators did not have enough methodological knowledge to carry out scientific psychological investigations.

There were a few exceptions, such as Dr. Horacio Rimoldi, who tried to instigate the application of statistical techniques to psychological investigations at the Laboratory of Experimental Psychology at the University of Cuyo, in the forties. However, his followers were very few. One of them is Professor Nuria Cortada, at present professor of Psychostatistics at the University of Buenos Aires. As have many other worthy scientists, Dr. Rimoldi had to go to other countries in search of an adequate field. He emigrated to the United States, where, after his work at the University of Chicago, he became an experimental psychologist of international fame. Thus it is possible to understand why critical quantitative methodology, which is characteristic of modern parapsychology, was not widely known in our country. Its development in parapsychology among us was a kind of outpost of scientific methodology in psychological studies, as our psychologists did not have a clear notion of its importance. The teaching of psychology was almost exclusively philosophical or clinical. Even today our psychologists are not taught how to investigate, and it is within this context of psychology in our country that the way parapsychology developed is particularly meaningful. Once again, to outline the development of parapsychology in our country we have to outline the methodological struggles between different groups, as well as the investigations that were frustrated for lack of an adequate methodology.

We shall now take a quick look at this development during the last four decades. We believe that in this way we will be able to present a panorama of the present state of parapsychology in Argentina and of its possibilities in the future.

THE THIRTIES: METAPSYCHICS AND SPIRITUALISM

The first attempts to introduce parapsychological studies in the Argentine university took place about the time that the Laboratory of Parapsychology of Duke University was established in the United States. In fact, on November 24, 1931 the first Institute of Psychology was created in the University of Buenos Aires. The Institute was part of the Faculty of Philosophy and Letters. The Institute was to carry out investigations in different areas, such as general psychology, psychological pathology, psychometry and psychotechniques. To each of these was assigned a special section of the Institute. One of these sections was in paranormal psychology; this was the name by which parapsychology was known by then.

Parapsychology in Argentina appears then joined to psychology within the state university from the beginning, which is easy to understand. In our country there were not such ideological struggles as there were in other countries where psychologists were divided into opposing schools. Psychology was then open to all theories. On the other hand, Dr. Enrique Mouchet, who was Head of the Institute of Psychology, knew the works of such metapsychists as Osty and Richet. He had attended sessions of some clairvoyants who were well-known in Argentina, such as Miss Ilma Maggi, and séances with spiritualist mediums, and he had come to the conclusion that it was necessary to start scientific investigations in this field. For this reason he included paranormal psychology in the syllabus of the Institute, and included these studies in the course of psychology he was teaching at the Faculty of Philosophy and Letters.

Dr. Mouchet was not the only Argentine scientist who promoted parapsychological investigations in the thirties. There are others worth mentioning.

1. On August 12, 1932, Dr. Fernando Gorriti, a psychiatrist, who was Vice-director of the Institute for the Insane, gave a lecture on "metapsychic forces" in the Popular Institute of Lectures, which was owned by the newspaper *La Prensa*. The lecturer was introduced by Dr. Gregorio Aráoz, one of the important personalities in Argentine medicine, who pointed out the need for "confirming the existence of 'metapsychic events,' and, if the results were positive, of seeking an explanation of them."

2. On April 7, 1932 Professor Dr. Gonzalez Bosch, who was Chief Director of the Hospicio de las Mercedes and taught psychiatry to a whole generation of Argentines, carried out some tests of ESP with a well-known psychometrist of Cordoba, Enrique Marchesini. These tests were attended by several professors of the Faculty of Medicine.

3. On April 25, and June 28, 1932, Dr. Efron, an outstanding psychiatrist, gave lectures on "distance communication" by a cross-correspondence technique, and on telekinesis, in which he reported his personal observations during a trip across Europe, where he had got in touch with Dr. Osty, of the International Metapsychic Institute of Paris. These lectures were also given at the Hospicio de las Mercedes and were attended by outstanding personalities of Argentine science.

4. On October 26 and 30, 1933, Dr. Eduardo del Ponte, Professor of Biology at the University of Buenos Aires, lectured about parapsycho-

logical subjects which he had included in his syllabus. Experiences of psychometry and clairvoyance were studied with "gifted" Mrs. Ofelia G. de Ricur and Dr. Luis María Ravagnan, who, right after his personal experiences with ESP, became actively interested in psychology and later became Professor of Psychology both at the University of Buenos Aires and at the University of La Plata. These lectures were attended not only by students, but also by authorities and such university professors as Dr. Juan Nielsen, who was then Counselor of the University.

5. Engineer José Fernández, who was Professor of Physics at the Universities of Buenos Aires and La Plata, studied ESP experiences of "gifted" subjects. He also participated in a public debate which took place on July 19, 1935, in the Modern Theatre of Buenos Aires. Among the audience were several well-known parapsychologists as well as critics of parapsychology. Engineer Fernández presented a defense of metapsychics and reported on the works of Crookes, Richet, Osty and others. He also related his own experiences with clairvoyants, among whom was his wife, Amanda Ravagnan de Fernández, sister of the above mentioned Dr. Ravagnan. He accepted the so-called "metapsychic" phenomena as fact and defended a spiritualistic interpretation of them.

As we see, there were then in Argentine very good opportunities for parapsychology to become a recognized branch of psychology and to be investigated at the University. We have mentioned important personalities in the field, such as Aŕaoz Alfaro, Bosch and Mouchet, who worked at the University and were interested in metapsychics. We have to add the name of Professor Dr. Nerio Rojas, whose interest in this subject led him to attend the sessions Osty presented at the International Metapsychic Institute of Paris.

In September of 1939, Dr. François Moutier, professor at the Faculty of Medicine of Paris, gave a lecture on metapsychic phenomena at the Faculty of Humanities of Buenos Aires. Thus, the works of metapsychists were well known to important Argentine scentists. According to these, metapsychics appeared as a new science neatly separated from occultism and spiritualism, though it had emerged from them. It was because of this division and because metapsychics was separated from occultism, that Argentine scientists began to be receptive to parapsychology. But the Institute which had been created in Argentine in the thirties was to run a very different course from that of Duke University, which had been established by Dr. Rhine in the United States at about the same time. The latter developed and became an active center of modern parapsychology, while the former remained inactive. It failed because it had been premature and because methodology had been inadequate. Toward the end of the thirties interest in parapsychology at the Argentine University had almost disappeared. This was not confined to our country, for it reflected a world process concerning this subject. You will all remember the historic lecture Professor William McDougall gave at Clark University in 1926, when after pointing out the fact that parapsychology was not an easy field for investigation, he said that it required the highest degree of scientific spirit and a good training in scientific methods. Metapsychics had failed because its qualitative methods, which were not adequate for dealing with the elusiveness of psi phenomena, had not been able to surmount the obstacle of scientific criticism. ("Moral certainty," which Bergson proposed as a truth criterion, cannot be a scientific criterion). To remove this obstacle it was necessary to consider criticism and to deal with the elusive character of these phenomena with statistical methodology. That is to say: it was necessary to create modern parapsychology, which is based on that critical attitude and on that methodology.

At the beginning of the thirties, while the university kept silent about parapsychology, there were a few active spiritualist groups. They were in search of an adequate methodology. Engineer José Fernández, to whom we have referred, gave great impetus to this movement. In May, 1933, he founded the ATMAN Spiritualist Circle and he attended the meetings of another spiritualist group, the Psyke Circle. These groups met periodically for séances with clairvoyants and mediums. The answers given by the subjects were registered. Judges evaluated these answers and classified them as right, doubtful, or wrong. In fourteen sessions that took place between June 12, 1937 and October 13, 1939 the number of answer items given by the subjects was 1,966, out of which 1,872 were hits, which is 94.99%. By assigning to each "right" answer an a priori probability of $p = 0.5$, engineer Fernández concluded that the significance of the whole result was $P = 10^{-300}$. In 1941 Engineer Fernández reported these experiences in a pamphlet entitled *Clairvoyance and Probability*, which was published by the Sociedad Constancia. Later he reported them in a lecture he gave at the Argentine Scientific Association (September 19, 1941), which was later published as a pamphlet under the title *The Statistical Method Applied to the Study of Cryptesthesia Phenomena*. Engineer Fernández' conclusions could not have been acceptable from a scientific point of view. The sessions from which data had been gathered lacked elementary critical precautions: possible sensory signs were not controlled and blind techniques were not used in the evaluation of answers. Besides, the estimation of the probability of success for each answer $p = 0.5$ was too arbitrary and the mathematical model which was used to estimate the significance of the whole result ($P = 10^{-300}$), the Gaussian distribution, was not applicable in this case. The model is based on the assumption of the independence of answers, which analyzed data did not satisfy, as many of them originated in the same universe of speech and so were correlated. Nevertheless, Engineer Fernández' works have an important significance within the historical context because they are the first attempt to apply statistical methods to the study of ESP in Argentine. Though controls did not meet the required level in parapsychology, we can find in these works the search for a new methodology. Rhine's works, which were unknown in Argentine thus far, are mentioned in them.

THE FORTIES: METAPSYCHICS AND SPIRITUALISM

During the first years of this decade parapsychological activities were almost paralyzed in Argentine. The war polarized attention and closed all channels of information. But when it was over, activity returned. During the last years of the decade three important events took place with reference to parapsychology: (1) The Medical Association of Metapsychics was created; (2) the Government tried to control spiritualistic practice, which it considered a "social evil"; (3) the Argentine Association of Parapsychology was created; its first members belonged to an important Argentine spiritualistic association. The three events were not independent of one another; we shall consider them in a chronological order.

On October 27, 1946, a group of physicians created the Argentine Medical Association of Metapsychics in the city of Santa Fe. Its chairman was Dr. Orlando Canavesio, a young psychiatrist who had taught psychiatry at the University of Cordoba and who was interested in metapsychics. Dr. Canavesio was preparing his Ph.D. thesis and was particularly interested in obtaining electroencephalographic records of the parapsychologically gifted. In 1942, with the cooperation of two professors of the Faculty of Medicine of Buenos Aires, he obtained the record of a famous clairvoyant, Eric Courtenay Luck, who was known as Mr. Luck. Subsequently, he went on with these experiences and obtained the electroencephalographic record of another gifted psychic Mr. Alfredo Parodi in Rosario (Santa Fe) in 1947. He reported his findings to the First International Conference of Parapsychological Studies in Utrecht, and to the Interregional Meeting of the Associazione Italiana Scientifica di Metapsichica in Bologna, both of which took place in 1953.

In October, 1947, the Argentine Medical Association of Metapsychics issued a publication, the *Revista Medica de Metapsiquica* of which three numbers appeared up to December, 1948. This review published seven of Dr. Canavesio's papers. As far as we know, he was the only member of that Association who investigated parapsychology. Two of his articles: "Historiando la metapsíquica" and "La ciencia metapsíquica parapsicológica" are of general knowledge; a third one, "Metapsíquica, su esquemática y desarrollo" aims at outlining the problems of parapsychological investigation and at delineating the different features to be studied. In "La utilización de la radiestesia por los gobiernos argentinos" Dr. Canavesio reports that the Government of the Province of Santa Fe engaged a radiesthesist of Córdoba, Mr. Armando King, to find water in the town of El Tostado, where lack of water had become a great hardship for its inhabitants. In another paper, "Historia metapsíquica del metagnóstico mister Eric Courtenay Luck," he reports the family history ways of operating and personal characteristics of this well known Argentine clairvoyant. In "Electroencefalografía y metapsíquica" he describes the electroencephalographic record of an Argentine psychometrist, Mr. Alfredo Parodi. These data were presented at the conferences of Utrecht and Bologna. Finally, in "Los desvíos del espiritismo; su solución," Dr. Canavesio explains the meaning of the control of spiritualistic practice imposed at the request of the National Government. Dr. Canavesio developed most of his activity during the forties. Later he worked in the Argentine Institute of Parapsychology, which was founded in 1953, and in 1957 he worked again among physicians and tried to promote new activities in the Medical Association of Metapsychics. This Association, which was located in Santa Fe, became almost inactive when Dr. Canavesio moved to Buenos Aires to take charge of his official functions. But in December, 1957, he was involved in an accident and died.

His last publication was a pamphlet, issued in 1957, entitled *Revista Médica de Parapsicología,* No. 4, in which he published the first part of his work "Electroencefalografía en los estados metapsíquicos." It contains an up-to-date version of those works which had been published in the *Revista Médica de Metapsíquica,* to which we have already referred. It is difficult to do a scientific evaluation of Dr. Canavesio's "Electroencefalografía de los estados metapsíquicos." The only report he published corresponds to the electroencephalographic record of the psychometrist Alfredo Parodi. The record is divided into four areas, two of which are specially interesting. The first is area A–B, which corresponds to the moment when the subject is about to attain the metapsychic state, with eyes closed and hands crossed on his chest. The second area, B–C, corresponds to the interval during which the subject is in the "metapsychic state," that is to say the state during which the unconscious activity of the subject's ESP reaches the object, apprehends it and elaborates the result which appears in the conscious and is communicated by the subject in subsequent stages. By finger movements the subject indicated when the first image started to appear and the metapsychic state ended. This corresponds to area B–C of the electroencephalographic record. Each record—there are seven of them—corresponds to a test of ESP with free answers.

The report comes to the following conclusions: (1) under state A–B it is possible to observe the alpha rhythm, which corresponds to normal rest, with an average frequency of 12 cycles per second; (2) under metapsychic state B–C the frequency could not be determined exactly, although in some records it is possible to observe that it gets to 11-13 cycles per second. Evident changes in the electric rhythm of the cortex are registered. It becomes irregular, and the voltage decreases by 50 to 70%.

A critical reading of this work shows that there is no evidence that can prove that the decrease of voltage and the irregularity of the rhythm bear any relation to the subject's ESP activity. This lack of evidence results from the fact that the qualitative methodology with which the tests were done does not make it possible to consider the subject's assertion as scientific data. On the other hand, even if we accepted that record B–C really corresponds to a metapsychic state, the experience would not prove that the changes observed in the record had any correlation with the attainment of the alpha state. This was proved by comparing the records of those tests in which the subject succeeded in his ESP activity, with others (of the same subject or of others) in which the subject failed in ESP, in spite of having paid attention to those images which came to his conscious mind. Only the finding of a statistically significant correlation between the changes in electric potential and rhythm of many records in area B–C and the changes (success-failure) in the result of the subject's tests in ESP would have justified affirming that irregularities and decrease of potential were an index of ESP activity.

What is important in these investigations is that Dr. Canavesio not only gave a strong impulse to parapsychological studies in the Argentine, but also that he was involved with Governmental activities related to metapsychics. Though these Governmental activities did not produce works of scientific value, they are important from a historic point of view, for they helped to make parapsychological studies legitimate.

On January 7, 1948 a decree of the Secretary of Public Health, Dr. Ramón Carrillo, created the Institute of Applied Psychopathology, which depended on the Secretary of Public Health of the State. One of the objectives of the Institute was to develop an "organized struggle against spiritualism," which was then considered a social evil because it was characterized by exploitation and fraud. The decree made it clear that "only those psychological events which enter within the context of a true scientific knowledge" would be studied. Dr. César Rafael Castillo was appointed Honorary Chairman of the Institute. To carry out the above mentioned objective the Institute of Applied Psychopathology formed a "Cabinet of Metapsychic Investigations" of which Dr. Orlando Canavesio was head.

The Cabinet of Metapsychics engaged Mr. Eric Courtenay Luck to carry out experiments. Other persons with relevant ESP aptitudes were Dr. Luis Acquavella, Mrs. Anne Carrel (widow of the renowned biologist Alexis Carrel), Mrs. Valentín A. King, Enrique Marchesini and Federico Poletti. During his work with the Cabinet, Dr. Canavesio made electroencephalographic records, but no parapsychological investigations of scientific value emerged. This was because their work lacked an adequate methodology, for they had used the qualitative approach that was typical of metapsychists.

The creation of the Cabinet of Metapsychics had an unexpected consequence which was important for parapsychology. The control of spiritualism which this institution developed caused unjustified restlessness among Argentine spiritualist associations, which believed that it was a menace to them. Under these circumstances, spiritualists turned to parapsychology in search of scientific support.

In 1949 the Argentine Association of Parapsychology was created. It brought Argentine professionals together, among whom there were many active spiritualists. Engineer José S. Fernández and kinesiologist Luis Di Cristóforo Postiglioni, who were the first vice-president and the general secretary of the A.A.P., were also members of the spiritualistic Association Constancia and of other spiritualistic associations. One of the objectives of the A.A.P. was to "establish guide lines for examining metagnomic subjects or mediums and to create an office for certifying qualified people, under the control or sponsorship of the authorities involved," which aimed at imposing some control on spiritualism. Another of the objectives—and this was very important for parapsychology—was "to study and investigate parapsychological phenomena . . . with emphasis on the development of statistical methods."

It was the first time in Argentine that an institution favored the application of statistical methods in a psychological area.

During its first two years of life, the A.A.P. mainly devoted itself to publishing activities. In 1949 it began to publish the *Bulletin of the Argentine Association of Parapsychology*, which issued only five numbers, the last one appearing in 1952. At the close of the forties the A.A.P. held a meeting at the Auditorium Birabén, which was attended by Dr. Carlos Ignacio Rivas, University Sub-Secretary of the State, representing the Minister of Education, Dr. Oscar Ivanissevich. During this meeting Eng. Fernández reported on statistical methods applied to parapsychology at Dr. Rhine's Laboratory, and kinesiologist Di Cristoforo Postiglioni gave a lecture on "Objective Metapsychics."

THE FIFTIES: TOWARD MODERN PARAPSYCHOLOGY

a) *Investigations*

At the beginning of the decade Eng. Fernández experimented with Zener cards, the subject being his son-in-law, Ronald Warburton. After 2,500 tests of clairvoyance, they obtained 1,209 hits ($CR = 35.45$; $P = 10^{-300}$); with 750 tests in precognition with pre-shuffled cards, they obtained 216 hits ($CR = 6.03$; $P = 10^{-9}$). It was the first time significant results—in this case highly significant—were obtained in Argentina with the Zener cards.

But to arrive at a scientific interpretation of these results was difficult. By then, the members of the A.A.P. already knew the critical controls required for ESP tests. Fernández himself had received from Rhine the book *Extrasensory Perception After Sixty Years*, published in 1940, which he circulated among his friends. But the fact was that from Rhine they took only the mathematic formalism, ignoring its spirit of criticism. The application of the Gaussian model to the analysis of these data could not be called inadequate, as was the case in the investigation we referred to earlier. In both cases a value of $P = 10^{-300}$ was obtained. The analysis proved that there was a cause, different from chance, that determined the subject's hits. But what was that cause? Experimental conditions did not make it possible to affirm with scientific certainty that the cause was ESP, since there was an absolute lack of the most elementary and usual controls. As for the experiment in precognition with the pre-shuffled cards, the report does not say who shuffled the cards or what technique was used, or if at the end of the operation any random cut was done. This was Eng. Fernández' final conclusion: "Precognitive aptitude is thus perfectly proved." A scientist, however, would not have so easily considered this conclusion to be the only one or even the most likely, according to the empirical data reported.

At the time of Eng. Fernández's first experiments, we became members of the Argentine Association of Psychology. Shortly after we began to take part in these experiments and became members of the Main Council. Eng. Fernández's first studies of the gifted Ronald Warburton were followed by others in which Dr. Canavesio and I took part.

My first work in the A.A.P. took place in the years 1951 and 1952. We reached the conclusion that Warburton was extraordinarily gifted, since he was able to obtain high results with the Zener cards for years. But it was not possible to use his talent for investigations of a scientific value, because difficulties had arisen within the group about the need for systematic studied planned with pre-fixed objectives and experimental controls. On one occasion R.W. guessed twenty-five cards of a new deck we had received, and obtained 22 hits (CR = 8.5). We suggested that he wear gloves and repeat the test. He accepted and repeated his performance: 22 hits. Afterwards we urged him to try again, but this time blindfolded, as well as wearing the gloves. To our surprise, his performance was even better under these conditions: 25 hits in 25 tests (CR = 10). On these occasions he tried to identify the positions of certain pictures in a deck with a technique which Eng. Fernández had called "penetration clairvoyance," and he obtained a highly significant number of hits. Eng. Fernández reported these tests in a pamphlet, *Experimental Psychology,* which was published in 1953; we reported them in our *Introduction to Parapsychology,* a pamphlet which was published in 1954.

During this decade we carried out three investigations. The first, about which we have reported in the pamphlet *Introduction to Parapsychology,* was done with a well known clairvoyant, Mr. Conrado Castiglioni. In the hall of the Buenos Aires Theatre, at the end of his professional performance, we conducted the "empty chair" test (la "chaise vide"), with four empty chairs which had been previously selected. Castiglioni described the occupants before the chairs were occupied by people from the audience. From 45 computable predictions, he obtained 37 hits; if to each hit we give an a priori probability of p = 0.5, we obtain a high significance (P = 10^{-6}) for the whole result. In June 1955 we conducted another investigation. We carried out a series of tests with mediums who belonged to different spiritualistic groups. The idea was to determine: (1) if the psychological characteristics of spirit personifications differed from the medium's when in a normal condition, and (2) if it was possible to obtain any evidence that information was due to any form of paranormal knowledge, through identifying these personifications by tests. We used a battery of parallel forms of Jung's directed association test, which was applied to each medium under normal condition and to every personification the medium expressed while in trance. Several psychologists and professionals, such as Jaime Bernstein, Enrique Butelman and Pedro Rapela, took part in the experiment. Mr. Naun Kreiman, who was a member of the Instituto de Enseñanza Espírita, Director of the review *The Idea* (which was published by the Argentine Spiritualistic Confederation) and a member of the Council of the above mentioned Confederation, was the most active of those who took part. Mr. Kreiman had assumed a critical attitude toward spiritualism, which he later abandoned to become an active investigator in parapsychology. Through his aid we were able to get in touch with some of the spiritualistic centers; his experiment with mediums in trance was very useful to us for the application of tests to "spirits."

Altogether we examined fifteen mediums and we applied forty-two directed association tests, out of which fifteen were applied to mediums in normal condition and twenty-seven to "spirits." The final conclusion was that "spirit" answers differed in no way from those of the medium under normal conditions. As for the aim of finding evidences of paranormal knowledge, the result was negative because the "spirits" refused to give proof of identification.

The three investigations I have mentioned were imperfect from a methodological point of view. We realized this when we got our colleagues together for a critical discussion of this work. The test of the "empty chair," which was similar to that carried out by Osty with Ludwig Kahn and by Tenhaeff with Gerard Croiset, was imperfect. The evaluation of the subject's answers, for example, was not done "blind." On the other hand, the test of statistical significance we used had the same faults we found in Fernández's work in the thirties. As for the investigation with mediums in trance, we did not note the concordance between the "spirits'" answers and the mediums' which should be estimated by independent observers by "blind" methods. Nevertheless, this was the best we could—and knew how to—do at the beginning of the fifties.

In 1957 we started on a more important work, which aimed at controlling ESP through statistical procedures. It was based on what we called the "focusing method," which was later applied by Milan Ryzl in Czechoslovakia, in some of his experiments with Pavel Stepanek. This work was subsequently confirmed by Pratt in the United States. In these experiments the "focusing effect" was found to operate.

The hypothesis on which the "focusing method" was based can be explained as follows: if the same deck of cards sealed in envelopes is repeatedly presented in ESP tests, and if a certain picture is named in relation to a certain envelope with a frequency that is higher than that expected, then that picture will correspond to the card within the envelope.

To confirm this hypothesis we made an experiment with two decks of Zener cards. Dr. Luis Boschi (who was skeptical about ESP) put one deck of cards (deck 1) in envelopes, in such a way that the envelopes could not be opened without the experimenter's noticing it. I repeated the operation with another deck (deck 2). Both decks looked identical. The aim of the investigation was to reveal the pictures of the 25 cards Boschi had put into the envelopes (deck 1), through analysis of the answers given about each envelope in many runs. Deck 2 was used as a control. We tried with many subjects, without obtaining significant deviations in the frequency of any of the five kinds of answers given by the subjects for the same envelopes. Then Warburton agreed to cooperate with us in the experiment. A few sessions later we noticed that, as we had expected, he associated certain answers with certain envelopes of deck 1. But when we opened the envelopes we discovered that the pictures which had been called more frequently did not correspond to the pictures enclosed in the corresponding envelopes. This association of wrong answers was also found by Ryzl and Pratt. But in our experience, the negative deviation—though it was suggestive—did not reach a level of statistical significance ($P = 0.01$), due to the fact that the sample was small ($N = 25$).

Warburton's intervention had very interesting features. He tried with the two enclosed decks, following his usual technique of identifying certain pictures through the deck (which Fernández called the "penetration" technique) and he obtained highly significant results. As you will remember, the subject sat before two enclosed decks: Deck 1, which had been put in envelopes by Dr. Boschi, and deck 2 which I had put in the envelopes. Though the envelopes looked identical, his hits on deck 2, with the above mentioned technique, had a significance of $P = 10^{-7}$. But with deck 1 the results were as expected. What was peculiar in the results was that with the "concentration" technique R.W. not only could identify the pictures correctly "through" the pile of enclosed and shuffled cards, but he could also distinguish those that had been put in envelopes by Boschi from those that I had put in the envelopes. He could repeat this difference even when we showed him the fifty envelopes, without our knowing which were Boschi's and which were mine.

The decade ended with an investigation of the possible mediation

of ESP in the diagnosis of a well known "chirologist," which was carried out by Di Liscia and which had a negative result.

b) *Associations*

Let me now refer to events which have personal implications and
about which it is necessary to speak, for they had important consequences for the development of parapsychology in our country. These
events shed light on the characteristics of that development.

Our interest in what we later knew as parapsychology dated from the
end of the thirties, when we were interested in spiritualism. At that
time we joined the "Spiritualistic Association Lumen," that was formed
by a group of scholars, among whom were many associated with the
university. The members of the Association were interested in science
and philosophy, rather than in spiritualistic religion. They believed
that it was possible to prove spirit survival scientifically, and that on
the basis of this fact a new humanism could be built, based on science
rather than on religion. This group had broken away from Argentine
spiritualism, which drew inspiration from Alan Kardec. The "mediumistic" practices carried out in Lumen tended toward the development
of mediums as subjects for studies and experiments under scientific
control. They believed that they relied on the aid of a "spiritual direction," which came from the "spirits" of sages who had pursued the
same goal during their lives (they believed that the spiritual director
of their sessions was Gustave Geley).

But their ideals were higher than their spirit of criticism. On December 29, 1941, the Directive Committee of the Association decided to
dismiss me for they considered that certain controls we had proposed
meant a deviation in its objectives. This circumstance caused me to be
skeptical toward metapsychic phenomena (and not only toward their
spiritualistic interpretation), and for many years I almost lost my interest in them. For this reason, and because at that time I felt it necessary
to join the groups that fought Nazism and Fascism in our country, I
dropped the study of parapsychological phenomena for many years.

However, my interest arose once more at the end of the forties, when
I was struck by several clairvoyant experiences of my first wife, Elvira,
that made me think that there was something to it. I realized that it
was necessary for me to revise my skepticism toward parapsychology.
Then I got in touch with the Argentine Association of Parapsychology,
which was directed by Eng. Fernández. I also got in touch again with
the Lumen group, where I found that important changes had taken
place, which I had probably influenced through my former activities.
In fact, I learned that since December 1942 the members of Lumen had

decided "to separate from spiritualism and to adopt a new name which would define the character of the new association." The new name was "Lumen Association of Psychic Investigations and Philosophical Studies." The chairman, Mr. Benjamín Odell, favored my re-entering the Association, which I did in September 1951. We proposed studies to be carried out according to modern parapsychological patterns, which were accepted. Our first steps in Lumen and in the A.A.P. aimed at coordinating the efforts of all those who were actively interested in parapsychology, and at obtaining the means for accomplishing our projects. Lumen had those means which the A.A.P. lacked. It had a large conference hall and also laboratories for investigations. But it had very few members. Most of the university people were at the A.A.P. During 1952 and 1953 we merged both groups. The Lumen group incorporated the members of the A.A.P., which then dissolved. After the meeting of December 20, 1952, the "Lumen Association of Psychic Investigation and Philosophical Studies" became the present "Argentine Institute of Parapsychology," which adopted new by-laws. The new association was officially recognized on April 22, 1953. And almost immediately, on June 30, 1953 the members of the Argentine Association of Parapsychology became members of the Argentine Institute of Parapsychology. Now it seemed that Argentine scholars of parapsychology were finally gathered in one group.

But soon there were disagreements between those who wanted to keep parapsychology apart from ideological problems and the active group of spiritualists who came from the ex-A.A.P. Some of us disagreed with those who wanted to include in the Board of Honor some persons who had nothing to do with parapsychology. We did not allow lectures on "flying saucers" to be held at the Institute by persons who were not scientifically competent. Neither would we accept for publication papers which had not been previously examined and criticized from a scientific point of view. As a consequence of all this the two groups opposed each other, and as the spiritualists were in the majority, the work at the A.I.P. was guided according to their ideology. Let us see an example: with reference to the problem of survival, we all know that to this day science has not been able to say "yes" or "no" on an empirical basis. Science can only say "we do not know." Many of us held this position, which we expressed in a paper called "La posesión espírita: cuestión cerrada?" In this paper we pointed out that the parapsychological proof of the existence of non-physical entities permits us to affirm logically that survival is possible, but that there are no empirical proofs of this. This matter is still open to investigation. And this position cannot be called "materialistic," for it is not an ideological position. It is a methodological position. However, in Bulletin No. 1 (August 1955), we can read the following opinion of the A.I.P.: "under the present state of studies, the ideological opinion according to which it is impossible to say 'yes' or 'no' to such an important problem (survival) is not adequate any more. This behavior was fashionable among the metapsychists of the forties, and although then it was admissible, today it is anachronistic. . . . Those who believe so are *shameful dogmatists* who do not want to confess their materialism, thus leaving their dogma in the unconscious which they use for their nominative hypothesis." These pamphletarian epithets give an example of the tendency which prevailed at the A.I.P. If anyone did not consider the "truth" of spiritualism to be scientifically valid, he was called "materialist" (and shameful).

At the end of 1954, as we did not agree with what we considered a lack of scientific seriousness, Mr. Benjamín Odell, Mr. Julio C. Di Liscia and I resigned. We then sponsored the creation of a new group: the Association of Friends of Parapsychology, which started publication of the *Revista Argentina de Parapsicologia,* under my direction. The first issue appeared in July, 1955. This was the first review that contributed to the spread, in Spanish, of the spirit, methodology and works of modern parapsychology. Through its pages we made public the activities of the A.I.P. and for this reason we were forced to resign —Odell, Di Liscia and I—on December 13, 1955.

But our words had not been in vain. Others joined us in our criticism, among them the new vice-president of the A.I.P., Dr. Héctor Meson, who also resigned. On December 1, 1955 Eng. Fernández resigned, together with most of the members of the former A.A.P. Dr. Meson, who was appointed temporary chairman of the A.I.P., called an assembly on December 16, 1955. At this assembly I was appointed president, Dr. Meson vice-president and Dr. Di Liscia secretary. Dr. Orlando Canavesio, who had been excluded from high responsibilities in the A.I.P., was appointed a member of the Board. Other members of the Board were important university professors, among whom were Dr. Gino Germani, Head of the Institute of Sociology at the University of Buenos Aires, and Dr. Jaime Bernstein, Head of the Institute of Psychology at the University of the Litoral (today Rosario University). Other members were Professor José M. Feola, who is at present on the faculty of the University of California at Berkeley and Chairman of the California Society for Psychical Study, Inc.; Professor Nuria Cortada, who taught psycho-statistics at the University of Buenos Aires; and Professor Enrique Butelman, who was director of psychology at the University of Buenos Aires. Many of them could not work in parapsychology, as they were absorbed by their work at the university; however, they helped to give parapsychology university status.

In fact, almost at the same time an important event took place: according to Decree No. 1,755 of January 16, 1956, parapsychology was incorporated in the syllabus of the Faculty of Philosophy, Letters and Educational Sciences of the University of the Litoral, as a course that was compulsory for psychology students. Now parapsychology had achieved the status it deserved for its significance to psychological studies. The program, which included parapsychology as a course, was developed by a group of professors and students.

c) *Publication*

The first stage was over. The second stage to come, as important as the first, was that of publication, which took place in the second half of the decade.

We have already mentioned the *Revista de Parapsicología,* which appeared in 1955. In 1957, we published a paper called "La percepción extrasensorial" in the *Revista de Educación* published by the Ministry of Education of the Province of Buenos Aires. It was the first time a paper on parapsychology was published in a government review. We have to mention our book *En los límites de la psicología (desde el espiritismo hasta la parapsicología),* Buenos Aires, Periplo, 1954, for it was the first book on this subject ever written in Spanish. Since 1955 editors have been publishing many books on parapsychology. In June, 1955, Paidós—the most important publisher of psychology books in Latin America—started a Library of Parapsychology, under my direction. The series started with *The Reach of the Mind,* by Rhine, which was followed by other works by Rhine, and books by Amadou, Ehrenwald and Tyrrell. Other publishers, such as Ediciones La Isla and Troquel began to put out works by Tocquet and Sudre.

During 1956 many courses and lectures were held. Dr. Miguel Figueroa Roman, who was Head of the Institute of Sociography and Planning at the University of Tucumán, lectured on "Introduction to Parapsychology." Two courses, about parapsychological techniques and about the relationship of parapsychology to psychoanalysis were held at the A.I.P. In addition, eleven lectures about parapsychology in relation to other disciplines, such as philosophy, pathology and sociology, were given by university professors. At the same time the A.I.P. started an annual course of parapsychology, with Dr. Orlando Canavesio as the lecturer until his death in 1957. Afterwards we taught this course. These were the activities within the A.I.P. In 1958 we gave a course on "Tests in Parapsychology" at the University of the South (Bahía Blanca), which became part of the course "Methodology of Scientific Investigation" in that university. This was the first course on the subject given in a state university. Others were given at such institutions as the Medical Circle of Psychiatrics and Neurosurgery and the American Federation of Clinical Hypnosis. In 1959 we were invited to lecture on parapsychology at the Faculty of Philosophy of the University of the Litoral. Later we learned that the course had been under the surveillance of the academic authorities of that Faculty. It had been a sort of "test" by which they wanted to decide if, from 1961 on, parapsychology would or would not become a course of the fifth year of the curriculum of psychology. It did, and the course was given from that year on.

Before finishing with this outline of the fifties, we have to refer once more to Eng. Fernández. In August, 1957, a spiritualistic group guided by Eng. Fernández started its activities under the name of Argentine College of Psychic Studies. Those who established it declared that the College was a successor to that Spiritualistic Circle of 1933, to which we have already referred. This group issued a bulletin called *Noticia Psi,* in which they reported their experiments. In the two issues of August 1957 and June 1958 they report tests on ESP with Zener cards, in which Dr. Ronald Warburton acted as subject, and also on free callings in which Mrs. María Amanda R. de Fernández acted as subject. The results and the conditions under which the observations were done were similar to those we have referred to, with one exception: the last bulletin reports nine tests on ESP with Warburton as a subject. These tests were done with the "penetration technique" on a deck of Zener cards which were enclosed within their original box—all nine tests were hits. It was the first experience the group did with Warburton without having the faces of the cards exposed, and the result was highly significant.

Eng. Fernández published four pamphlets: *Parapsicología Experimental,* 1953; *Nuevos problemas filosóficos de la parapsicologia,* 1954 (this paper was forwarded to the First Argentine Congress of Psychology, which was held in Tucumán); *Fundamentos científico-filosóficos de la supervivencia con reencarnación* (with Kin. Luis Di Cristóforo Postiglioni), 1956; and *Parapsicología y realidad del alma,* 1958 (this was a lecture given at the Institute of High Studies in Montevideo). His last work contained two essays: "Tiempo y precognición" and "La reencarnación," besides some of his former ones. It was published as *Más allá de la cuarta dimensión,* Buenos Aires, Constancia, 1963. Eng. Fernández died on March 14th, 1967, aged 74, when he was preparing a work on *Elementos de parapsicología* with his son-in-law, Dr. Ronald Warburton. His death was a severe loss for Argentine parapsychology.

THE SIXTIES: EXPANSION AT THE UNIVERSITY AND EXPERIMENTS

a) *Associations*

At the end of the fifties the first stage ended with the creation of the A.I.P., which brought together those men who were interested in modern parapsychology, and the establishment of the first Chair of Parapsychology at the University. During the sixties parapsychology expanded in the universities, and the men of the A.I.P. played an active role in this process. It is necessary to say, however, that our activity at the universities was not confined to parapsychology. Due to our knowledge of statistics and scientific methodology, we were asked to teach methodology to psychology students. This was because the teaching of psychology in our country was influenced principally by philosophical and clinical schools, and ours was one of the few groups that knew and applied methodology in investigation.

In 1961 we were asked to lecture on parapsychology for fourth year students of psychology at the Litoral University. During the course we discovered a serious difficulty. The students lacked a solid methodological background. Their knowledge of the subject was not sufficient, was abstract, and inadequate for the requirements of our course. For this reason we had to include some items of psychological statistics in our syllabus. As the students had been trained almost exclusively in clinical psychology, parapsychology was something strange to them. But then, the authorities of the Faculty decided to provide a scientific background at the beginning of the curriculum. In 1962, we were asked to take charge of a course on psychological statistics, which was taught to first year students. In this course, we included many parapsychological examples. In this way parapsychology ceased to be something "strange" in the curriculum and became another branch of psychology. Besides, the students realized that the methodology parapsychology required was the same as that required by scientific investigation in all the branches of psychology. After this course, the psychologist Mirta Granero, whose interest in parapsychology had led her to psychology, got interested in psychological statistics and in scientific methodology. From 1964 on she took part in the development of parapsychology in Rosario City.

In 1964 I was given the Chair of Psychological Investigation Methodology at the University of Buenos Aires. The following year I was appointed Head of the Department of Psychology by the Board of Professors. In that year a committee formed by student, professorial and graduate delegates decided to include parapsychology as a course. For this reason I held a seminar on "Methodology and Techniques in Parapsychological Investigation." Thus, our discipline was also incorporated in psychological studies at the University of Buenos Aires.

Another field of action during the sixties was that of private universities. The process in this field was similar to the process that had taken place at the state universities. As a result of this the teaching of parapsychology was incorporated in the teaching of scientific methodology in psychology. In 1966, Horwitz and Di Liscia were appointed professors of parapsychology at the Argentine Social Museum University, while Kreiman—who had specialized in statistical methodology—and I were appointed professors of psychological statistics. In 1967 the psychologist Ana María Perrotta, who had been our pupil at the Litoral University, was given the Chair of Parapsychology at Kennedy University, a private institution.

In 1961, Dr. Bruno Fantoni joined the A.I.P., and the following year became a member of the Board. From then on he was very active within private universities. He lectured on parapsychology at the Psychological Sciences Private University (Buenos Aires, 1962), at the Argentine Army High School of War (Buenos Aires, 1965), at the High Catholic Seminary (La Plata, 1967) and in other institutions such as the Medical Association of the Alvarez Hospital. Since 1964 he has been in charge of the annual course at the A.I.P., where Horwitz and Di Liscia lecture on more specialized subjects. Dr. Fantoni is also well known in Brazil, where he has given courses and lectures. But his most important activity in parapsychology is the chair he has held since 1963 on the Faculty of Philosophy at the Argentine Catholic University (Buenos Aires). His course there corresponds to the fourth year of Psychology.

b) *Public Information*

Fantoni, Di Liscia and Horwitz held lectures and courses in different institutions, as well as on radio and TV. On some occasions there were ESP tests on TV. In 1966, the psychologist Susana Pensa (a former pupil of Fantoni's at the Catholic University) and I conducted a GESP test on TV, in which TV watchers acted as subjects and sent their answers by mail. This test has not been analyzed as yet, as we lack the means to do so. On the other hand, Mirta Granero gave courses, lectures and speeches on radio and TV in Rosario.

As for publications, the output was rather poor. The A.I.P. had to suspend the publication of the *Revista de Parapsicología,* because it did not have the financial means to continue it. However, Kreiman with the aid of his wife, Mrs. Dora Ivnitzky de Kreiman, published the *Cuadernos de Parapsicología,* of which approximately fifteen issues appeared between December, 1963, and June, 1966.

In addition, a number of papers were published. Two were Fantoni's: "Parapsicología y psicología," in the *Revista Argentinade Psicología* (March 1966); and "El objeto de la parapsicología," in *Revista de Parapsicología* of the A.I.P. (June 1967). As for me, I also published two papers: "Los tests de parapsicología" (which was included as a chapter of a book published by Kapeluz, Buenos Aires, 1961, as *Los tests,* by Béla Székel and others, and which deals with the principal psychological tests), and "Contribución de la parapsicología al conocimiento del hombre" which was published by the *Revista de la Universidad de Buenos Aires* in 1966. It was the second time Argentine universities included parapsychological subjects in their publications. In 1966, some of my pupils at the Rosario University published four of my papers, which were to be used within the University; these papers were: "Experimentos con tests de dibujos," "Problemática especial de los experimentos con respuesta libre y colectivos—técnicas de Pratt-Birge y Greville"; "Experimentos con cartas reloj—técnicas de aproximación al objetivo"; and "Experimentos de PK con escala de posición graduada."

c) *Investigations*

The decade started with an investigation of the determining factors in injuries suffered in fire-walking ceremonies with which certain groups celebrated Saint John's Day in Argentina. During 1961 and 1962 Di Liscia and Horwitz observed the ceremony, and in 1962 we were able to carry out an experimental reproduction of it, for which we recorded such data as temperature and size of the bed of wood embers, number of steps and time of each passage, etc., and the presence (or absence) of injuries in those who walked barefoot on the fire. The conclusion was that it was not necessary to have recourse to any sort of parapsychological hypothesis to explain the absence of injuries. Though this investigation did not bear any relation to our own line of work, it was interesting for it helped to counteract in many people the superstitious belief these ceremonies were generating. Dr. Boschi and I fire-walked twice across the bed of wood embers, which was almost three meters long. It was really a highly shocking experience.

From 1963 to 1966 Di Liscia carried out several experiments: (1) on ESP at a distance of 2 km.; (2) on "dermo-optic perception"; (3) on PK with subjects who had been classified into two groups: sheep and goats. Results were not significant. In 1965, Di Liscia cooperated in the "Antártida Experiment," to which we shall refer later.

Kreiman engaged in active research. He carried out several exploratory investigations with many subjects, of which we have to mention two, because the problems investigated were very interesting. The aim of the first was to determine if, when ESP was functioning, the subjects were driven to modify their call-habits or patterns. Kreiman had observed that some subjects acquired call-habits: they called certain pictures after certain others, and this call-habit was characteristic of each subject. Then he decided to find out if those subjects maintained the same call-patterns in the ESP series in which they obtained significant deviations, as well as in those in which they obtained the expected results. None of the subjects obtained any result which had individual significance, so that there was no need to analyze their call-patterns. But in one subject it was possible to observe that he seemed to obtain hits with a significant positive deviation when he gave his answer after having "thought" it carefully (and after having chosen it among other answers he also "thought"). These calls were named "intended calls" as opposed to "non-intended calls," which the subject gave spontaneously. Then a new test was carried out with this subject, which consisted of 41 runs with "intended calls" and 9 runs with "non-intended calls." As was expected, the average of hits in the first case was significantly higher ($CR_{dif} = 2.51$; $P = 0.0063$) than in the second. In the second experiment a child—who competed with others—was tested under two conditions: in the first—which was called "spontaneous"—the subject chose the day to do the test and on that day he did as many runs as he wanted; in the second—which was called "compulsory"—the day of the test and the number of runs had been previously fixed. In the "spontaneous" series the result was higher than expected ($CR = 3.10$), while in the "compulsory" series it was as expected.

Mirta Granero continued her research in Rosario. During 1962-1963 she carried out 637 runs with Zener cards, with 36 subjects, and obtained significant results with two of them. Then, with these two subjects, she made two series of tests, at distances of 150 m. and 3 km. Every day, she held a closed deck of Zener cards in her house, and the subject tried to perceive the cards, whenever he felt like it, and afterwards he sent the results to her. With both subjects she obtained highly significant positive deviations. In one case it was $CR = 5.7$ for

37 runs; in the other it was $CR = 3.9$ for 25 runs. The tests were carried out in the last six months of 1963. When she repeated the experience with the same subjects, but at a longer distance, the results were as expected. In 1966 she experimented with a handicapped child, and obtained evidence of psi-missing when the child was competing ($CR = -2.83$). But in 1969 Granero succeeded in finding a gifted subject: a professional from Rosario who had remarkable ESP aptitudes for drawings and other free-call tests. In that year Mirta Granero and I started on an experiment to which I shall refer later. During this decade, besides many informal tests, we carried out five formal investigations which were sponsored by the Psychology Department of the Faculty of Philosophy (Litoral University). The first took place in 1962. Mr. José Martin, of Rosario, who for the past years had been studying an interesting "medium," Mrs. Adela Albertelli, cooperated with us. While in trance, the "medium" produced writings in languages which were absolutely unknown to her, such as English, German, Hebrew, Chinese, and even a strange, almost pictographic writing which the Hungarian Society of Psychic Investigations identified as belonging to a gypsy dialect of the country. Martin had found that the medium's writings usually corresponded to something that had been published in foreign magazines that she could have actually seen. We thought this could be a remarkable case of hypermnesia and tried to confirm this hypothesis by giving the subject (for controlled, short periods of time) sequences of words in different languages that were unknown to her, and by motivating her to retain these words. We had weekly sessions with the "medium" for several months. Martin and Mirta Granero were present at the sessions. However, we could not induce her to reproduce the same words in trance.

In that year—1962—we planned a re-examination of the data we had obtained in 1956, when we had tested 302 pupils of a primary school with randomized ESP cards enclosed in opaque envelopes, by the "focusing" method. This re-examination aimed at confirming some of Van Busschbach's findings about interpersonal relations (teacher-pupil), and Schmeidler's correlation between attitudes (sheep-goat) and scores. The re-examination could be done because the IBM Trade Corporation collaborated with us in the use of its computers. Through variance analysis, significant differences were found in the sheep-goat scores, which confirmed Schmeidler's results. The paper was published in the *Journal of Parapsychology*, June 1965. It was the first paper written by a Latin American to be published by a foreign review of parapsychology of high scientific level.

In 1964 we carried out an investigation in Rosario with a remarkable sensitive, Mrs. Ofelia B. de Scheafer, whom José Martin had discovered. We held six sessions of "psychometry" (object-readings) with her, during which we gave her six objects (keys) which had been provided by six persons who were not present at the sessions. The free calls were evaluated—with the cooperation of Jorge Bisbini, of the A. I. P., by the Pratt-Birge method. The analysis of data was done with the Greville method and the result, though suggestive (P = 0.02), did not reach the significance level. This was the first time these analysis techniques were applied in Latin America.

In 1965 we carried out an investigation which aimed at verifying if the old guessing technique known as I Ching, of which Jung has spoken favorably, really provided significant information to those consulting it. It was found that such people considered the answers of I Ching as very significant when related to their personal troubles; but when they selected their corresponding answer-items by "blindly" marking them within a set of non-corresponding items, the number of correct choices was as expected.

However, Di Liscia, M. Granero and I carried out our most ambitious investigations in 1965 and 1969. In 1965 it was an investigation of long distance ESP, which was international, for groups of subjects belonging to twenty different countries took part in it. We called it the "Antártida Experiment" because for 64 days Zener cards were exhibited under different conditions at the Station of the Antártida Naval Base, which belongs to the Argentine Navy. The cards were exhibited for 24 hours and had to be perceived by the subjects in their different countries. Approximately 200,000 answers were obtained. But circumstances to which we shall refer later caused the Institute of Calculus of Buenos Aires University, where the data were being processed, to interrupt its work in 1966. Thus the experiment remained unanalyzed. At present work is being done on it at the Computing Center of Santa Fe Province; we expect to receive the results shortly.

As for the experiment of 1969, it consisted of a series of 90 ESP tests by a high scoring subject, on free drawings which were exhibited in a nearby room, under different conditions. Answers were evaluated by the blind method, by judges who worked independently of one another and by rank order method. The analysis of the data, which required non-parametric statistical techniques, was finished in 1971, and the results were very significant. They prove that the subject identified the object-drawings correctly by GESP, as well as under clairvoyance condition, that is to say, without M. Granero seeing them.

Further analysis revealed interesting information on the way the subject's ESP operated.

d) *Two negative facts*

As we have seen, parapsychology had developed in Argentina during the sixties. It had been incorporated as a course in five Argentine universities and for the first time experiments of high level design had been carried out in our country under strict scientific controls. But there were also two negative facts: (1) parapsychology disappeared from State universities; and (2) the number of persons who were actively interested in parapsychology increased very little.

In 1967, after the coup d'Etat with which a group of Army officers took over the political power of the country, parapsychology disappeared from State universities. And this happened at the time the Dean of the Faculty of Philosophy of the Litoral University, Professor Guillermo Maci, had given us a hall for installing a research laboratory, which was to be under the jurisdiction of the Chair of Parapsychology. One of the first acts of the new Government was to take over State universities. When this happened, almost all the professors of all State universities resigned. This answer to the government's decree seemed—at least at that moment—inevitable from a moral point of view. But the effect it produced was not precisely the expected: by resigning, we had intended to prevent some measures, which instead were taken very soon. The takeover of the universities led to a series of measures which resulted in a progressive deterioration of academic and university life. One of these measures was to emend the psychology syllabus arbitrarily and without consulting anybody. Since 1966 the syllabus in psychology has changed—always arbitrarily—every time a new ruler replaced his predecessor, which has been commonplace since 1966. As a consequence, parapsychology was eliminated in State universities.

As for the small increase in the number of persons actively interested in parapsychology, this can be explained as follows: when the A. I. P. was formed in 1953, its approximately 100 members were only passively interested in parapsychology; they limited themselves to "seeing and listening." Only a few of us felt a real active interest, and we spent all of our free time in learning and investigating. At the end of the fifties only four of us remained: Di Liscia, Kreiman, Horwitz and I. We hoped that if we held a series of courses and lectures, the number of followers would increase. But the truth is that in spite of our labor, only two persons have followed us during the whole decade: Dr. Bruno Fantoni in Buenos Aires and Mirta Granero in Rosario.

Several thousand people attended our courses and lectures during this time, but most of them did not approach parapsychology with a scientific interest. They were spiritualists who came in search of a confirmation of their own beliefs, and who disregarded our approach to parapsychology, for they realized that scientific parapsychology did not confirm their beliefs. However, this scientific approach which discouraged spiritualists, appealed to people with a scientific mind. Many of them, who had expected nonsense from us, changed their minds and attitudes and became convinced of the importance of parapsychological studies. But they could not start investigating, because this field did not offer good monetary possibilities.

At the university, some of the students who had to take parapsychology, as was required by their syllabus, were really only interested in clinical psychology, or in educational psychology, or in industrial psychology, which offered them better opportunities for professional work. But none got interested in parapsychology, which did not offer such possibilities. The study of parapsychology did not even offer the possibility of becoming a "professional investigator," as this career did not exist on the faculty. (The fact is that we had introduced it into the program when we were head of the department of psychology in 1966, but this did not last, due to government takeover.) Thus, only very few could be actively interested in such a specialized field, which demanded study and effort without giving much in return.

e) *The seventies: prospects*

It seems now that there are a series of favorable conditions which can counteract the facts we have referred to. At the end of 1968 the A.I.P. moved to a new building, in a good location in town. This fact seems to have been important, for during 1969 and 1970 we noticed the influx of new people—most of them young—to the courses Fantoni and Di Liscia held. This year—1971—a group of young people are following courses in parapsychological investigation, with Kreiman and me; some of them were moved by their interest in parapsychology and entered psychology after abandoning other studies. It is the first time that we have been able to observe such an active interest in young people, and this leads us to be optimistic about the future.

In the young students we observed something we had already observed in some of us: it seems that there is a process which takes them from parapsychology to psychology, and not from psychology to parapsychology. It seems that an active and lasting interest in parapsychology is related to a primary interest in the knowledge of man's inner nature. Parapsychology is, of course, that branch of psychology which proposes the greatest challenge and at the same time the most promising prospect for that knowledge. But it also seems that if that original interest lasts, it soon becomes necessary for knowledge to integrate parapsychology with general psychology. In our country it seems to be this way: parapsychology is one of the leading roads to psychology. During the last two years the interest in parapsychology has increased in Argentina to high levels—higher than ever. This year Mirta Granero and I started a short course at the Faculty of Engineering at Córdoba city; the course was so crowded—more than 800 persons—that it was necessary to move to another place. Father Oscar Gonzalez Quevedo, who is active mainly in Brazil, held short courses in the Argentine cities of Tucumán and Buenos Aires, which were also attended by a large number of people. Father Quevedo intends to fight, through parapsychology, the superstitious beliefs arising from spiritualistic and occult practices.

But this extraordinary interest involves a serious danger: the multiplication of humbugs. For lecturing on parapsychology has become a profitable business for some people, which is the more dangerous because the parapsychologist's activity is not controlled in our country. In these years many "free courses" in parapsychology or in psychometry as well as courses in astrology have become prolific. We had the opportunity of meeting some persons who introduced themselves with a diploma of "parapsychologist" they had received from these "courses." The A.I.P. will have to face this fraud.

Also within the universities this decade seems to offer a promising prospect. In 1970 the new Dean of the Faculty of Philosophy of the Rosario University, Professor Luis Arturo Castellanos, called on us to direct the curriculum of psychology in that Faculty, and to take charge of the Seminar on Parapsychological Investigation Methodology. At that time parapsychology was undergoing a serious crisis in the universities, as a consequence of the last government takeover. There were more than ten vacant chairs, which we filled with carefully selected professors. The psychologist Mirta Granero was appointed to the chair of General Psychology in June 1970.

In 1970 Mirta Granero and I included parapsychological items in our syllabus. She included extrasensory perception and the usual techniques for its investigation and I included examples of parapsychology in my syllabus of Psychological Investigation Methodology. These examples are used to illustrate the operative definition of scientific concepts and the techniques to verify hypotheses. Thus, these courses were returned to the Rosario University, arousing great interest in the students.

In 1970 I also published two books which demanded many years of preparation: *Methodological Problems and Myths in Psychology and Psychotherapy* (Problemas y mitos met dológicos de la psicología y la psicoterapis) and *Methodological Fallacies and Myths in Psychology* (Falacias y mitos metodológicos de la psicología), which will be used as textbooks by students. In these works I approach the foundations of the different psychological schools, and I point out the differences between scientific schools and branches; at the same time, I develop some items of parapsychology.

However, the future of parapsychology in the university is still uncertain, specially after the last takeover. In fact, the new authorities which were appointed in 1970 after our return to the university, made an important change in 1971: the Department of Psychology, which had been part of the Faculty of Philosophy of Rosario University, was separated from it and turned into a High School of Psychology and Educational Sciences, which is under the jurisdiction of the university. This change, and the appointment of a Delegate as Head of the School, made the position of Director—which I was holding—disappear; so that at present I only keep my Chair.

At present the future remains uncertain. We expect changes of all sorts, but there is no news so far.

Still, it is our firm belief that whatever may happen within Argentine State universities, parapsychology will regain the place it deserves for its significance in the psychological field and for man's knowledge.

THE DEVELOPMENT OF PARAPSYCHOLOGY IN HOLLAND

Jan Kappers

INTRODUCTION

In writing this brief summary of the history of parapsychology in the Netherlands, I had to start somewhere and select those facets which seemed most important to me. This means that in outlining the main features of what happened, I may have omitted some persons or investigations. But in the course of time other writers will fill in any important omissions. Moreover, history can only be viewed objectively in retrospect.

I will not mention the early Dutch mesmerists, but start with the last decades of the last century. In comparison with the surrounding countries, parapsychology in Holland developed slowly. Apart from the positivistic outlook of science, which hampered the development of psychical research in every European country, one special factor played a part here. Occultism was mainly the interest of ideological groups, principally spiritualists and theosophists, more bent on conversion than on convincing argument. This explains, perhaps, the strong resistance of the average Dutchman at the turn of the century to even the mere mention of paranormal phenomena. At that time a strong revival of religious thinking and feeling took place in the Protestant and Roman Catholic churches. Clerical parties were formed and succeeded by united efforts in replacing the liberal establishment in almost every aspect of public life. The Socialist and Communist parties, which together never carried more than one-third of the votes at the elections for Parliament, were then in their infancy and in rebound strongly antireligious.

THE FORERUNNERS

No wonder that the pioneers of parapsychological research in Holland were found among the artists and students, always most open to new ideas. I will cite four of these early researchers.

Best known is Frederik van Eeden (1860-1932), physician, author and poet, who became interested in psychical research and psychiatry. He was acquainted with Frederic Myers and had several sittings with the medium Mrs. Thompson. His most valuable contribution to the field was "A study of dreams" (*Proceedings of the Society for Psychical Research 26* [1913], p. 431), wherein he coined the term "lucid dreams," that is the type of dream in which the sleeper knows that he is dreaming. This state of consciousness seems to border upon out-of-the-body experiences. Tart thought it so important that he included it in his book "Altered States of Consciousness," and C. Green cites it amply in her study of "Lucid Dreams." Van Eeden seems to have had personal experiences of astral projection and incorporated them in a novel *The Bride of Dreams* (1918).

Dr. K. H. E. de Jong (1872-1960), a classical student, was in close contact with Mrs. E. Calcar, author and editor of a spiritualistic periodical *Op de Grens van Twee Werelden* (At the Border of Two Worlds). He chose as subject for his doctoral thesis, the mysteries of Isis (De apuleio isiacorua Mysteriorum teste), in which he made use of the findings of Myers in such well thought-out terms that it was whole-heartedly accepted. Another Dutch classical scholar, Leopold, had his thesis on Cicero's "De Divinatione" rejected, it being considered that nothing could be explained by non-existing telepathy. Next, de Jong wrote a standard work on antique mysteries (Das antike Mysterienwesen), 1909, in which he made it clear that some hitherto unintelligible texts could be explained by out-of-the-body experiences and other paranormal phenomena. De Jong later became the second lecturer in parapsychology at the University of Leiden (1940-1960), and contributed many scholarly books and articles on the subject of psi.

Dr. P. A. Dietz (1878-1953) studied biology at the University of Groningen, where in 1900 he attempted to organize a students' society for psychical research. Nothing lasting came from this, but Dietz did not lose interest and he was the first investigator in Holland to try card experiments, mostly with himself as a subject (1916–1917). On 4712 calls with playing cards, he obtained 128 hits (expectation 91; $CR \pm 4$), but never published his results. Later in life, he took up medicine, qualified as a medical doctor in 1924, and set up as a neurologist in the Hague in 1925. In 1928, with W. H. C. Tenhaeff, he founded the periodical *Tijdschrift voor Parapsychologie* to which he contributed numerous articles, covering the whole field, as he did in his books. In "Wereldzicht der Parapsychologie" (Parapsychological View of the Universe), he tried to bring out the most important conclusions from parapsychological facts as a basis for our idea of the cosmos. He coined the terms paragnosy for psychical phenomena and parergy for physical phenomena. In 1931 he was appointed a lecturer in parapsychology at the University of Leyden, the first such appointment in Holland. He was a brilliant speaker, who attracted crowds of students. In 1940 he retired for personal reasons.

Florentin J. L. Jansen (1881-   ), son of the artist H. W. Jansen, is a meteor in the parapsychological sky. We know little about him, but while still a medical student, in 1907, he established in Amsterdam what may have been the first parapsychological laboratory in the world. He also founded a quarterly periodical (*Driemaandelijkse verslagen van het Psychophysisch Laboratorium te Amsterdam*). In August 1906 he published in a spiritualistic magazine a program for his investigations, remarkable for its critical and mature thinking. He intended to build a bridge between psychical and biological sciences and to verify the findings of the British Society for Psychical Research by reproducing the phenomena. He worked with the sthenometer of Joire and showed that a "force nerveuse, capable de s'extérioriser de l'organisme humain" could not be demonstrated with this. He investigated with 83 subjects the existence of the Od of Reichenbach and found 12 of them capable of discerning when the current in an electromagnet was switched on. This was a remarkable result, but the safeguards against sensory cues did not meet modern standards. Most interesting were his experiments on mental suggestion. His subjects succeeded several times in transferring rather intricate drawings. Jansen had to discontinue his efforts because of lack of money. He then attempted to incorporate his laboratory in a "Company for Biological Research Ltd" and to issue a German translation of his publications, but with no success. He did not reappear in the history of parapsychology. He immigrated to Buenos Aires in 1912, and the last we know of him is that he was active there as a physician in the twenties.

I will now mention a few others active in this initial stage of parapsychological research.

Marcellus Emants (1848-1923), author of naturalistic novels, who wrote strongly antireligious poems in the eighties, became interested in Eusapia Palladino. With the physiologist van Rijnberk, he performed some experiments with Eusapia and became convinced of the genuineness of her performance. In 1903 in an article in the Hague Journal *Het Vaderland* he proposed the founding of a Dutch Society for Psychical Research. Although he was a rich and independent man, his record as an atheist may have prevented the realization of his project. G. A. van Rijnberk (1875-1953), professor of physiology in Amsterdam, dedicated a chapter of his treatise on physiology to physical paranormal phenomena. With regard to parapsychology, he was a split personality. He wrote articles in a weekly magazine under a pseudonym, and criticized these same articles in the *Dutch Medical Journal* of which he was an editor for thirty-five years.

At least two spiritualists of the "reserved" type helped to prepare the way for parapsychology in Holland.

The engineer Felix Ortt (1866-1959), prolific writer on a variety of subjects, developed the philosophy of pneumatic-energetic monism, holding that spirit reveals itself under the double aspect of energy and entelechy. In later life he contributed many articles to parapsychological literature. He stressed the importance of a theory concerning the drops in temperature in relation to physical phenomena, which indeed had not been sufficiently taken into account so far. In 1949, to round off his life work he wrote *The Super Cosmos,* with the subtitle "Philosophy of Occultism and Spiritualism." Maintaining the ideas of substantiality and causality, he postulated that in the case of an apport, the object exists, before it appears in a closed room, in some other continuum (the supercosmos). However, as C. H. van Os, professor of mathematics, pointed out in a critical review, in the light of modern physics, in which objects may have a limited and very ephemeral life, there need be no prior existence.

Another spiritualist to be mentioned is Captain H. N. de Fremery, who wrote a manual of spiritualism (1904), and was a regular contributor to the *Tijdschrift* before the Second World War.

THE FOUNDING OF THE DUTCH SOCIETY FOR PSYCHICAL RESEARCH

In the autumn of 1919, at the instigation of Professor G. Heymans (1857-1930), of Groningen University, a number of interested persons met in Amsterdam to discuss the foundation of a Dutch SPR. Heymans was the first psychologist of importance in the Netherlands and a well-known philosopher as well. His interest was in a psychical monism. He believed there existed a close parallel between the findings of parapsychology and the consequences of psychical monism. He dealt with this idea in "Psychische Monismus und 'Psychical Research' " (*Zeitschrift für Psychologie,* 1912). He established a laboratory in 1892 and a school and had many followers. His word carried weight. On April 1, 1920 the constitutional meeting of the Dutch SPR was held in Amsterdam. The organization was officially named

"Studievereniging voor Psychical Research." Heymans became president. Many important people joined the new society. The membership looked very promising. There were critical scientists, well-known scholars, prominent spiritualists (such as de Fremery) and theosophists (Poortman and Denier van der Gon). But in many respects the birth of the Foundation must have been most ill-starred because from the very beginning the Society was shaken by quarrels and conflicts.

The experiments with van Dam

The work of the Society started with what was, for the time, an outstanding piece of experimentation.

In the spring of 1919 a man, calling himself Rubini, came over to Holland and gave performances of an allegedly telepathic nature in many Dutch towns. Presumably, the phenomena could be explained by so-called muscle-reading. But at Groningen A. van Dam, an undergraduate student in mathematics and physics, was duly impressed. So much so that he tried to imitate Rubini and discovered that he possessed telepathic powers without the need of any direct contact with the sender. When the staff of Heymans's laboratory heard of this, van Dam was invited to be a subject in a series of experiments in telepathy. Blindfolded he had to select one out of 48 squares on a board. The target was chosen at random and the experimenters (Heymans, Brugmans and Weinberg) "willed" him to pick the correct squares. He guessed correctly in 60 of the 187 trials (expectation: 4). I won't go into details. The investigation has been published in the *Compte-Rendu du Premier Congrès International des Recherches Psychiques,* Copenhagen, 1921, and S. G. Soal wrote a critical analysis of the experiment in his *Modern Experiments in Telepathy.* I think it extremely unlikely that the results can be explained by sensory cues, but the setup was not up to our present standards.

Van Dam lost his gift very quickly and was never able to perform again.

The first crisis in the Dutch SPR

It soon became apparent that the rift between the hard-boiled scientists and the more descriptive-speculative wing of the Society was unbridgeable. The medium Peters came from England, and de Fremery had a sitting with him, which was considered partially very successful. In a séance at Groningen in October 1920, Wiersma, Brugmans and such others as J. C. Kapteyn, the leading astronomer of the time in Holland, did not get any results. Peters complained of the cold reserve of the circle and said he could not work without sympathy.

Other sittings followed with similar results. In the course of years, things deteriorated. The Society acquired a poor reputation among promising subjects. Sensitives refused to cooperate; almost no spontaneous paranormal cases were reported. An inquiry conducted among 700 doctors and ministers brought only two responses about observed paranormal occurrences. For everyone concerned, it became apparent that for psychical research, the Dutch SPR was not the place to go. The number of members dwindled and publications became sparse. When Heymans retired in 1926 and was replaced by L. Polak, his successor at Groningen, things became worse. Polak did not believe at all in the possibility of telepathy as this was in contradiction with his scientific beliefs, based on a special form of psychic monism. More open-minded members protested and Polak resigned. But the state of affairs was such that the secretary, H. M. van Dijk, proposed to dissolve the Society. Some members argued another course and carried on. An interested member, the lawyer P. W. de Koning from Amsterdam, became president and salvaged the situation; that was in 1927.

A more prosperous decade

At that time, parapsychology in Holland received a new impetus from the sphere of freemasonry. Dietz and W. H. C. Tenhaeff, a prospective psychologist, founded the periodical *Tijdschrift voor Parapsychologie* which soon incorporated the official publications of the SPR. Things moved fast now. On the initiative of Poortman, Tenhaeff became secretary of the SPR and began his never-ending crusade all across Holland, lecturing for every society, scientific or nonscientific, that was prepared to listen to his popular discourses about parapsychology. It can't be doubted that the immense interest in parapsychology in Holland was generated by Tenhaeff, whom I once termed the bell-ringer of parapsychology in Holland. For instance, in 1931 he gave 54 lectures for university extension classes, let alone his other lectures, and a lecture by Tenhaeff is a night-long affair. The Society's membership increased, and its library grew.

The *Tijdschrift* prospered. Although Dietz and Tenhaeff were its main contributors, it published important articles by many others. I mentioned already de Jong, Ortt, de Fremery, and will later name a few whom I consider of outstanding importance.

But at this point, I would like to speak of J. J. Poortman. He came from the school of Heymans, but, being a philosopher, he developed his own philosophy, starting from the basic paradox that the pure self cannot be known essentially. As this is true for everyone, Poortman stated that that which is the center of our being is always the same supra subject. This appears in a countless number of individuals (infra subjects), as the self is wrapped in a number of material cloaks of diminishing density. Dr. Poortman's work, unfinished at his death, was about hylic pluralism. He claimed that this might be the foundation of a theory of paranormal phenomena, as indeed it might be. Poortman was a founding member of the Dutch SPR, the only one left after half a century. Another of his contributions to parapsychology is a study on the "Feeling of being stared at." Through his relations with Leyden University, he opened the way for Dietz to become a private lecturer in parapsychology there in 1931. From then on, parapsychology was taught at Leyden University. The importance of this was stressed by Dietz in a masterly public lecture, "The struggle of parapsychology."

Where one sheep goes another follows. The following year, Tenhaeff became a private lecturer at Utrecht University.

Relations between Dietz and Tenhaeff soon become very strained and in 1936 Poortman took over the secretaryship of the *Tijdschrift*, to keep things in balance.

So far the contributions to the *Tijdschrift* consisted mainly of descriptive and speculative articles, summaries of certain aspects of parapsychology, and reports and reviews of investigations. Now, a longing for clearly-defined experiments emerged. A small laboratory was opened, courtesy of Dr. Spoor, in an unused annex of an Amsterdam hospital, with Tenhaeff as the psychologist and L. J. Koopman as the technical manager.

In the following years, sittings using token objects with five or six sensitives were held, a study of dowsing was undertaken and, more important perhaps, the neurologist L. J. Franke started an EEG investigation of hypnotic and trance states.

Meanwhile, the physicist Denier van der Gon wrote about physics and parapsychology and the use of instruments and measurements. But the most interesting findings of this period came from engineer J. M. J. Kooy (now Dutch space travel expert) and notary J. C. M. Kruisinga. For years, they investigated precognitive elements in dreams and found that by rigorously noting every item, hundreds of pertinent observations could be made. Some of these are noteworthy. Most predictions came true within 48 hours, seldom later. Elements of daily life in dreams were as often derived from the future as from the past. Of great significance was a very marked decline effect in Kruisinga's series. This brings one to suspect that the Dunne effects are not as generally found as Kooy thought. They don't come automatically; if they did, there could be no decline effect.

The second crisis in the SPR

Shortly before the war, Dietz retired from corporate life and gave up his position as a lecturer in Leyden. K. H. de Jong replaced him. There is no need to go into details about the Dietz-Tenhaeff controversy, but it is clear that the full-time parapsychologist Tenhaeff did have more contacts and influence in the Dutch SPR than the spare-time parapsychologist Dietz. After the death of his wife, Dietz was too old and tired to fight back. Then came the German occupation and, in 1941, the Dutch SPR was suppressed. The library was confiscated and taken to Germany where it was destroyed. Only the periodicals were saved. The work came practically to a standstill, although Tenhaeff continued lecturing and tried to elicit war impressions from sensitives and spontaneous cases.

When liberation appeared close, some prominent members met in Amsterdam to discuss the re-establishment of the Society. And shortly after the war, the Dutch SPR was reconstructed and within a few years counted a thousand members. But in reality the losses were severe. Several important workers had lost their lives in the resistance movement; others died in the war; and still others were alienated by the Dietz affair.

One new writer on parapsychological topics came to the foreground: G. Zorab, whose study *Het opstandingsverhaal in het licht der parapsychologie* (the Resurrection in the light of parapsychology) in its original Dutch version (1949) is of outstanding quality. But for the rest, the Dutch SPR became identified with Tenhaeff.

The period from 1945 to 1960

In the first six volumes of the *Tijdschrift* published after the war, aside from book reviews and in obituaries, 731 pages are from Tenhaeff, 202 from Zorab, 303 from other Dutch contributors, and 66 from foreign authors. Except for some dowsing experiments and some observations on the sensitive and healer Gerard Croiset, no experimental work was done, partly because of lack of money and opportunity, but also because Tenhaeff believed in the so-called qualitative method and thought of experiments with statistical analysis as being only auxiliary.

This fomented some unrest and several teams sought opportunities to start experiments. In 1952, at the instance of many members, a scientific advisory committee was set up which gave impetus to many investigations. In the beginning this was done with the cooperation of Tenhaeff; later, after the creation of the special professorate for the Dutch SPR in Utrecht, in the face of his growing opposition.

In 1950 F. A. Heyn and J. J. Mulckhuyse tried to repeat the well-known experiment of Whately Carington (use of drawings as test material) with Zener cards. A vast number of subjects all over Holland guessed the card J. J. M. exposed daily in his study. No significant results were obtained. In 1951 G. Zorab and H. A. Nanning did a radio experiment, also without significant results. In 1952 J. G. van Busschbach started his study of extrasensory perception in the classroom, which, in 1957, would bring him the first McDougall Award.

In 1953 A. Mak started his investigation of "objective" clairvoyance. His subjects guessed the color of marbles directed to the left or to the right in a special apparatus. Only the total score was given, not the correctness of the individual guesses. Nobody ever knew which guess was correct or incorrect. Thus telepathy was ruled out. As is often the case in group experiments, positive results were cancelled by negative ones. I took part in the investigation and, in retrospect, I think it would have been better to use an analysis of variance. Although no impressive experimental work was done in Holland, the important proceedings that took place abroad, the tireless lecturing and writing of Tenhaeff, stimulated by the advent of a few remarkable paragnosts, bore fruit. After strong opposition from several sides, the Dutch SPR was given the right to establish a special professorate in parapsychology at Utrecht and the University took care of establishing a small laboratory in 1953.

For various reasons, but also to underline the importance of Utrecht for parapsychology, the First International Conference of Parapsychological Studies, sponsored by the Parapsychology Foundation, was held in that city. It brought together 63 members of 14 nationalities and various disciplines for a lively discussion of psi problems. This conference brought new impetus to research in Holland and, for several Dutchmen, international contacts in the field started there. The importance of American and British studies with the aid of statistics was better understood and stimulated work in that direction. But lack of money prevented many experiments. To be noted is the work of J. D. A. M. de Neijn van Hoogwerff on clock-tests published in 1956.

Generally speaking there was a growing chasm between Tenhaeff's Institute of Parapsychology and most of the other workers. In the Dutch SPR a lot of time was frittered away by endless discussions and internal conflicts.

The third crisis in the SPR

In 1960 the tension in the Dutch SPR came to a head. Part of the members thought work no longer possible there and left. They set up study groups in several towns with a joint periodical, *Spiegel der Parapsychologie* (Mirror of Paraspchology). For some years much research was done in the spare time of the participants. To maintain interest in parapsychology in the general public, lectures were given regularly. From this time on, as much parapsychological work was done outside the SPR as inside it. Therefore I will discuss this separately.

INVESTIGATIONS AFTER 1960

To obtain money for parapsychology, Kappers set up in 1959 the Amsterdam Foundation for Parapsychological Research (ASPO). Many professors of both Universities of Amsterdam joined the Board of the ASPO, and the vice-chancellor of Amsterdam University, Professor J. Kok, became chairman. The Foundation obtained some private funds and Kappers started an investigation of the influence of psychedelics on ESP, in cooperation with the psychologist S. R. van Asperen de Boer and a continuing change of psychiatrists. Reports in the literature had given them the impression that psychedelics would facilitate psi. They did get some results with LSD, but this is a powerful drug and subjects are not very cooperative. So, with a grant from the Netherlands Organization for the Advancement of Pure Science, they continued the investigation with psilocybin. This time, P. R. Barkema was the psychiatrist. They compared subjects under normal conditions and during psilocybin intoxication, and had a small control-group of sensitives under normal conditions. In all three groups they found significant indication of psi operating, but there was no difference in performance, and they concluded that psilocybin did not facilitate psi.

In the late fifties Kappers set up a committee in Amsterdam to investigate the occurrence of spontaneous paranormal phenomena. The starting point was to find out the frequency of psi occurrences in daily life. A pilot inquiry was made and, based on its results, a questionnaire was sent to 8,000 randomly chosen inhabitants of Amsterdam over 21 years old. The response was so overwhelming that the verification took years and the compilation still longer, so that Kappers has not yet been able, notwithstanding much cooperation, to publish the results. He was able to present a preliminary report at the 1964 convention of the Parapsychological Association in Oxford: Almost 1% of the population had had an important paranormal experience one or more times in life, and another 2% had had less important experiences. At least one of every 1,200 has had out-of-the-body experiences. This proves that paranormal phenomena are not rare, and show the importance of psi research. The psychologist R. Greiner compared 20 people who had had spontaneous experiences with 20 people who did not have such experiences but who were interested in the investigation and 20 people without experiences and without interest. He could not find significant personality differences. The inquiry and Greiner's follow-up were made possible by grants from the Parapsychology Foundation.

In 1963, by courtesy of Dr. Milan Ryzl, J. Barendregt, P. R. Barkema and J. Kappers had an opportunity to conduct an experiment with Pavel Stepanek in Prague which gave highly significant results. Later, J. G. Blom, an engineer with the Phonetics Laboratory of the University of Amsterdam, repeatedly cooperated with G. Pratt in his experiments with Stepanek. Blom developed and published a method to account for code conversion in card tests. He also conducted a television experiment in psychokinesis with an apparatus wherein steel balls balancing on pins are to be willed to the left or to the right. Unfortunately this effort was not successful. The same could be said of a follow-up investigation by Blom and Kappers with a subject of the psilocybin series, who had scored significantly on card tests at first (with allowance for code-conversion), but had no success the second time. Enthusiasm waned in the study circles, as most of these efforts and many more were undertaken part-time by people under pressure of work in their own full-time occupations. Some even considered quitting parapsychology. But then, something happened at the universities. Almost at the same time, in 1967, at five different universities, groups of students took an interest in parapsychology. It may have been curiosity about the use of psychedelic drugs for producing altered states of consciousness that fostered this movement. At three of these universities, permanent student societies were set up and several investigations were started. Periodicals were printed. In Amsterdam, at the instigation of Kappers, R. Esser undertook a pilot study to reproduce the findings of D. Dean with the use of a plethysmograph, and some results were obtained. Later, attention focused on the van Busschbach's experiments and two groups headed by B. Camstra and D. Bierman set up vast programs with school children.

In Amsterdam, all the students are now grouped in the Study Centre for Experimental Parapsychology (SCEPP).

In Utrecht, the group under the psychologist L. Pannekoek conducted card, picture and PK experiments, so far without significant results, and interest there seems to be shifting to an investigation of astrology.

A common characteristic of the student groups is that, with all their enthusiasm, they are strongly conscious of methodology. SCEPP has a methodology committee that checks all proposed investigations. In Amsterdam, a close cooperation between SCEPP and the study group has been established.

THE INSTITUTE FOR PARAPSYCHOLOGY IN UTRECHT

The main efforts of the Institute have been (a) the investigation of the personality structure of gifted paragnosts, (b) some research on paranormal healing, and (c) the publication of case studies of clairvoyants. The hope that the laboratory would carry out a program of experiments has not been fulfilled.

a) *Personality structure of paragnosts*

The outcome of this investigation compares with other findings as Eysenck noted in a review of parapsychological studies on this subject (*Journal* of the SPR, June 1967, p. 59). Tenhaeff has given, writes Eysenck, "personality tests to such persons which reinforce this impression of somewhat unstable extraversion. However, the tests used in his research are entirely of a very subjective, interpretive character, and it would not be wise to accept their evidence without many qualifications." Another possible criticism is that the experimenters do not indicate how the paranormality of the subjects was established. Kappers did several experiments with a subject included in the investigation without any significant results, while other experiments with a subject excluded from the investigation produced very good results.

b) *Paranormal Healing*

A special group for research on paranormal healing was established, but although many important political and industrial men joined the Board, lack of money and opportunity frustrated this effort. An investigation of a healer, initiated by Tuyter as a pilot study, did not have any follow-up.

It is understandable that much attention was given to paranormal healings. Gerard Croiset, an outstanding paragnost as well as a very successful healer, has been for many years a subject of Tenhaeff. Unorthodox healing is of great social interest as M. van de Vall showed in a study of "The Public and the Magnetizer" (*Tijdschrift voor Parapsychologie*, November 1955, p. 236). Shortly after the war, Musaph carried out some experiments with Croiset and thought that the patient's reaction was a response to his personal expectation of the healer and not to the actual acts of the healer. But then Musaph did not take into account the possibility of telepathy, which can't be screened out. But, as Kappers argued, although this problem warrants investigation, it is not for parapsychology to take the lead. Unfortunately, the efforts of Tenhaeff with healers were used against the Institute many years later by opponents at the University to thwart a continuation of the Institute and the nomination of a medical man to a newly created chair in parapsychology.

c) *Case studies of clairvoyants*

Perhaps the most important contributions of the Institute to parapsychology are the case studies of such sensitives as G. Croiset, P. J. C. Seelen, and W. Tholen. The study of sensitives requires a special approach to obtain their cooperation for a period long enough to observe their capabilities and make use of the "Verstehende Methode" to interpret their communications. In this, Tenhaeff succeeded very well in several cases. The foremost objection to this procedure is the extreme subjectiveness inherent in the method. Gratifying therefore is the fact that the results, especially with Croiset, could be objectively demonstrated with chair-experiments. The paragnost foretells who will be the occupant of a randomly chosen chair in a room where a lecture is to be given at a later time. Of course it is essential that the audience be randomly seated. Repeatedly, remarkable results were obtained in this type of experiment.

To conclude this brief survey, something must be said about the man who contributed more books and articles on parapsychology in Holland than any other and gave his attention to every aspect of parapsychology: Dr. W. H. C. Tenhaeff. A selection from his publications is difficult. Perhaps his books on spiritism and war prognostications belong to the best. Dr. Tenhaeff attempted to relate paranormal phenomena to concepts of various schools of psychology and, repeatedly, the theory he decided on could have been the starting point of clearly defined experiments to confirm or invalidate a hypothesis. He chose not to do so. As de Neyn van Hoogwerff pointed out in a recent study, this leads to dogmatic formulations and "puts the openness of his scientific investigation under restraint." Tenhaeff continued along the course set in the twenties by himself, Dietz, de Jong, Ortt, Poortman, etc., which was to describe, interpret and investigate historical cases. This explains why he selected for his inaugural address as a professor, a spontaneous case of a 17th century navigator, instead of sketching the vast areas of research which could link parapsychology to the other sciences. Thus he did not keep up with the rapidly developing psychical research in Holland, which is strongly influenced by the methodology of the Amsterdam School. This is one of the reasons that he could never train successors for his chair. The threat that Utrecht University will close down the Institute and incorporate parapsychology into experimental psychology is the extreme reaction to a one-sided view of the investigation of parapsychology.

In the opinion of the present writer, a solution must be found so that parapsychological research in Holland can be independent as well as multi-sided.

PARAPSYCHOLOGY IN ITALY TODAY

Piero Cassoli

When on August 29th, 1957, Mrs. Garrett greeted the small group of Italian people who took part in an International Research Coordination Meeting, she addressed Dr. Marabini and me—a very active tandem up to that moment in the field of experimental psychical research—and, looking into our eyes, said: "You, Dr. Cassoli, will continue studying and researching in parapsychology. You, Dr. Marabini, will not." It was the last time I saw this extraordinary person, who has forever left her trace on the history of parapsychology. With this reminiscence I would like to pay homage to her clairvoyant faculties. Indeed, thick clouds gathered over our Center in Bologna; members were divided over methodological problems that even risked—and I could not permit that—questioning the existence of parapsychology itself, and Dr. Marabini left the national parapsychological stage. At first, helped by Dr. Buscaroli, then by Dr. Inardi, present President of the Center, I continued working amid the difficulties, the disbelief, the distrust and continuous professional injury, for what in my opinion is, today more than ever clear, this wonderful but grievous ordeal, the study of parapsychology in Italy.

It is true, as Professor Servadio says, that in parapsychology as in every science, "life starts today," but it is also true, as he adds, that "it is the experience of yesterday which makes that of today possible."

In Italy, the coordinated planned study of our subject started in November 1901, when Angelo Marzorati founded the Societa di Studi Psichici (Society of Psychic Studies) in Milan, and started a series of experimental researches with the mediums Politi, Eusapia Palladino and Lucia Sordi. Among members, I will mention such well-known personalities as the anthropologist, psychiatrist and criminologist Cesare Lombroso; the physiologist Filippo Bottazzi; and the neuro-psychiatrist Enrico Morselli, whose book *Psicologia e Spiritismo* (Psychology and Spiritism) is certainly a classic in our field. I must also cite Luigi Barzini, Antonio Fogazzaro, Luigi Capuana, Ernesto Bozzano, Antonio Bruers, William Mackenzie, and Rocco Santoliquido who were interested in parapsychology at different levels.

In Rome, in 1937, four well-known scholars, Ferdinando Cazzamalli, L. R. Sanguineti, Giovanni Schepis and Emilio Servadio founded the Societa Italiana di Metapsichica—SIM (Italian Society of Metapsychics), which, on January 23rd, 1941, was recognized by a State Government decree.

In 1946, after the war, a section of SIM led by Professor Cazzamalli left the Society and formed the present Associazione di Metapsichica in Milan—AISM (Italian Scientific Association of Metapsychics). Later on the Societa Italiana di Metapsichica changed its name to Societa Italiana di Parapsicologia—SIP, using the term parapsychology instead of the more traditional metapsychics.

In 1948, the Centro Studi Parapsicologici (Center for Parapsychological Studies) was established in Bologna. The founders were Dr. Buscaroli, Dr. Marabini and Dr. Cassoli. At first it was a section of the AISM of Milan; then it led an autonomous life asserting itself as the most active center, particularly in the experimental field.

In 1959 in Naples, the Review *Uomini e Idee* (Men and Ideas) started publication. In 1965 it was replaced by *Informazioni di Parapsicologia* (News of Parapsychology), as an organ of the Centro Italiano di Parapsicologia (Italian Center of Parapsychology), a new association that joined the other three already in existence.

At the end of 1968 there was established in Pavia the Centro Italiano di Studi Metapsichici (Italian Center of Metapsychic Studies), with a more limited program: the organiaztion and study of psychic healers in Italy.

Finally, in Rome, in 1960 the Facoltà di Scienze Psichiche e Psicologiche (Faculty of Psychic and Psychological Sciences) of Academia Tiberina was established.

This concludes the historical survey of the associations interested in parapsychology in Italy.

I think it is appropriate now to give an idea of the work of each of these associations and of the trend, too often not very clearly stated, of the association itself or its members. The order of precedence coincides chronologically with the appearance of each on the Italian stage, keeping the Center I represent, that of Bologna, until the end.

Societa Italiana di Parapsicologia—SIP (Italian Society of Parapsychology). Present President: Professor Stefano Somogy of the Faculty of Statistic Science of the University of Florence. Address: Via dei Montecatini 7, Rome. Periodical: *Rassegna Italiana di Ricerca Psi-*

chica (Italian Review of Psychic Research), four monthly issues grouped in one or two volumes.

After a period of intense activity before the Second World War, the Society slowed down, with brief revivals, as is usual in our field, this being tied in with the activity of such scholars as Egidi, Tron, Mancini, Perrone, Schepis, and Nestler. The work of Professor Servadio who, I think, is today celebrating his twentieth participation in the Conferences of the Parapsychology Foundation, has always stood out for its continuity and important contributions to international meetings. We see his articles (the most recent on healers, psychedelic substances, Voodun and Comblé rites) in the Review of the Society. But Professor Servadio's activity embraces general parapsychological activity both in Italy and elsewhere, so it is superfluous for me to emphasize his contribution here.

SIP has the cooperation of a very qualified journalist and scientific writer: Dr. Leo Talamonti, author of *Universo Proibito* (Forbidden Universe), a very popular book in Italy (Sugar, 1966, Mondadori, 1969). I would say that the SIP's present contribution is only cultural and informative (Journal and annual series of lectures); no known experimentations, no or very few on-the-spot investigations of so-called spontaneous phenomena.

As our purpose here is to inform you of the trends of the different groups and societies in their respective geographic areas, I should add that except for the attitude of a few members of the SIP, we can observe from the latest issues of the Review a particular trend toward interest in books and subjects dealing more with "related fields" than with "the scientific approach to parapsychology." The Society does not even seem interested, as other associations are, in obtaining funds for research, or in attempting to persuade the University to establish free university courses or a chair in parapsychology.

Before going on to the Italian Scientific Association of Metapsychics in Milan, the second chronologically, I would like to mention a Roman institution:

Accademia Tiberina. President: Professor Igor Istomin-Duranti. Address: Via del Vantaggio 22, Rome.

The Accademia Tiberina carries out didactic activity in different areas, including the psychological field in general, with the Facolta di Scienze Psichiche e Psicologiche (Faculty of Psychic and Psychological Sciences) at the head.

It is a sad fact that in Italy we found it necessary to establish such a "Faculty" outside of the University, because of the insensitivity of the academic world, which even today has difficulty in catching up not only with new trends, but also with students' demands. Indeed, in many universities, psychology is not taught; it is considered an optional subject.

In Italy out of 22 universities where medicine is taught, only five Faculties of Medicine have chairs of psychology; and only three universities have a course in medical psychology. It is impossible to obtain a university degree in psychology because we do not have a Faculty of Psychology and there are no departments of psychology.

This lack has been made up through the "good will" of the "Faculty of Psychic and Psychological Sciences" I just mentioned. But what we want particularly to emphasize is that the teaching course, divided into a normal course of three years and a course of specialization, provides also for the teaching of parapsychology with duplicated lecture notes, lectures and groups of experimentation.

I personally got in touch with a peripheric section of the "Accademia," that of Padua, which, before becoming a section of the Accademia, was already known in Italy through the publication of a survey on the "Centro di Ricerche Biopsichiche" (Center of Biopsychic Research), edited by Mr. Giorgio Foresti. This Center was active in research relating to spontaneous phenomena, and one of its Council members, Ing. Aldo Berlanda, was one of the few Italians to witness the "psychic surgery" of the famous medium José Arigò in Belo Horizonte in Brazil. Today, the aim of the Center in Padua is mostly directed toward filling the need for teaching psychotherapy in Padua and in Venetia, and it tries to cooperate at an academic level with Italian and foreign associations having the same interest. Mr. Giorgio Foresti is helped in his work by Ing. Aldo Berlanda and Mrs. Carla Berlanda, a doctor in pedagogy. The address of the Center is: Via Dante 13/A, Padua.

Associazione Italiana Scientifica di Metapsichica—AISM (Italian Scientific Association of Metapsychics). Present President: Ing. Ettore Mengoli. The Honorary President is now Professor W. H. C. Tenhaeff. Address: Corso Firenza 8, Genova. Periodical: *Metapsichica,* official organ of the Society and of our Center in Bologna; two issues, January–June and July–December.

In Milan, headquarters of the Center, Mr. Luigi Occhipinti, who is a lawyer and one of the vice-presidents, carries on active work.

This association was founded in 1946, breaking away from the SIP in Rome because of friction between the then President Professor Ferdinando Cazzamalli and some members, and officially assumed the denomination "scientific." Now it carries on social and official cultural and information activities (through two annual interregional meetings and the Review), while leaving investigation or experimentation to the individual researcher. But I must say that the activity of the Society regarding diffusion of information and relations with all the other national and foreign associations is of enormous value. For this, special praise is due Ing. Mengoli who is the animator. This activity was reported in the Review *Metapsichica,* which, I think, after the *Parapsychology Review* is one of the best for up-to-dateness and wealth of news. The Review also avails itself of the cooperation of a keen parapsychologist, Professor Vincenzo Nestler, whose knowledge of parapsychology is surpassed by few other persons in Italy.

Dr. Giuseppe Crosa of Genova, a psychiatrist, is one of the two Vice-Presidents of the AISM. He is known for having taken part in several international Congresses (Konstanz, Kyoto, Moscow, Freiburg) and for introducing into Italy the autogenous training of Schultz. Lately he became interested in the phenomena of the paranormal tape recording of Kostantin Raudive, and in the Rol case, a much debated instance of complex and polymorphic phenomena, still talked about in the press. Dr. Crosa also studied the phenomenon of psychic healing and collected numerous case histories of subjects with mediumistic painting ability. He organized three meetings on parapsychological topics in Campione d'Italia (1968-69-71).

Another cooperator of the AISM is Dr. Giorgio Alberti, a young doctor who, in Milan, obtained his doctoral degree discussing a thesis on "Methodological Criticism of the Experimental Parapsychological Method" with Professor Cesa-Bianchi, professor of psychology at the University of Milan (Faculty of Medicine). Dr. Alberti was still a student when he was entrusted with the supervision of a group of eight students who asked that parapsychological subjects be included in their curriculum. He carried out this task both at didactic and experimental levels. Working with Dr. Alberti, the student Franco Guarnieri, physics major in his senior year, taught a course on experimental PK, and will present his doctoral thesis on this subject. This year at the Institute of Medical Psychology, Professor H. Bender was invited to give a lecture on spontaneous PK at which he showed three films (Kulagina, Ted Serios, and the Rosenheim case). Another serious and active collaborator is Mr. Nicola Riccardi, who recently concerned himself with the so-called Rol phenomena and with physical phenomena.

Centro Italiano di Parapsicologia—CIP (Italian Center of Parapsychology). Address: Via Calascione 5/A, Naples. President and editor of the Review: Architect Giorgio di Simone. Periodical: *Informazioni di Para-*

psicologia (News of Parapsychology). In 1959, in Naples a review of philosophy, science and metapsychics started publication under the title *Uomini e Idee* (Men and Ideas). In 1965, the review was first changed into a literary review and later gave way, in the parapsychological field, to the present *Informazioni di Parapsicologia*.

CIP is active in cultural, informative and experimental programs. Recently, Professor Di Simone agreed to edit for a Roman publishing house a series of books entitled *La Ricerca Psichica* (Psychic Research). He will start with the reprint of rare and out-of-print books, and follow with books on modern parapsychology. Recently, the Center promoted an inquiry into interesting cases of paranormal phenomena with a well thought-out questionnaire. This was widely accepted here and abroad.

CIP continues to maintain relations with academic authorities and others, attempting to get subsidies and obtain a chair of parapsychology. But in vain—all doors remain closed.

It is true that it appears more and more clearly from the Review, that some doubts may be raised about the trends of this group. Indeed, in January 1969, it published a very extensive report of many hundreds of sittings carried out with a person who, Di Simone says, "I will call the 'medium' because I cannot violate a pledge of secrecy of his identity, and this has prevented us up to now from imposing a rigorous scientific control of his faculties."

The communications come from a "dimension X" and are given by an "Entita A." The author realizes the danger he is running and concedes this over and over again. We acknowledge this. But we hope that Professor Di Simone will admit that it is not with this kind of material that we can hope to enter the university. The author intends, according to the program he sent us and which we are now illustrating, to carry out experiments on "spectra of voices" through comparative analysis with the medium's voice. This is an incorporation phenomenon not one of "direct voice."

The tenor of the communications from the so-called "Entita A" are, as you may suppose, of a spiritual nature; they attempt to explain moral, ehtical, cosmological and scientific problems.

Another collaborator of the CIP is Mr. Corrado Piancastelli who was—and is—interested in the so-called "San Gennaro's blood miracle"; his pamphlet on this puzzling phenomenon gives a thorough description of it.

Centro Studi Parapsicologici de Bologna—CSP (Center of Parapsychological Studies in Bologna), Via Tamagno 2 (the President's home). President: Dr. Massimo Inardi. Periodical: *Quaderni di Parapsicologia* (Notebooks on Parapsychology). I personally edit the review and direct the group on experimentation. My address is Via L. Valeriani 39, 40134 Bologna. Professor Enzo Nardi, a lawyer and full Professor of Roman Canon, is our Honorary President. He published, some years ago, a book on *Haunted Houses and Old and Modern Canon* which is, in my opinion, still basic today, if one is interested in the legal details of rent agreements where a "haunted house" is concerned. CSP now has 110 members. Reports of its activities from 1956 to 1961 were published in *Minerva Medica,* the most important Italian medical review. Then, and this was a big mistake, we gave up such academic aims in order to establish, jointly with the other associations in Rome and in Milan, a review that came to an end with the death of Professor G. Schepis. The CSP now cooperates with *Metapsichica* of the AISM. It will try to publish in the *Notebooks on Parapsychology* reports of experimental work, texts of important lectures (given in Bologna during the academic year), and the contributions of its scholars to Congresses and meetings.

Two and a half years ago, the Group of Study and Experimentation was formed. Today it comprises twenty members, graduates and students in physics, biology, medicine, the humanities. In order to join the group, one must be qualified to take part in experimental activities. The applicant must possess a general knowledge of parapsychology; he may present a short thesis with his comments to the Group in session.

Competence is necessary because the Group receives numerous requests from subjects who want to be examined, or for information on alleged paranormal phenomena taking place in Italy or abroad. In such cases, we form a Commission of three or four, led by an expert (up to now, most of the time, my wife) and start the so-called preliminary or explorative examination. If the phenomenon appears worthy of consideration, if it is publicly known, then I intervene personally and investigate the case to the best of my ability (check and control period).

I will mention briefly some of the studies that have up to now given the best results.

Many years ago, we studied at length (for three years) one Maria Gardini, a palmist, using more and more rigorous controls to prevent the so-called "sensorial cues," going so far as to put the subject, examined by the palmist, behind a wood screen (a cabin-shaped construction) from which only the hands came out. The results were always positive and they have been published in two works.

In the past we also carried out GESP experiments, using as "targets" events really lived by people who operated as transmitters or agents. The results were presented at a Congress held in Bologna at the local Neuropsychiatric Clinic.

I also engaged in a series of experiments in precognition using pre-ferred targets, that is to say, chosen by the twelve subjects at the begin-ning of the experiments (which lasted six months) and which would always be mixed in their single pack. The data, although negative, were considered interesting by Professor A. Naddeo, professor of Sta-tistic Sciences at the University of Rome, and Mr. Alberto Agnetti worked on these data to make them the subject of his graduation thesis "Statistical Criticism of an ESP experiment." This was the first thesis on a parapsychological topic discussed in Italy (1961-1962). My wife and I led this work on precognition with the help of a subsidy from the Parapsychology Foundation.

I also went to Greece for a preliminary examination of the phenom-enon of fire-walking, again with funds provided by the Parapsychology Foundation, and reported on my trip here in Le Piol. The results were positive and probative.

We followed up with an experiment in fire-walking here in Bologna, with two subjects of Naples who claimed to be able to repeat the Anas-tenarides performance, but the result was completely negative.

We organized two surgical operations performed under hypnosis (appendectomy and tonsillectomy) with controls excluding any possi-bility of fraudulent (pharmacological) intervention, and obtained posi-tive and really exceptional results. Professor Servadio was present.

More recently, we initiated experiments in influencing the growth of fungi by the laying on of hands. After many trials, in which I also served as subject, it seems we found a subject giving positive results.

Dr. Inardi, my wife and I were present at one of the "exploits" or "performances"—I cannot call them experiments—of the famous Dr. Rol of Turin. My preliminary report, already published, bears the title "G. A. Rol, a Great Medium or a Great Illusionist?" The impos-sibility of applying even the slightest control prevents me from express-ing any judgment. I can only say that what we saw that evening was something akin to the miraculous. In our many years of activity, we have examined about one hundred subjects, and the on-the-spot investi-gations of alleged paranormal phenomena have been many (some far from Bologna and for periods of many days). We have uncovered many tricks, some trivial, others complex and shrewd.

The last investigation worthy of interest was the so-called "case of the bells of Carpegna." Carpegna is a small village in the center of Italy, close to the Republic of San Marino, where there is a priory of Franciscan Friars. In November 1970, in the cloister and inside the priory itself, people began hearing the sound of bells, sometimes loud, sometimes soft, exactly like the sound of the bells of the bell-tower.

But the priory bells actually remained perfectly still and silent. With the cooperation of an electronic technician and a physicist, we explored every corner of the priory for two days and conducted some experiments. We did not uncover any tricks or presumed medium. The phenomenon stopped three days after our departure only to start again later and continue sporadically up to Easter. We will publish a report on this subject after we have studied the collected data.

Also in November 1970 we came across a case of presumed "spiritualistic painting." As the subject lived in our town, we were able to follow up the case, using controls, for about four months, that is to say, until the phenomena ceased. The subject is 57 years old, a dental mechanic, who had never painted in his life. On the night of March 19, 1970, an irresistible impulse compelled him to get up and paint. Since then and for the whole year, almost every night (at 1 or 2 o'clock) he got up and produced a painting. With the aid of hypnosis we obtained some results, even after the end of the spontaneous phenomenon. Of this case also I will write a report this year.

At present I am investigating a poltergeist case in Rimini about which it is still too soon to speak.

Apart from these five associations, I would like to mention, though I think few are unaware if it, that the review *Luce e Ombre* (Light and Shadow), founded by Marzorati with Ernesto Bozzano as a collaborator, is continuing its program firmly though with difficulties. Everyone knows the spiritualistic leanings of Dr. Gastone De Boni and of many of his collaborators, among whom I would cite Jacopo Comin, one of the few "scholars" already mentioned as exceptional experts in parapsychological bibliography. The trend, the aims, the dangers are clear. We have a deep friendship and esteem for Dr. De Boni and his work; we would like to help him still more. But in no way can we agree to his standards of control of the phenomena.

There are still three matters to speak about concerning parapsychology in Italy. One is a thesis (the third) by Mr. P. Curci on "Extrasensorial Perceptions and Psychopathology," which was discussed in Modena with Professor Rossini; no relations between capacity and psychopathology have been found here, either.

The second matter puzzled me. On October 17, 1969, in Rome, at the Accademia Alphonsiana of the Pontifical "Università Lateranense," the opening lecture of a course in parapsychology directed by the Reverend Father Professor Andreas Resch, was presented. The course was included in the first academic semester 1969-1970, and seminary directors and Catholic priests of every race and country took part. Perhaps it will be useful if I make a list of the subjects which were treated: 1. Conceptus paranormale; 2. Paranormalia in historia et scientia; 3) Phaenomena parapsychica (levitation, haunted houses); 4. Phaenomena parapsychologica (stigmata); 5. Phaenomena paraphisica (materializations); 6. Phaenomena paranormalia mere intellectualia (intuitions, prophecies, precognitions); 7. Faticitas phaenomenorum paranormalium; 8. Explicationes et theoriae.

I must say that I don't like to present this news as a conquest or as an Italian contribution to the achievements of parapsychology here and in the world.

On the other hand, I can proudly announce that on September 25, 1971, a symposium on parapsychology, sponsored by the SIP (Italian Society of Psychiatry), and in which directors of university institutes and head physicians in hospitals will take part, will be held at the psychiatric Clinic of the University of Modena. Professor Emilio Servadio will speak on "Parapsychology and Psychoanalysis," and I will speak on "Limits and Subjects of Parapsychology." I think this symposium marks an important stage in the achievements of parapsychology in Italy.

And so I have finished. I think I have answered the questions I was asked when I had the honor to be invited by the Parapsychology Foundation to this meeting. Anyway, I would like to answer these questions in a brief, concise way:

1. Which scientific doctrines are concerned with psychical research?

Here in Italy, for the moment and in a marginal way, psychology, psychiatry, hypnosis, psychoanalysis (Servadio and Gaddini are at this time the most directly interested) and statistic sciences.

2. Are the different groups scientifically oriented or do they tend toward occultism, spiritism or related fields?

All groups, except the review *Luce e Ombra* (Light and Shadow), declare that they follow scientific aims and methodology. Almost everyone includes, more or less clearly, some trends which do not follow the Galilean method, the experimental one. Immodestly I would say that the CSP has never deviated from the scientific approach.

3. Is there an increase of interest among students and young people?

Without a doubt, there is a great increase. The study groups in Milan (Dr. Alberti) and our study group show evidence of this. Also in the other societies, there is an increasing demand for information and requests for membership by young people. Two months ago, for example, I was invited to a university college to give a series of lectures on parapsychology. The invitation came about at the express demand of the students.

4. The Parapsychological Association became a member of the Amer-

ican Association for the Advancement of Science. Does this represent progress in the acceptance of parapsychology as a scientific doctrine? Is it true for you, too?

I have always stressed that fact whenever possible. But for the moment, the fact is known to only a few and has not yet influenced the acceptance of parapsychology as a scientific doctrine. This acceptance is spreading here, in other channels, as, for example, in the press which devotes much space to it, with many articles by Professor Servadio, a pioneer—as always.

I thank you for your kind interest and hope I have been sufficiently thorough. We Italians will gratefully accept any help from any of you that will contribute to the success of parapsychology in Italy.

PARAPSYCHOLOGY IN FRANCE

Yvonne Duplessis

Parapsychology is not accepted as a scientific discipline in France today, nor is it part of the curriculum of any university in the country. Professors and students are interested in the subject, but they pursue their studies clandestinely. Some investigators who have done considerable research and conducted experiments in parapsychology have requested anonymity for fear that otherwise their academic progress would be jeopardized. A striking example was the 12th Annual McDougall Award to two French researchers whose true names were never revealed, at their request. And yet, the fact is that parapsychology in France today, as in the past, has involved representatives of many scientific disciplines, including physicians, physicists, chemists and engineers among others. It is also noteworthy that in recent years, particularly the past two, more and more students have been meeting in formal and informal groups for the purpose of discussing their studies and experiments.

In 1971, students founded the Groupe d'Etudes et de Recherches en Parapsychologie (G.E.R.P.). Through this organization, they hope to exert the kind of pressure that will result in the acceptance of parapsychology as an integral part of the university curriculum.

Now, I will report briefly on experimental research. Since the results of most research work in France have already been published in the *Revue Métapsychique,* I shall deal with the more recent studies which have not yet been published.

Psychokinesis

1. *Animal Parapsychology.* The G.E.R.P. students have conducted laboratory experiments with white mice in a manner similar to Dr. Helmut Schmidt's work in the U.S.A. to discern possible psychokinesis (PK) effects in these animals. However, it must be pointed out that with the G.E.R.P. students, the generator of randomness was electronic and thus different from the one used by Dr. Schmidt, that was based on radioactive emission. It may be that comparison of the two

types of generators could possibly give a more precise evaluation of the nature and efficiency of the psi phenomena produced.

2. *Vegetal parapsychology.* Dr. and Mrs. Paul Vasse observed the effect of thought on germination and the growth of plants. Eight of their experiments were remarkably significant. However, when these experiments were repeated by others, there were varying degrees of success and sometimes negative results. More recently, Dr. Jean Barry and his collaborators made a statistical and comparative study of the psychokinetic effect on a culture of fungi in vitro.

Experiments in psi missing were conducted in 1965 and 1966. Experimenters were chosen from both sheep and goats. Psychical and physiological states were noted before each trial. There were nine experiments in 1965, and another nine in 1966.

For each trial, the total results were compared with the control fungus by the calculation of variance. The results for some of the experimenters were quite significant.

Among other researches conducted in the Laboratory of Dr. Barry in Bordeaux, I will note the telepathic experiments with the plethysmograph. Some of these were long-distance experiments between Dr. Barry (the sender) in Bordeaux and Professor Douglas Dean (the receiver) in the U.S., at the Newark Engineering College, New Jersey. Statistical results were significant.

3. *The PK Effect on Material Systems*

The engineers Mr. De Cressac and Mr. G. Chevalier have constructed equipment for the study of the PK effect. The engineer, Mr. René Pérot constructed a machine for throwing dice. All these experiments were conducted under the same conditions, once a week, utilizing the same target: No. 3. Mrs. Pérot, a subject in her husband's experiments, scored highest with a C.R. of 21 in 1956-57 in a total of 5,568 trials.

Discussion

The notable difference in the scores obtained by Mrs. Pérot and the two other subjects is that her results confirmed those she obtained during ten years of experiments in clairvoyance. These results in turn confirm the original hypothesis offered some years ago by Professor J. B. Rhine in his own well-known experiments. Parenthetically, it should be noted here that Mr. G. Clauzure of the Laboratory of Parapsychology in Bordeaux, headed by Dr. Jean Barry, has also conducted experimental research on the PK energy of the unconscious. The results are noteworthy for they showed that a subject who had scored

33 on 180 throws, scored 48 out of 180 throws after training, the probability actually being 30 for 180 throws.

Clairvoyance

A variety of important experiments in clairvoyance have been undertaken in France in recent years, and they will be noted briefly here. The physicist, Dr. R. Dufour, has engaged in research on clairvoyance and psychometricity. Dr. Dufour worked with a group of about ten persons once a week on his experiments. In his research Dr. Dufour utilized an apparatus which revealed a so-called automatic manifestation, which in turn has great interest for psychoanalysts.

Parapsychological phenomena associated with blindness

For the physiologist Ch. Féré (*Sensation et Mouvement*, 1887) all sensory excitations have comparable physiological effects, of which he has measured the variations. The sharpness of a sense, he believes, can be reinforced by the excitation of another sense. For example, the sound of a tuning fork lowers the level of perception. There is also the possibility that a sound induces a color, as in the phenomenon called "color hearing," which is the most frequent of the "synesthesias." Furthermore, peripheric excitations have repercussions throughout the nervous system by increasing the energy and reinforcing all the psychical activity.

Thus, we have investigated the concentration of the sender on peripheric excitations. Although auditory and olfactory excitations have given some results, the best ones have been induced by the tactile impressions of the sender, for example, when he touched a three-dimensional picture.

We have also conducted experiments with blind subjects. Having no sight, they have developed the sharpness of their other senses and they are very attentive to their internal feelings. Most blind people have a highly developed visual imagination. Some have colored dreams and often they also have "color hearing."

GESP and Blindness

We have been experimenting since 1966 with two blind students and with Mr. Jacques Berthaux who became blind thirty years ago. Since he is a sculptor, we have had an opportunity to investigate the interrelationship of creativity and GESP. (We reported these first experiments at the Thirteenth Annual Convention of the Parapsychological Association. Our experiments reveal that "inward speaking" is well developed among blind subjects. These subjects are also better senders than receivers, but it seems difficult for them to synchronize their movement with that of a non-blind person.

Effects of Light and Colors on Blind Subjects

The forerunner of research on eyeless vision in France was Jules Romains of the Académie Française. In 1920 his book, entitled *La Vision Extra-Rétinienne et le Sens Paroptique,* was first published, and it was reissued in 1964. Mr. Romains honored us by coming to one of our meetings in Paris at the Centre d'Information de la Couleur in April 1971 and observing our experiments.

In these brief notes I have mentioned the relatively modern experiments in psychical research in France. It is essential that I allude also to the earlier history of this science in France, where parapsychology is actually a division of metaphysical studies and derives from some of the early work of Professor Charles Richet, the Nobel Laureate in Medicine and Physiology in 1913. Richet, as we all know, included in his studies the physical phenomena exhibited by mediums and the manifestation of what we now call psi phenomena. Professor Richet was elected President of the Society for Psychical Research, London, in 1905, and some French correspondents of the SPR in that earlier period included Th. Ribot, H. Taine, Dr. P. Janet, and Ch. Féré. In 1913 Henri Bergson was elected President of the SPR, thus strengthening the ties of French thinkers internationally with psychical research. (See *Parapsychology Review,* May-June 1970, for reprint of the Bergson address.) One of the most significant developments in the advance of psychical research in France was undoubtedly signalled by Jean Meyer's founding of the Institut Métapsychique in 1919. Its first Honorary President was Charles Richet, who became active president in 1930. Other presidents have been Dr. Moutier and René Warcollier, the chemical engineer. He was succeeded in 1934 by Dr. Ch. Roux. Some of the first directors were Drs. G. Geley and E. Osty, and the mediums studied during those early years of the Institut included F. Kluski and J. Guzig. Thus, the studies of the blind, of clairvoyance, of psychokinesis and other phenomena mentioned earlier in these brief observations are a natural historical development which began at the turn of the century. As I conclude, I must note that the founder of the Parapsychology Foundation, Eileen J. Garrett, was one of the pioneer publishers in America who first brought to the attention of the American and international audiences the work of René Warcollier and of the other French pioneers.

PARAPSYCHOLOGY IN CANADA

J. M. O. WHEATLEY *

In Toronto, both at the University of Toronto and off-campus, there are now signs that parapsychology will be more energetically and widely studied in the near future than has previously been the case. While I know of no plans to introduce full-blown courses in parapsychology at this institution (unfortunately our students lack opportunity to take the sort of basic course in parapsychology that has lately proved so popular in neighboring Buffalo, under Douglas Dean's tutelage), the Department of Philosophy is launching a new undergraduate course next year in which extrasensory perception will be considered at some length. Advance registration for this course indicates an unusually high class enrollment: much higher, in fact, than had been anticipated. Next year, also, I shall be giving a graduate seminar in philosophy of parapsychology, and, as far as I know, it will be the first time that a course in that subject has been offered at this University at the graduate level.

It does seem that more philosophers hereabouts are expressing interest in parapsychology, although I strongly doubt that this is a result of the recent "recognition" of the Parapsychological Association by the American Association for the Advancement of Science. Contributions from this and nearby universities have lately included a number of papers that deal, if not directly with problems in the philosophy of parapsychology, then with matters that are of interest and importance to philosophers of parapsychology. For example, I may cite an intriguing article on death by James Van Evra (University of Waterloo), who develops "a view in which death is seen to be a state which characterizes absoultely nothing, and hence requires no commitment to the belief in selves which survive death" ("On death as a limit," *Analysis* 31 [April, 1971]: 170-176), and two cogent papers by Douglas Odegard of the University of Guelph: "Disembodied existence and

* Professor Wheatley, unable to be present, mailed in his report in the form of a letter to the Parapsychology Foundation.

central state materialism" (*Australasian Journal of Philosophy* 48
[1970]: 256-260) and "Persons and bodies" (*Philosophy and Phenom-
enological Research* 31 [1970]: 225-242). In the first, Odegard attempts
to refute the view, which he finds in D. M. Armstrong's recent work
on *A Materialist Theory of the Mind*, "That central state materialism . . . can consistently allow the possibility of disembodied existence" (p. 256); and in the second, he argues that the propositions " 'It
is possible for any person connected to a body to become disconnected
from it' and 'No person connected to a body can be identical with that
body' must both be true" (p. 242).

As for experimental and other research at the first-order level, as
distinct from the philosophical, most of it is taking place off-campus.
Within this University, I understand, a little experimental research is
being done by individual students in the Department of Psychology,
but undertakings of seemingly greater promise are being made elsewhere. Two research organizations, each at least partly concerned with
parapsychological problems, have very recently been formed in Toronto, and evidently both have been active during the past year. One
group is the Toronto Society for Psychical Research, whose president
is Allen Spragget, a journalist of many parts and the author of the
widely-read book *The Unexplained*, and whose members (approximately 200) are investigating, among other things, ESP and PK, altered
states of consciousness, spontaneous cases, and psychic photography.
The other new organization is the New Horizons Research Foundation,
an institution whose fields of study, in addition to parapsychology,
include archeology, anthropology, and religion. The noted parapsychologist George Owen is Director of New Horizons and is also an
Honorary Councillor of the Toronto Society. Research has reportedly
been energetic and productive, and autumn publication of preliminary
results is expected.

The style, strategies, and goals of these new research endeavors will
obviously differ appreciably from those of an earlier tradition of psychical research carried out in Toronto and other Canadian centers, which
concerned itself primarily with the question of survival and was of the
mediumistic genre. The most recent example is the work of the Clendennings, a sedulous and talented family who devoted many years in
this city in the 1950s and 1960s to an inquiry into survival, an inquiry
described in *The Search*, by Gertrude Clendenning (London, 1968).
The reports and conclusions of this book may be compared to the remarkable results obtained by Thomas Glen Hamilton (1873-1935), that
indefatigable physician, educator, legislator, and psychical researcher
whose studies in deep-trance automatism, described in a book published

in Toronto in 1942, *Intention and Survival* (J. D. Hamilton, ed.), surely earned him the title of most outstanding pioneer in psychical research in Canada. His labors in this field, and their outcome, have just lately been rechronicled by his daughter, Margaret Hamilton, in a book entitled *Is Survival a Fact?* (London, 1969). On this question, she, and the Clendennings, and Dr. Hamilton himself all seem to agree that it is. And all three of these books, *Intention and Survival, The Search, Is Survival a Fact?*, are impressive, interesting, and careful records. The first is especially striking. Still, despite the convictions of their authors, many of us can read them, and shelves of more or less similar works, and remain thoroughly unconvinced about personal survival. Part of the reason, it would seem, is that in confronting the survival question we are facing one of those comparatively rare subjects (and here the contrast is with evolution, memory, "ordinary" paranormal phenomena, etc.) where we first need to know *how* before we can acknowledge *that*. In the matter of survival, indeed, perhaps we are constrained to understand how it could possibly be a fact, before we can even *believe* that it is one, for if it were a fact, then I suppose this would entail a need for us to reclassify as "paranormal" what we regard as "normal," and vice versa. Anyhow, the cited books are of little help in elucidating a theoretical framework that would afford a grasp of how a person possibly could "live after dying." To my mind, they don't make this idea any more intelligible or less bizarre. The "survival hypothesis" itself can hardly change the enigmatic quality of some of the putative evidence that they offer, for that "hypothesis" appears just to lack any explanatory force.

PARAPSYCHOLOGY'S CENTURY OF PROGRESS

Joseph H. Rush

INTRODUCTION

Parapsychologists soon will celebrate a hundred years of professional existence. During that period, the field has progressed from an exploratory anecdote-collecting enterprise to an emerging experimental science that is gaining increasing acceptance among more sophisticated scientific groups, and in academic circles generally. The University of Colorado, for example, now offers a course in ESP; and I have for the past two years assisted in such a course in the adult education program of one of the local school systems. The admission of the Parapsychological Association to membership in the American Association for the Advancement of Science in December, 1969, was a major indication of the changing attitude of scientists toward the field.

However, little professional psi research is currently being done in the western mountain region from which I come. The outstanding exception is the study of the apparent materialization of mental images on photographic film by Ted Serios, which Jule Eisenbud has investigated for several years. His work has been widely publicized through his book [1] and in journal articles, so I shall not dwell on it here.

Because of the scarcity of professional parapsychological work in my part of the country, I must depart somewhat from the primarily geographic emphasis of this conference. As an observer and sometime participant in this uniquely exciting field, I want to summarize what appear to be the more significant research trends of recent years, and to try to evaluate the present status of parapsychology as an emerging science. Finally, I will note some tendencies that I believe should be modified in the interest of further progress. My comments will relate primarily to the developments in the U.S.A., though by implication they will apply generally to Western Europe also. Psi research in the Communist countries has developed along significantly different lines, and my knowledge of it is not sufficient to justify including it.

Thouless recently published an excellent commentary on parapsychology in recent decades.[2] He noted that the outstanding developments since about 1945 have been the shift of emphasis from "proving" psi phenomena to exploring their characteristics, and the related adaptation of experimental methods and designs to this purpose. I shall not repeat his summary of psi characteristics that he considers established. Instead, I want to mention several categories of research that are especially significant or that appear to mark definite trends in parapsychology today.

RESEARCH TRENDS

Psychological and physiological correlates of psi

Parapsychologists have recognized increasingly that the psi manifestations are not a detached group of phenomena that can be studied in isolation. Rather, they are intimately involved with personality types, states of consciousness, motivations, personal relations, emotional states, physiological conditions, and other variables. Of course, such influences were recognized much earlier, and some of the pioneer work at Duke University involved exploratory tests of the effects on psi performance of drugs, motivation, and personal relationships. What is new is the rising emphasis on such investigations. During the past two years, for example, more than a third of the experimental reports in the *Journal of Parapsychology* have involved the evaluation of such correlates either incidentally or as their primary purpose.

Attempts to explore the relations between states of consciousness and psi performance appear to be especially significant; they build upon a long tradition as to the efficacy of meditation or dreaming as media for psi experiences, and they offer the possibility of conditioning a person for psi performance by management of his state of consciousness. Such investigations include the work of Ullman, Krippner, and Feldstein [3] on induction of telepathic dreams, that of Osis and Bokert on meditation,[4] and studies of the relation between the electroencephalographic (EEG) "alpha state" and ESP scoring by Rex and Birgit Stanford [5] and Honorton.[6]

Various information supports the hypothesis that the state of passive alertness in which the brain-wave pattern is dominated by the "alpha rhythm" is characteristic of meditation, and is favorable to psi experience. Research in this direction has increased sharply since the recent discovery that many persons can learn readily to go into or out of the alpha state at will if they are given feedback from the EEG so that they know what they are doing (e.g., Kamiya [7]). It would be naive to expect that just anyone could become psychic by turning on his alpha rhythm. More probably, the alpha state is but one of several psychological factors that facilitate psi. Nevertheless, the ability to monitor and control this state appears to be a significant step toward psi-training and the consistency of performance of which all parapsychologists dream.

Hypnosis has shown evidence since the early years of psi research of a potential for putting a person into a state favorable for psi performance. Later experiments by Vasiliev,[8] Ryzl, [9, 10] and Casler,[11] for example, support these indications. Nevertheless, hypnosis is little used by parapsychologists in the West.

Subliminal response mechanisms

This area is mentioned, not because it is a favored trend, but because I believe the work that is being done is especially significant. Subliminal or autonomic psi manifestations have been recognized for many years. Mediumistic trance, automatic writing, the planchette and Ouija board, all have figured in reports of psi communications; and a class of phenomena of which the poltergeist is typical appears to represent similarly unconscious PK performance.

Psi experiments in which the subject must report a consciously-formulated impression such as a card symbol are notoriously unreliable. Scores usually are low and subject to unpredictable fluctuations. Psychological considerations suggest that a substantial portion of the difficulty lies in the mediation of subliminal impulses or information into conscious awareness, and that the psi process might operate more reliably if it were "read out" through its effect on some autonomic indicator.

In recent years, Dean [12] has reported successful experiments in which psi effects on the capillary circulation have been monitored by the plethysmograph. Further pursuit of this and other autonomic response mechanisms might prove rewarding, particularly since recent research has demonstrated that the autonomic system is trainable by procedures similar to operant conditioning of the voluntary system.

Physical correlates of psi

Perhaps the most fundamental question concerning the psi phenomena is whether they are amenable to physical laws or limitations. Efforts to detect any relation between scoring level and distance between subject and target have been inconclusive, and material shields or barriers have not been shown to influence scoring significantly.

Osis and Turner [13] combined the results of thirteen reported experiments involving various distances, and found a consistent tendency toward reduced scores with increasing distances. They noted that the rate of decline was much less than the familiar inverse-square relation.

However, such a relation was not to be expected, because ESP tests measure information transfer, not field strength, and for other reasons.

Osis and Fahler [14] compared scoring with variables of distance (4,000 miles), time (precognition), and distance-and-time jointly. Only the latter condition yielded significant results, but these were at the .0007 level of probability. This curious result merits much further work. Recently Osis and Turner [15] have reported an unusually elaborate effort to detect a distance effect on clairvoyance scoring at distances up to 10,500 miles on the earth's surface. The results suggest a decline of scoring with distance, but more extensive experimentation is needed to resolve the question.

More distance may be needed also. It is most unfortunate that no use has been made of the space flights for psi experiments, except the test initiated by one of the Apollo astronauts (results unpublished). Earth may be simply too small to clarify the distance effect, if it exists.

Forwald has reported extensive PK experiments with tumbling cubes,[16] in which he finds evidence of orderly relations between the magnitude of PK effect and the material and thickness of foils covering the cubes. If these results can be confirmed by other experimenters, they will mark one of the most important milestones in psi research.

Theoretical developments

We still appear to be far from achieving a theoretical model that can relate the psi phenomena intelligibly to other areas of understanding. Most efforts at such inclusive theories are either empty plays on words or operationally meaningless invocations of a fourth dimension, vibrations, fields, or other ill-defined concepts. Nevertheless, the accumulating evidence on various facets of psi manifestations continues to stimulate new viewpoints and hypotheses, each of which adds its bit to the insight that eventually will flower into a fundamental theory. Without attempting a comprehensive survey, I want to mention several such contributions.

Psi-missing has been one of the most puzzling aspects of psi behavior. A decline of scoring to chance level appears intuitively plausible; but why should a subject use his psi capability to "fail" a test? Sometimes a series of runs or trials shows a steady decline right through chance level and on down to a significantly negative level. J. B. Rhine has examined many experiments that show psi-missing, and has reached several significant conclusions.[17] He finds that psi-missing occurs almost exclusively as a position effect in a series of runs under certain conditions, or when the subject is trying for two aspects of a target situation (in which case he tends to hit on one and miss on the other), or when the subject is experiencing anxiety or similar stress. From these and other considerations, Rhine concludes that psi-missing can be practically eliminated by attention to experimental design. Further, and most significant, he argues that the association of psi-missing with identifiable subjective conditions means that the "psychological conditions of psi-missing instead of psi itself" are responsible for unstable psi performance.

This distinction, if it is valid, is most important. It implies that a kind of impersonal medium of information (ESP) or action (PK) is accessible to the individual mental complex, and that this medium is not the capricious, uncertainly-functioning entity that psi usually implies, but is inherently reliable. The capricious, unpredictable aspects are identified with the same psychological processes that mediate other experience. "Psi" in this sense would appear to be analogous to the role of light in vision—impersonal, pervasive, independent of the subjective processes it stimulates, yet essential to visual cognition.

Psi phenomena appear irreconcilable wtih the more familiar concepts of physics. If they are to be accounted for at all in physical terms, the accommodation must be sought in those fringe areas of physics where current theory departs most radically from common sense: i.e., in relativity and quantum theory, which deal in multidimensional spaces and violate our ordinary notions of time. Attempts to invoke space warps, time travel in a fourth dimension, and the like to rationalize psi remain in the realm of science fiction. In recent years, the quantum theory of small-scale events has come in for more serious consideration.

The physicist Pascual Jordan [18, 19] proposed that the complementarity principle, a cornerstone of quantum theory, may apply to some psychological phenomena as well. Physicists have discovered that atoms or other small bits of matter behave in some respects like particles in the ordinary sense, but in other respects like systems of waves. The complementarity principle, in simple essence, states that the wave and particle aspects of matter are complementary. The bit of material may exhibit either aspect, depending on its situation and the means used to observe it; and the more definitely wave-like it appears, the less it exhibits the characteristics of a particle. Yet these are fundamentally equivalent ways of perceiving the same bit of matter.

Jordan argued that the conscious and unconscious aspects of mind are complementary in this sense, and therefore should be symmetrically related to the external world. He noted that we take for granted the social interaction of conscious minds through their sensorimotor systems, but assume that the unconscious is individual and private. "Dreaming of a table, I do not expect other persons to dream about the same table; but perceiving a table, I think it natural that other persons . . . perceive it." [18] Yet, he continued, if the symmetry demanded by the complementarity principle applies, then interaction at the unconscious level also must be assumed—implying the kinds of phenomena familiar to parapsychologists.

Wolfgang Pauli, another quantum physicist, collaborated with C. G. Jung on a voluminous work [20] dealing primarily with psychological and psychoanalytical concepts. However, their study has many implications for parapsychology.

C. T. K. Chari,[21] however, examined the implications of quantum theory for psi, particularly precognition, and found no justification for expecting an explanation of psi phenomena from this approach.

Several years ago, I developed some theoretical speculations [22] concerning psi which do not attempt to find an explanation in physical terms. These ideas are concerned mainly with the associative peculiarities of psi phenomena and with the probable complementary interaction of psi and the sensorimotor system.

The broadest approach to a fundamental theory of psi that I have seen is that advanced by LeShan.[23] His work is based upon a comparative study of mystic and psychic experiences, and of the development of modern science from sensory perceptions of the world. He is led to believe that psychic and mystic experiences are essentially identical and are characteristic of a state of consciousness that is basically different from the ordinary waking state. He then proposes his own principle of complementarity, an elaboration in some sense of that of Jordan. He holds that the world view derived from ordinary sensorimotor experience and that revealed in mystic experience are both valid, equally "real" intimations of the world; they are different because they derive from different means of apprehending the world. Psi phenomena then are anomalous only in the ordinary state of consciousness. They are normal functions in the mystic state.

Further, LeShan develops the remarkable observation that the world view of modern physical science, though derived from ordinary sensorimotor experience, nevertheless is no longer expressible in commonsense terms. Instead, it becomes ever more like that of the mystic.

This approach is exciting. It makes no attempt to pour new wine into old bottles. Rather, it offers a bold synthesis of some outstanding peculiarities of mystic experience, psychic phenomena, sensorimotor experience, and abstruse scientific theory, drawing them together in what seems to me the most promising approach to the rationalization of psi that has been proposed.

THE SCIENTIFIC STATUS OF PARAPSYCHOLOGY

Parapsychology stands in a peculiar relation to "establishment science." The evolution of this relation, and the emotional attitudes of both opponents and proponents of psi, have seemed to me almost as intriguing as the psychic phenomena themselves. The perennial controversy and the slow struggle of parapsychologists for professional status have demonstrated to any thoughtful observer that the evolution of science is not as it is depicted in textbooks! Most scientists clearly are conservative, stubbornly resistant to radical ideas, and have a deep emotional commitment to the current belief system. As I remarked in an earlier paper,[24] "The progress of science remains a tangled and erratic process in which the midwife and the undertaker play essential roles."

Recently a historian of science, Thomas S. Kuhn, published a book[25] that should be read by every parapsychologist. *The Structure of Scientific Revolutions* seems to me to clarify the evolution of science as no previous work has done. It does not deal directly with parapsychology; but the principles it elaborates apply with peculiar relevance to this field. In brief, Kuhn conceives of the evolution of an area of science as comparable to that of a religion (my analogy). A new and compelling revelation (e.g., Newton's *Principia*) inspires a growing body of devotees, who apply themselves to exegesis of the new faith. They explore its implications, elaborate theoretical details, devise new experiments to confirm them, and develop a body of literature that ideally is designed to answer all questions in terms of the basic revelation.

But their very thoroughness inevitably exposes inconsistencies (e.g., the anomaly in the apsidal motion of Mercury), and heresies arise. When the anomalies become numerous and significant enough, the traditional faith breaks down and a period of confusion and uncertainty ensues. This is then resolved by a new revelation (e.g., Einstein's relativity theory), and the cycle is repeated.

I am deliberately oversimplifying Kuhn's concepts. But one of his essential points is that "normal science"—which means nearly all science, commonly called "orthodox"—is essentially conservative, and its activities are motivated by the desire to confirm and vindicate the basic theoretical model or "paradigm," not to refute it. " 'Normal science' does not aim at novelties of fact or theory and, when successful, finds none." [26] Yet it is betrayed by a paradox: the very refinement and precision attained in the elaboration of the prevailing paradigm lead inevitably to the detection of anomalies that lead to its downfall. As Kuhn says,

The more precise and far-reaching that paradigm is, the more sensitive an indicator it provides of anomaly and hence of an occasion for paradigm change. . . . The very fact that a significant scientific novelty so often emerges simultaneously from several laboratories is an index both to the strongly traditional nature of normal science and to the completeness with which that traditional pursuit prepares the way for its own change.[27]

No more beautiful example of this tendency could be found than the work of the physicist Heinrich Hertz on electromagnetic waves. Maxwell's electromagnetic theory was the triumphant culmination of decades of evolution of the wave concept of light, and Hertz's experimental demonstrations finally confirmed it. Yet in the course of these very experiments Hertz discovered the photoelectric effect, which proved to be irreconcilable wtih the wave theory.

When the transition to a new paradigm develops, Kuhn maintains, it comes about not because of a direct rational decision that a proposed new paradigm accords better with observed data than does the old. Rather, it involves a subtle and gradual shift of conceptual viewpoint, of the whole intellectual context, so that what had seemed outrageous or absurd becomes obvious. The peculiar effects associated with amber and lodestone were undeniable, but they were intellectually meaningless until the context of electromagnetic phenomena had developed sufficiently to give rise to a relevant theory. Bertrand Russell once remarked that belief in witchcraft declined, not because of any specific demonstration to the contrary, but because of the shift to a rational climate of thought in which such a belief became absurd.[28] A committee of the French Academy once refused to credit reports of meteorites because there were no stones in heaven. Later, when the fancied distinction between terrestrial and celestial substances had broken down, stones from heaven became acceptable. Such diverse phenomena as hypnosis and ball lightning have undergone similar shifts in acceptability, more because of changes of intellectual context than of demonstrative proof.

But what of a field that has not yet achieved a satisfactory theoretical model, or paradigm? This question is of special interest, because it applies obviously to parapsychology. Typically, the prehistory of a science begins as "natural history," when a few people become interested in certain loose categories of objects or phenomena and try to assemble accounts of them in some meaningful order. The meaning inevitably reflects the collector's preconceptions. I am reminded of a small girl who asked her librarian for a book called *Alice in Africa*. The librarian checked the catalog. "I'm afraid we don't have that book," she said. "Would you like to see another book about Africa?"

"No. I'm reading books about Alices."

The embryo science begins with a collection of "Alices." In psi research, these involved tales of haunted houses, prophecies, dowsing, second-sight, miraculous healing, spirits of the dead, magic and witchcraft, mesmerism, personal magnetism, auras, veridical dreams, etc. The pioneers of the Society for Psychical Research took a long step toward development of a science when they chose to concentrate upon incidents bearing on the nature of human personality and especially the survival of death. Unfortunately—as often happens—they chose the area that by hindsight appears least amenable to definitive investigation.

During the past century, the field has exhibited a classic succession of the stages of development that Kuhn attributes to the pre-paradigm period of investigation. In the early decades, hypotheses were nearly as numerous as workers, and small groups coalesced around exponents of one emphasis or another. Some studied "mediums," others experimented with hypnosis, while still others explored the novel application of statistics to low-yield experiments. Publications was mainly through books that expounded both the observations and the individual philosophies of the authors, though the society journals gradually gained currency.

The past half-century has seen a distinct shift from collections of strange experiences to "controlled" experiments, a sure sign of progress toward a mature science. But we still don't know what to control, or how. Much of the early literature includes details that now would not be considered significant, but omits other details that we would like to know. The latter deficiency extends to recent experiments as well as anecdotes; without a basic theory, a paradigm, one doesn't know what details are relevant. Gradually, however, the field of active interest has narrowed and shifted focus (not many people are working on spirit survival nowadays); professional publication has shifted largely from books to journal papers, and reports have become steadily more esoteric and limited in scope. There is steadily less preoccupation with questions of philosophy, validity of methods, or "proving" psi than in former years, and more emphasis on delineation of its involvement in various relations. (I am speaking primarily of developments in Western Europe and America. The pattern appears to be somewhat different in the Communist countries.)

In all of these developments, we can see already the emergence of an incipient paradigm. No inclusive theory is yet available, of course; but several working hypotheses have quietly moved into general acceptance. Psi is not a sensorimotor function. It is not "mental radio."

It is nearly if not entirely independent of such physical parameters as time, distance, and material barriers. It is a common human trait, though with great individual differences in degree. It is intimately involved with the whole personality. It operates in animals as well as humans. It is fundamentally analogous to conventional transmission of information or energy. It appears in both sensory (ESP) and motor (PK) analogues.

All of these more-or-less tacitly adopted assumptions about psi inevitably influence experimental ideas and designs. They subtly limit the variety of experiments and the scope of theoretical thinking. This effect is of course an essential aspect of the development of a science. Learning what to ignore is nearly as important as learning what to observe. Yet no investigation is ever complete, or any theory entirely comprehensive. Clarification, objectivity, in a field always is gained at the price of discarding information that is considered insignificant or cannot be objectified. Inevitably, as parapsychology evolves toward an effective paradigm, it will neglect certain details that might—and eventually will—alter its concepts fundamentally.

In less than a century, parapsychology has progressed from no scientific standing at all to the development of professional societies and journals, an extensive literature, sponsorship by several universities and foundations, and acceptance in the most inclusive American scientific association. Yet the findings of parapsychologists are not generally accepted by other scientists, nor is the field accorded the academic status and financial support that its subject matter warrants.

I believe—and this accords with Kuhn's interpretation—that parapsychology is generally ignored not for lack of experimental evidence, but for lack of a theoretical model that can unify it and relate it to the established body of science. It is clear by now that the psi phenomena cannot be so related by simple accretion to existing science. They will require some radical adjustments of theoretical concepts and of the emotional attitudes that underlie them; and "normal science" never makes such adjustments until it is forced to by the accumulation of anomalies in its own province. Intrusions from without are ignored or explained away.

Yet the indifference of established science to parapsychology is not monolithic. J. B. Rhine once remarked to me that visitors to the Duke laboratory included more physicists than any other category of scientists, and that the physicists generally were more open-minded concerning psi than were their colleagues of other fields. My personal observations have supported this impression. That is not to say that physicists generally are convinced that the phenomena are genuine, or even that they are much concerned about the field; and some are actively hostile, as some were toward relativity and quantum theory in their times. But physicists have tended to be more tolerant of the implications of parapsychology than have scientists in other fields, and readier to acknowledge that psi may be a legitimate field for investigation. They also are more inclined to offer theoretical conjectures and hypotheses.

The reasons for this attitude among physicists seem fairly clear. For one thing, physics is the most esoteric and sophisticated of the sciences, and has demonstrated enough magic to establish itself beyond question. It need not be defensive. Further, the physicists already have had to forego commonsense intuition as a guide to reality. As LeShan noted,[23] their own theoretical models of reality resemble the visions of the mystic more than they do our common perceptual impressions.

ON AVOIDING TRAPS

Having pointed out the inevitable tendency in any research field to become over-committed to provisional hypotheses and concepts, I would like now to comment on several such intellectual "traps" that are noticeable in parapsychology.

The transmission analogy

Implicit in practically all parapsychological discussions and experimental designs is the assumption that information—a characteristic pattern or message—travels from one place to another. This concept is an obvious analogue of familiar communication systems, in which material or energy, or both, travel from sender to receiver. Letters, sound waves, radio waves, light, electrons in wires, any form of energy or material that is propagated from one place to another can be modulated with a message. "Mental radio" was an inevitable suggestion to account for telepathy. This idea is untenable for various reasons; but the basic concept of some kind of movement of something from target to percipient, or from PK agent to target, is tacitly assumed. If the analogy with known physical processes holds, the concept implies also a causal sequence: something that emanates from the sender or target affects the percipient in a meaningful way.

This transmission concept may be a trap. In appraising any psi hypothesis, one should ask first, What about precognition? And no transmission hypothesis can presently offer any pretense of an explanation of precognition. Information can be transmitted physically from one place to another (or to the same place) in future time: but it cannot be propagated backward in time to any practically significant degree by any means known to physics.

It is not easy to suggest an alternative approach. However, considerable evidence from both experiments and spontaneous cases suggests that past and future situations are symmetrically accessible to psi awareness. Also, as Gardner Murphy has pointed out,[29] it was noted even in the early days of the Duke University laboratory that psi responses often tended to resemble free association to the target more than specific recognition of it. In an earlier discussion,[22] I have gone into these aspects of psi in some detail, and have suggested that what comes to consciousness through the psi faculty is determined or selected more on the basis of associative similarity—an informational relationship—than of rational or causal relations.

Various experiments seem to indicate that psi cognition is "diametric," not "circumferential." [30, 31] In a blind-match card experiment, for example, scoring levels tend to be similar to those by open-match procedure. Yet a causal or transmission concept would seem to require that the psi process be circumferential: i.e., that the subject must independently cognize the concealed symbol on each target card, and that on the trial card. In an open-match procedure, he need cognize only the trial card. Logically, the probability of an extra-chance hit in the BM procedure should be the square of that observed in the OM test (implying usually insignificant scoring in BM), since the subject must "see" both cards correctly to get a hit. Yet the experimental evidence indicates that a given subject scores similarly on either type of test. This finding appears to indicate that psi is diametric: i.e., it somehow compares target and test cards for similarity without needing to know explicitly what symbol either carries. If this evidence is valid, it appears to rule out the circumferential, step-by-step process that physical concepts appear to require, and to support the concept of cognition of similarity *per se*.

However, an alternative hypothesis is possible. If the psi process works reliably up to the point of acquiring both target and trial symbols at a subliminal level and noting whether they coincide, but the low scoring level results from unreliable mediation of this information into conscious awareness, then OM and BM tests should yield similar scores. The work of J. B. Rhine on psi-missing that was mentioned earlier [17] tends to support this alternative.

Stereotyped methods

For more than thirty-five years, ever since the early work at Duke University established experimentation as the preferred approach to parapsychological research, most ESP experiments in the U.S.A. have been done with the so-called Zener cards. This device is highly advantageous, of course, in some respects; otherwise, it would have been abandoned. Yet its predominance even in current experimental reports suggests that it may have become a stereotype. Since stereotyped methods imply stereotyped thinking, it is perhaps desirable in the design of an experiment to consider whether Zener cards really are superior to possible alternatives.

It is remarkable that the Zener symbols have not been revised since they were first used. The basic geometrical similarity between the cross and square invite confusion if a percipient "gets" only a fragmentary impression of right angles; and experiments with drawings indicate that such fragmentary cognition is much more common than is a mental glimpse of the entire target pattern. Even the star has enough circular symmetry to risk confusion with the circle.

However, the danger in excessive dependence on the Zener cards is more fundamental. In the early evolution of any scientific discipline, some phenomena are noticed and groping, exploratory experiments are devised to isolate and analyze them. But, as the investigation becomes more sophisticated, experimental designs—based on expectations derived from experience—tend inevitably to define the phenomena that will be observed. As T. S. Kuhn comments, "In short, consciously or not, the decision to employ a particular piece of apparatus and to use it in a particular way carries an assumption that only certain sorts of circumstances will arise. There are instrumental as well as theoretical expectations, and they have often played a decisive role in scientific developments." [32] Enrico Fermi once remarked that he had missed discovering the fission of uranium by the thickness of a piece of foil in a detector chamber! His experimental design had not anticipated the possibility of nuclear fission.

It is difficult to say explicitly just what assumptions about psi are implied in the use of the cards, and of course impossible to know what aspects of psi functioning they may be missing. A clue may be found in the discovery by Ryzl and Pratt [33] of the "focussing effect." Only because they used unconventional two-choice cards in individually-identified envelopes were they able to isolate this curious effect. Also, drawing tests (in which the subject tries to sketch a target picture or drawing) have been little used by professional workers in this country. Yet they reveal detailed psychological peculiarities of the psi response that are not apparent in the all-or-none responses of card trials.[34, 35, 36] Probably they also offer a more congenial psychological situation for the subject.

The Zener cards or something similar were indispensable for demonstrating the occurrence of psi by rigorous statistics, and they still are a sensitive detector of low-level psi performance. However, scores might improve and new aspects of psi become apparent if more varied and psychologically more congenial techniques were widely adopted. In this connection, Gardner Murphy has commented: "It is only when baffling conceptual problems loom upon us that we have the courage and the imagination to invent a new method. Yet paradoxically much of the history of science is a simple matter of finding new methods." [29]

Excessive isolation of psi

Another trap may be an excess of zeal to isolate psi phenomena from sensorimotor contamination. When any anomalous effect is observed, it is entirely logical to try to isolate it in order to verify its occurrence and to determine its characteristics in as simple a situation as possible. But, when the phenomenon normally occurs in the context of a complex system with many concurrent, interrelated functions, as does psi, there is a risk of attenuating or distorting the manifestation one is trying to observe. It is a situation crudely analogous to trying to study the growth of a plant isolated from its root system.

Psi phenomena had to be effectively isolated from the sensorimotor (SM) system to demonstrate their occurrence unambiguously. Now it is time to recognize that psi normally is free to function concurrently with SM and other processes, and to consider whether psi performance might be enhanced and its governing principles possibly clarified by studying it in its natural context.

Many spontaneous case reports, and a few experiments, suggest a complementary relation between psi and SM functioning. This concept was suggested by the physicist Pascual Jordan [18] on theoretical grounds, and later by Gardner Murphy.[29] I have developed it at some length in an earlier paper,[22] and so will discuss it only briefly here. It is the concept that the interaction between a personality and its environment is normally dominated by the SM functions, but that psi enters in a complementary role, "filling in" under certain conditions when the SM capability is inadequate or inhibited. Crystal gazing is a familiar illustration. The psychic stares into the crystal ball until it "clouds" and a subjective vision takes shape. I propose that the clear, window-like crystal invites vision, it creates an expectation of seeing something; but nothing meaningful appears, and this frustration of normal vision is compensated by a subjective shift to the inner vision we call clairvoyance. Our senses have been habituated by long evolution to expect a stimulus to be accompanied by information, so that a stimulus carrying little or no information is an open invitation to compensatory fantasy or psi input.

The well-known experiment of Heymans, Brugmans, and Weinberg [37] suggests a similarly motivated psi intervention. The subject had to try blindfolded to point to a target unknown to him, while the experimenter was free to observe the subject's efforts but could not intervene in any normal way. In these circumstances, very high scores were obtained. Again, I propose that the situation amounted to an interrupted servo loop. Instead of a single personality seeing and acting on the visual information, the sensory function resided in one person and the motor function in the other. The motivation for psi intervention to complete the circuit must have been peculiarly intense.

I believe enough evidence is available to suggest that more experimentation designed to make use of this principle of psi-SM complementarity would be highly rewarding. Some experiments do involve the principle, but the involvement usually is incidental. Better results probably could be achieved if experimental designs were developed on the complementarity principle as a primary consideration.

Neglect of psychokinesis

During the past decade, the *Journal of Parapsychology* has published about 200 papers on ESP, and 45 on PK. Eight of the latter were theoretical.

Psychokinesis is not a favorite subject among parapsychologists, as Rex Stanford also has noted.[38] Why this is so is a matter for conjecture. Possibly there is a clue in the fact that precognition was represented by only 36 papers. Are parapsychologists "broad-minded in the groove," accepting the intuitively more plausible manifestations of psi but wary of the "unbelievables"? And why should PK appear less plausible than, for example, clairvoyance? In ESP manifestations, the terminus or focus of the process is a mind, and it is intuitively easy to believe that mysterious things can happen in a mind. What, if anything, the target object does to evoke the mental response is not apparent; it therefore poses no difficulty. But the terminus of the PK process is an inanimate object or system. A change of its state without physical mediation is a tangible insult to common sense, and therefore is much more difficult to believe than is a mental anomaly.

Whatever the reason, the stark fact is that research interest in PK continues to decline. Eisenbud [1] published reports adducing strong evidence for the genuineness of Ted Serio's psychokinetic photographs, which for several years he produced with gratifying regularity. Yet only one other research team in the country took the opportunity to experiment with Serios. To me as a physicist, such indifference is appalling. It carries the ominous implication that the theoretical paradigm already is taking shape, and that it is dismissing PK.

Just because PK is an influence on an inanimate system rather than a mind, it offers opportunities for sophisticated physical experimentation that ESP does not. I do not suggest that such investigations will elucidate psi; but they can be expected to yield some insight as to what happens physically in the vicinity of the PK target. That would be a great advance over what we know now. Forwald, for example, has reported a mass of experiments [16] indicating consistent relations between defined physical parameters in the target situation and the level of PK influence registered. It is of the utmost importance to determine whether these results can be repeated by other experimenters, for they bear directly on the question of whether psi processes are subject to physical constraints or limitations. (Do parapsychologists avoid PK because it threatens the "non-physical" nature of psi?)

Exaggerated emphasis on unconscious mediation of psi

Frequently in the parapsychological literature, we find strong emphasis on the fact that the psi processes are unconscious. The implication is that psi is in this respect different from ordinary SM cognition and action. This emphasis seems to me unjustified. *All* mental processes are without exception mediated unconsciously, even rational thought. But the scope of conscious awareness varies widely with the kind of process and the circumstances.

Even in the most intensely conscious activities, such as using eyes and hands in a delicate operation, the SM mediation of vision and manipulation is entirely unconscious. One is not aware of a field of radiation entering the eye, or of chemical changes induced by it in the retina, or of consequent neural impulses and the unimaginably complex processes in the visual center. One is only aware of "something out there." Similarly, one "wills" the hand to move in a certain way, and it moves. Subjectively, the intervening processes are as occult as those involved in ESP or PK.

The unconscious mediation of psi does not therefore appear to be unusual. It gives the illusion of an anomaly because it is not associated with any identifiable organ or channel. Sight is readily associated with eyes, and sound with ears. But we know only of diffuse and indefinite factors that influence psi functioning. Yet psi is no more an unconscious process than is memory, which also can "emerge" in consciousness in all degrees of insistence or subtlety, vagueness or clarity, diffuseness or specificity. In fact, memory appears to be the nearest analogue of psi in our ordinary experience.

The emphasis on unconscious mediation of psi can be a trap, because it tends to discourage attempts to bring the psi functions under conscious, reliable control. Most successful psi scorers are not conscious of their hits or misses. However, disciplined psychics apparently have some awareness of whether they are in a favorable state for psi experience, and whether they are getting significant imagery. Such examples, and a few experiments, suggest that psi facility should be trainable by proper methods. However, the few reported attempts to train subjects for better psi performance have involved hypnosis, meditation, or other procedures intended to enhance psi scoring indirectly by creating a favorable mood or state of consciousness, or to heighten motivation. Such approaches are important; but they are comparable to exercising to raise the blood pressure, or subjecting oneself to embarrassment to dilate the peripheral blood vessels. More direct approaches, if they can be discovered, should be more effective.

Until recently, it was believed that the autonomic nervous system was inaccessible to direct conscious control—i.e., to "willing" rather than indirect influence such as running to increase the heart rate. Recent work, however, has shown that many persons, if not all, can learn to control some of the deeply autonomic functions by volition alone *if* they are given some instrumental feedback so they can monitor the blood pressure or whatever other function they are trying to control.

Of course, yogis and some other meditative adepts have claimed such control for centuries; but they require years of devotion to subjective discipline to achieve it. We have, then, the traditional association of meditative disciplines with the autonomic system and with psychic powers; and we have the discovery of relatively simple ways to assert voluntary control over certain of the autonomic functions. The suggestion is inescapable that we may be near the discovery of similarly direct techniques for training persons in psi facility and conscious awareness of the psi process, provided we do not assume that the entire psi process is inaccessible to consciousness.

I offer these suggestions with some hesitation because of my peripheral position in parapsychology. Yet this lack of full-time involvement may be of some advantage in permitting a perspective that is not accessible to the professional research worker. Research enforces a narrowly specialized focus of attention as the price of success. Yet there is always the risk that an emerging science will narrow its field too much, to the neglect of essential aspects of its subject matter—as psychology did in the heyday of behaviorism. As the theoretical structure matures, it always excludes some known phenomena, and discourages the pursuit of some that are only suspected, because they do not appear to fit the prevailing paradigm. Not many scientists are able to maintain the peculiarly schizoid state of mind that is necessary to keep a lively awareness of the existence of such unassimilated phenomena while making the intellectual commitment to the paradigm that is necessary to use it productively. Yet in parapsychology, of all fields, it is essential to keep the open view.

REFERENCES

1. EISENBUD, J.: *The World of Ted Serios* (New York: William Morrow & Co., 1967).
2. THOULESS, R. H.: "Parapsychology during the Last Quarter of a Century," *J. Parapsychol.* **33** (1969): 283–299.
3. ULLMAN, M.; KRIPPNER, S.; and FELDSTEIN, S.: "Experimentally-induced Telepathic Dreams: Two Studies Using EEG-REM Monitoring Technique," *Int. J. Neuropsychiat.* **2** (1966): 420–437.
4. OSIS, K., and BOKERT, E.: "Changed States of Consciousness and ESP." Abstract, *J. Parapsychol.* **33** (1969): 360–361.
5. STANFORD, R. G., and STANFORD, B. E.: "Shifts in EEG Alpha Rhythm as Related to Calling Patterns and ESP Run-Score Variance," *J. Parapsychol.* **33** (1969): 39–47.
6. HONORTON, C.: "Relationship between EEG Alpha Activity and ESP Card-guessing Performance," *J. Amer. Soc. Psych. Res.* **63** (1969): 365–374.
7. KAMIYA, J.: "Operant Control of the EEG Alpha Rhythm and Some of its Reported Effects on Consciousness," in *Altered States of Consciousness*, edited by C. T. Tart (New York: John Wiley & Sons, 1969), pp. 507–518.
8. VASILIEV, L. L.: *Experiments in Mental Suggestion*. English translation (Church Crookham, Hampshire, England: Institute for the Study of Mental Images, 1963).
9. RYZL, M.: "Training the Psi Faculty by Hypnosis" (edited and reviewed by G. W. Fisk), *J. Soc. Psych. Res.* **41** (1962): 234–252.
10. RYZL, M., and RYZLOVA, J.: "A Case of High-scoring ESP Performance in the Hypnotic State," *J. Parapsychol.* **26** (1962): 153–171.
11. CASLER, L.: "The Improvement of Clairvoyance Scores by Means of Hypnotic Suggestion," *J. Parapsychol.* **26** (1962): 77–87.
12. DEAN, D.: "The Plethysmograph as an Indicator of ESP." Abstract, *J. Parapsychol.* **25** (1961): 280.
13. OSIS, K.: "ESP over Distance: A Survey of Experiments Published in English," *J. Amer. Soc. Psych. Res.* **59** (1965): 22–42.
14. OSIS, K., and FAHLER, J.: "Space and Time Variables in ESP," *J. Amer. Soc. Psych. Res.* **59** (1965): 130–145.
15. OSIS, K., and TURNER, M. E., Jr.: "Distance and ESP: A Transcontinental Experiment," *Proc. Amer. Soc. Psych. Res.* **27** (1968).
16. FORWALD, H.: *Mind, Matter, and Gravitation*. Parapsychological Monograph No. 11 (New York: Parapsychology Foundation, 1969).
17. RHINE, J. B.: "Psi-missing Re-examined," *J. Parapsychol.* **33** (1969): 1–38.
18. JORDAN, P.: "Reflections on Parapsychology, Psychoanalysis, and Atomic Physics," *J. Parapsychol.* **15** (1951): 278–281.

19. ————: *Verdrängung und Komplementarität* (Repression and Complementarity). (Hamburg-Bergedorf: Strom-Verlag, 1947).
20. Jung, C. G., and Pauli, W.: *The Interpretation of Nature and the Psyche.* English translation (New York: Pantheon Books, 1955).
21. Chari, C. T. K.: "Quantum Physics and Parapsychology," *J. Parapsychol.* 20 (1956): 166–183.
22. Rush, J. H.: *New Directions in Parapsychological Research.* Parapsychological Monograph No. 4 (New York: Parapsychology Foundation, 1964), p. 12.
23. LeShan, L.: *Toward a General Theory of the Paranormal.* Parapsychological Monograph No. 9 (New York: Parapsychology Foundation, 1969).
24. Rush, J. H.: "The Rediscovery of Mind," *The Humanist* (1960), No. 3, p. 144.
25. Kuhn, T. S.: *The Structure of Scientific Revolutions,* 2nd ed. (Chicago: University of Chicago Press, 1970).
26. *Ibid.,* p. 52.
27. *Ibid.,* p. 65.
28. Russell, B.: *The Impact of Science on Society* (New York: Columbia University Press, 1951), p. 7.
29. Murphy, G.: "Progress in Parapsychology," *J. Parapsychol.* 22 (1958): 229–236.
30. Foster, A. A.: "Is ESP Diametric?" *J. Parapsychol.* 4 (1940): 325–328.
31. Osis, K.: "A Test of the Relationship between ESP and PK," *J. Parapsychol.* 17 (1953): 298–309.
32. Kuhn, T. S.: *op. cit.,* p. 59.
33. Ryzl, M., and Pratt, J. G.: "A Repeated-calling ESP Test with Sealed Cards," *J. Parapsychol.* 27 (1963): 161–174.
34. Warcollier, R.: *Experiments in Telepathy* (New York: Harper & Brothers, 1938).
35. Sinclair, U.: *Mental Radio* (London: T. Werner Laurie, 1930; rev. ed. Springfield, Ill.: Charles C Thomas, 1962).
36. Rush, J. H., and Jensen, A.: "A Reciprocal Distance GESP Test with Drawings," *J. Parapsychol.* 13 (1949): 122–134.
37. Heymans, G.; Brugmans, H. J. F. W.; and Weinberg, A. A.: "Een experimenteel onderzoek betreffende telepathie," *Mededeelingen der S. P. R.* 1 (1921): 3–7.
38. Stanford, R. G.: "'Associative Activation of the Unconscious' and 'Visualization' as Methods for Influencing the PK Target," *J. Amer. Soc. Psych. Res.* 63 (1969): 338–351.

PROTOCOMMUNICATION

ANDRIJA PUHARICH

Progress in parapsychology and the advancement of the epistemo-logical problem, it seems to me, are dependent on solving the *modus operandi* of certain phenomena:

1) The Origin of Life
2) Replication in the Life process
3) Sensory Perception
4) Memory in Brain
5) Artificial Perception and Intelligence
6) Direct Brain Perception
7) Direct Brain Action
8) Memory in Nature
9) Precognition

I feel that these phenomena have a common thread the pursuit of which has been my life's work. I shall describe what I have done and what others have done to untangle this thread from nature's fabric. Although this exploration is fragmentary and presented with utmost reserve, I believe that it may serve a useful function in stimulating discussion and experimentation.

1. *Problem of the Origin of Life*

The consensus of scientific opinion [1,3] is that life originated on primitive earth from four atoms, C, O, H, and N which produced four molecules, CH_4 methane, NH_3 ammonia, H_2O water, and H_2 hydrogen. These molecules are known to exist in interstellar space.[4,5] These four molecules have also been formed into amino acids under laboratory conditions.[6-8] Twenty amino acids are the molecular foundation of all proteins. The unique feature of amino acids produced in living things is that they are all levo-rotary, i.e., they will rotate plane polarized light waves to the left. [9,10] In trying to understand this asymmetrical feature of life energies, I observed that all of the antagonistic physiological pairs of atomic elements are polarized magneti-cally.

Physiological pairs can be ranked by nuclear magnetic incre-
ments of 0.4 Bohr magnetons, μ. All the values for μ are ground
state values.[11] From the data we can make some deductions. First, we
observe that the four atomic letters of life show a set of unique
magnetic moment polarizations:

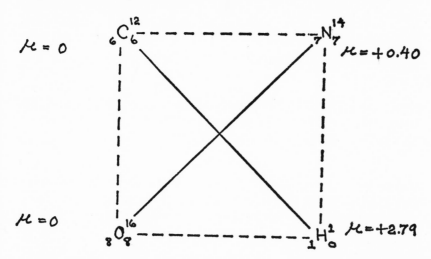

We shall refer to this asymmetrical magnetic polarized group as the
COHN set. The COHN set magnetic moment asymmetry within amino
acids may account for the l-amino acids of life. We can briefly characterize this asymmetry with the example of glycine, one of the sim-
plest of amino acids and the one produced in the greatest abundance
in the laboratory re-creation of life origins. The chemical formula
below is from Pauling.[12]

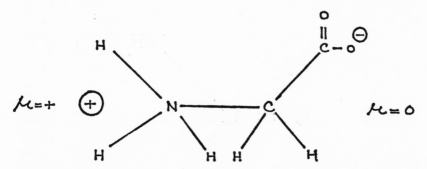

The base NH_3^+ group has a positive electric charge. The acidic
COO^- group has a negative electric charge. But note that the mole-

cule is also polarized magnetically with the $NH_3{}^+$ group carrying $+8.8\mu$ while the COO^- group has zero magnetic moment. In this molecule the positive electric pole, and the positive magnetic moment are on the same end of the molecule, and rotation of this group may account for the optical rotation of amino acids.

I believe that this "life" asymmetry reflects the weak violation of parity that exists in the cosmos. I further believe that this violation is related to the preponderance of hydrogen atoms in the cosmos (90% by count) [13] and preponderance of hydrogen atoms in the human body (63% by count).[14] This possibility focussed my attention on the role of the proton in life processes.

This analysis begins with the pair oxygen and hydrogen and their combination in water; and the pair carbon and nitrogen and their combination in amino acids and in nucleic acids. We shall develop the role of OH as the electron fuel cell of the organism, [15] and HOH as the proton matrix end product of fuel cell hydrosynthesis and what this means for the storage of memories originating from life experience. We shall develop the role of CN groups as building blocks of proteins and nucleotides which become the memory bank for phylogenetic and ontogenetic experience.

2. *Replication and Control in Life Processes*

Cell division has two important goals, one is to perpetuate the species, and the other is to carry on orderly growth and repair in an organism. This process is under the control of the DNA system which is made up of four nucleic acid sentences whose active components are the 2 purine bases, adenine and guanine, and the 2 pyrimidine bases cytosine and thymine.[16] It is of interest that these bases are made up of molecular building blocks that exist in interstellar space, NH_3, OH, and HCN.[17] In fact, these molecules were used by Wohler in 1828 to synthesise the first "'organic" molecule, urea:

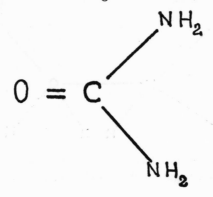

which is a building block of all the purines.[18] The DNA molecule is a double helix in which the two nucleotide strands are held together by hydrogen bonds. The hydrogen bonds hold together the base pairs guanine: cytosine (GC); and adenine: thymine (AT). What is of interest is that this simple four letter code GC and AT, replicated in unit aggregates of molecular weight of the order of 100,000,000 contains complete instructions and operational control necessary to build a human body. Not only does this system contain an awesome stable memory capacity and accuracy in carrying out instructions, but it must also be responsive to very small signals that tell it "GO" and "NO-GO" for growth and repair.

In normal cell division the combination of the sperm and ovum triggers cell division. The start of DNA division is heralded by the appearance of a centrosome body. This latter body splits in two and the chromosomes containing DNA line up transverse to the lines connecting the two centrosomes. A classic spindle formation of microtubules occurs which is clearly visible under a microscope. At this point the hydrogen bonds holding the two strands of the DNA double helix cleave and the cell divides with a full complement of chromosomes going to each new cell.

Now we do not know what tells the DNA hydrogen bonds to divide, because the same effect can be artificially induced with electric pulses of the order of 30-40 volts.[19] The hydrogen bonds are of interest in that one of them is composed of the COHN set in the form,

$$C = O:H:N$$

(The dots (:H:) represent electron lone pairs) and the other is composed of the NHN set in the form

$$N:H:N$$

In both bond sets the proton of the hydrogen atom is in a resonant state with the electron "lone pairs" on each side of it which gives the bond great stability. What kind of command is given which breaks this proton resonance stability in such an orderly way? The centrosome bodies behave like repulsive magnetic poles and the protons of the hydrogen bond system tend to line up in the interface repulsion region of low energy. The protons of the double helix ladder are paired in such a way that their center of momentum falls on the low energy interface where repulsive (magnetic) forces meet. This sets up a possible mechanism for super-conductivity at body temperature [20] and protons can shift like a zipper opening up the ladder of H bonds.

After the protons shift up the ladder one step and the magnetic repulsive force separates the two strands of the double helix the mechanism for super-conductivity collapses. Now in order to under-

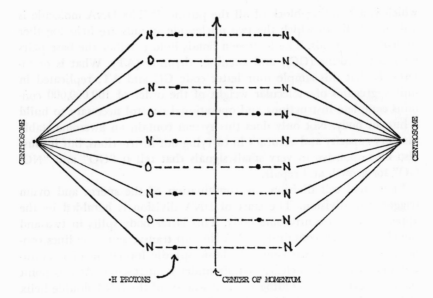

stand this phenomena of cell division more fully let us consider what happens when we block cell division.

This can be reversibly accomplished in any system of dividing eggs by replacing about 20% to 30% of the water of the medium with deuterium oxide, D_2O.[21] While cell division is arrested as though a motion picture of the process had stopped it, the metabolic activities of the cell go on. If the D_2O is removed from the medium, cell division will resume normally. This is a phenomenon of great interest because the D_2O has counter-manded the "GO" command to divide with a reversible "NO-GO" command. Where does it act? Normal H_2O and D_2O differ only in that the hydrogen atom contains a neutron in addition to the proton. Thus the mass of the hydrogen atom is doubled; hence the term "heavy water." The essential difference between H_2O and D_2O is not chemical but nuclear. It turns out[22] that the neutron (n) has a spin opposite to that of the proton (p) where

$$n = -1.91 \mu$$
$$p = +2.79 \mu$$
$$\text{and,} \ _1H_1^2 = +0.85 \mu$$

The result is that the neutron's magnetic spin tends to cancel the magnetic spin of the proton. It is my considered opinion that this spin "shielding" effect is large enough to cancel the protonic "GO" command to divide. What we do not know is the locus and origin of the "GO" command except that it is probably protonic. But we shall pursue this question later. What is of interest is the role of water in the GO, NO-GO control mechanism.

Let us look at a situation where there is potentiation of the "GO" command in cell division and the growth and repair process. Grad [23] of McGill University has clearly shown that if a healer "treats" distilled water in glass bottles, and such treated water is used on plants, there is a significant potentiation of the growth process. Sister Justa Smith [24-26] has shown that distilled water treated by a healer's hands will significantly increase the hydrolytic action of the enzyme trypsin. The healer's "treatment" is exerted solely on the water, and the effect is most likely to be on the proton moments of the resonant hydrogen bonds of the water molecules. Further research should be directed to looking for nuclear magnetic resonant shifts either in magnetic field, or radio frequency. We shall return to the role of water in bio-control systems later. There remains the mystery of the "GO" command in egg division which I do not believe is a simple question of sperm and ovum meeting nor of electroshock stimulation of an ovum.[27] The life pattern of the Pacific salmon illustrates the larger framework of the problem.

The salmon hatches in an inland fresh water lake or pond in the spring of the year. It finds its way to the open sea by the autumn, and then moves as far as 4000 miles in the open sea from its place of birth. Five years later it begins the return voyage to its place of birth and arrives in time for optimal conditions for egg hatching. It finds a mate en route, and the two salmon ritually lay the eggs and fertilize them and then die within four to seven days. This annual event which has gone on since time immemorial has these problems for us:

What is the nature of the imprinting on the egg (at time of fertilization?) that brings the salmon back to this spot five years later? This imprinting requires a precise fix on a point on an earth that is spinning in orbital motion. The instructions require a timer for maturation, mating, and return in the right timing for optimum weather for egg hatching. The instructions require a command to go to the sea, navigate out and return in synchrony with physiological changes required for fresh to salt water adaptation. The final timing is of course the prescribed death following egg production and fertilization.

I believe that a solution of these problems should be a top priority for parapsychology because it comes close to the heart of the mystery behind the general phenomenon. I believe that the postulate of proton superconductivity is a necessary condition for such rapid and complex imprinting of the fertilized egg. The super-conductivity hypothesis is supportable for protons based on the theory of nuclear spin thermodynamics in the rotating frame.[28] This theory describes the mechanism whereby proton spin systems attain spin temperatures in the region of 1°K while the solid they are in is at room temperature (300°K).

3. Normal Sensory Perception—Audition

Within biological systems one of the more highly developed environmental information transfer systems is the neural network. I shall use the acoustic neural system as a model for these systems. Let us consider the perception of a 1 KHz sine wave, air-conducted tone by a human at the threshold level of sensation. The interface between the biosystem and the air is the ear drum which transmits the analog wave into the system with a displacement of $10-^8$ cm = 1Å (0.3Å = radius of a hydrogen atom). The 1 KHz wave is then transmitted by ossicular coupling to a fluid medium, the cochlear perilymph which transfers the wave or energy to the Basilar Membrane (B.M.). At the threshold of hearing the 1 KHz sine wave displaces the B.M. about 10^{-11} cm.[29] The radius of a nucleus—e.g., proton is 1.5×10^{-13} cm.[30]

Note: The distance from O to N in the COHN system ranges from 2.60 Å to 2.90Å.

$$\text{Average} = 2.72 \text{ Å in alpha helix}[31]$$

This mechanical displacement of the B.M. is transferred to the auditory sensor—the hair cell wherein the 1 KHz sine wave undergoes transduction to produce an analog 1 KHz sine electrical signal—the cochlear microphonic signal.[32] Up to this point the information transfer process is linear. But the hair cell is now excited to generate a chemical pulse which it discharges across the synapse (Deiter) at the first order auditory neuron.[33,34] Encoding occurs, and the information (1 KHz sine wave) is now transferred along the nerve as a series of time distributed digital pulses, the classical "action potential" electrical pulses.

The actual mechanism of auditory encoding at the Deiter's synapse is not known in spite of great efforts to solve it.[35] What I present here is a highly speculative solution for which we can make certain assumptions. The first is that hair cells can resonate to one cycle per second intervals over the range of 16 Hz to 30 KHz.[36,37] The second assumption is that the higher the audio frequency the greater will be the current density flow for the constant level voltage of each action potential pulse.[38]

As the hair cells go into vibration in resonance with the 1 KHz signal, the acoustic phonon displacement of 10^{-11} cm is sufficient to strain the $C=O:H:N$ set to open the membrane gate for the sodium pump. As the current flows (the higher the frequency, the higher the current density) it will set up a magnetic field.[39] The magnetic field will be picked up by the hydrogen proton of the $C=O:H:N$ set and cause it to precess. The higher the magnetic field the higher the frequency of precession.

The magnitude of the current density across the membrane will determine the number of molecules of chemical transmitter such as acetylcholine that will be released at the presynaptic membrane.[40] Thus we have two parallel related events:

1) Energy release (current density) linear to audio frequency which triggers chemical transmitter molecules.

2) Proton precession triggered by the magnetic field generated by current density—and such precession frequency is linear to audio input.

The acetylcholine activating the postsynaptic membrane transfers phonons of thermal energy to the axon whose energy is equivalent to the original acoustic phonon at the hair cell. This phonon repeats the events already described. It is to be noted that each $C = O:H:N$ set is activated serially, thus setting up the mechanism for a delay line which accounts for the slow conduction of the nerve impulse. The current density pulse besides metering out "quanta" of chemical transmitter material has another function, which is to act on perineural water shells with a hydrolysis-like action. This effect on water protons becomes, in my theory, the basis for memory. This topic will be discussed later as a brain effect when we consider more fully the subject of brain memory.

Within this model is the well-known sodium pump mechanism which maintains a DC barrier potential across the cell membrane.[41] With nerve excitation K^+ goes out of the cell, and Na^+ goes into the cell. Each of these ions has an opposing ion which acts to damp its action; K^+ is damped by Ca^{++}, and Na^+ is damped by Mg^{++}. What is not generally recognized is that K^+ has a positive (0.4) magnetic moment, and Ca^{++} has a zero moment; Na^+ has a positive (2.2) magnetic moment, and Mg^{++} has a zero magnetic moment. We would expect a short range transfer of magnetic information from the precessed proton to Na^+ and K^+ via the acetylcholine molecule.[42] This would tell the postsynaptic membrane whether it is to be excited, a process which opens the membrane to sodium ions, or to be inhibited, a process which closes the membrane to sodium ions.[43,44] This information would have to be delivered to the proton of the COHN system which acts as a gating switch on the postsynaptic membrane.

The information to be transmitted, a 1 KHz sine wave, must reach the temporal lobe cortex without distortion, and be stored in such a way that a person can vocally mimic this sound at some later time. Such storage may occur in a single nerve cell's membrane surrounding glial cells and water shells.[45] This would require domain formation (ferroelectric type) in which the proton magnetic moment poles are arranged in north pole and south pole regions.[46] Access to this memory bank requires that the action potential pulse and the proton magnetic dipole interact to perform such functions as write-in, read-out, numerical functions, store, hold, search, and erase.[47] The basic scheme of nature has the fixed hydrogen bond proton matrix scanned by travelling waves of electric pulses. The distinctive aspect of this scheme is that the protons form the storage, and hence the gestalt of the system; while input and output access is mediated by quantum electronic and photonic pulses.

We propose an extremely simple model and equivalent circuit of a unit element of the plasma membrane. The EMF source can represent any stimulus; the potential (DC) across the cathode-anode plates is determined by the polarized state of the dipoles; and its current flow by the depolarization release of potassium and sodium ions from the lattice structure of the plasma membrane. In the resting state of the nerve, the ferroelectric capacitor, C_0 is charged to a constant voltage, V, and the charge, Q, on the capacitor $= C_0V$. All linear current flow in the system is through the conducting fluids on both sides of the plasma membrane. However, the plasma membrane, on its outer surface, is covered by a coating made up of lipoid-protein layers. Conduction through this protein material is non-linear, and is represented by the $C = O:H:N$ element as a semiconductor.

It is postulated that nerve stimulation, or depolarization will only occur by a decrease in the capacitance of the ferroelectric capacitor, and this is fundamentally dependent on the dielectric polarizibility, ϵa of the plasma membrane. ϵa, is dependent on the electronegativity of the neutral bound atoms of the plasma membrane, and can be lowered by DC biassing, by the choice of AC frequency, by pressure (strain) effects, by change in chemical composition, hydration, hydrolysis, thermal variations, etc. We will illustrate this triggering condition with the not-so-obvious case of thermal fluctuation stimulation. We assume that there is a Curie temperature, T_c, transition point, at 38°C. A temperature change above or below T_c, will decrease the capacitance and this will cause a current to flow to the load, since current flow through the EMF source is blocked by the non-linear semi-conductor element. The capacitive discharge will in itself generate additional heat, and this represents part of the positive heat observed during the action potential phase of nerve firing. It has been observed in nerve firing that the positive heat phase is followed at times by negative heat, or absorption cooling effects. Thus the thermal cycle is completed by an increase in capacitance, causing a reverse flow of current through the load from the EMF source establishing the original charge on the capacitor. The net result is an AC output.

4. *Artificial Sense Perception*

My colleague, J. L. Lawrence, and I invented and developed an electronic system which makes it possible for a totally deaf person to hear speech sounds by Direct Brain Perception (DBP) using as stimulus to the brain an amplitude modulated alternating current carrier signal (AMAC). [48]

The AMAC signal is applied to the dry neck skin below the mastoid areas bilaterally via gold plated circular electrodes. This placement directs the AMAC signal to the brain stem region.[49] The deaf patient requires several weeks of electronic signal conditioning of such tissues with audio frequency band pure tone modulation before he can hear sounds.[50-52] One of the first measurable effects of such AMAC electronic conditioning is that a barrier potential of about 0.6 volts develops across the energized tissues. This is due to dielectric polarization of the cell membranes of all cells in the signal path.[53] Once a barrier potential is present across tissue, one can evoke the following effect: One of the AMAC energized electrodes, when it is lightly stroked over the skin, produces the sensation of hearing both in the deaf and in normals.[54] During the hearing attendant upon skin-stroking one will observe on the oscilloscope that the sine wave carrier signal injected into the head becomes half-wave rectified with the positive half-wave being clipped. What tissue mechanism detects AMAC signals?

Detection occurs when the keratin of the skin is stretched by the stroking action.[55] The coils of the alpha helix configuration of the keratin are held together by hydrogen bonds.[56]

Under the combined effect of the barrier potential forming a DC bias across the carbonyl-H-imide bond, and the stretching of the distance across the H bond, the $C=O:H:N$ system becomes a semiconductor which rectifies the sine wave carrier.[57] Commoner has shown that stretching of such proteins in a nerve fiber also produces an electron spin resonance signal during neural conduction.[58]

The production of speech hearing capability in a deaf person by means of direct brain electro-stimulation has revealed some significant data about information processing. Empirically we found that the deaf hear words optimally at a carrier frequency of 20 KHz with amplitude modulation of audio signals (double side band) where the half-power band pass is about 3 KHz.[59] This passes about 1.5×10^7 bits per second of information to the brain. This compares favorably to normal hearing where some 3×10^7 auditory nerve fibers with an average time constant of 5×10^{-3} sec. yields 6×10^7 bits of information per second.

Secondly, the power spectrum of the AMAC signal shows that the power pulse height of the side band curve is inversely proportional to frequency, and this accords well with the classic Fletcher-Munson curve for threshold of hearing. Thirdly, all evidence pointed to current pulses as being the signal mechanism of electrostimulation of hearing.[60]

Fourthly, actual hearing of tones in the deaf is due to a beat frequency detection effect. For example, if a 100 Hz tone is the stimulus signal, it is impressed on a 20 KHz carrier signal. Thus the head neurons see the following signal: 20 KHz + 100 Hz = 20,100 Hz: 20 KHz − 100 Hz = 19,900 Hz. The 20,100 Hz and the 19,900 Hz beat against the center frequency of 20,000 Hz and the result is that the deaf person "hears" 100 Hz. Certain proton nuclear magnetic resonant (NMR) signals in the nerve system may be of this nature where the actual perceived signal may be a side-band signal. For example, Nelson has shown that the HCH group of ethyl alcohol has a NMR at 200 MHz, but that each proton has a separate side band line 7 Hz above and below the center frequency. These side bands are due to proton-proton spin couplings.[61] Such proton-proton spin couplings may have great importance in memory induction.

5. Memory in Brain

We have shown in the skin-stroking effect that both the carrier potential across the $C = O:H:N$ set and stretching the H bond length produces semiconduction, and also gates AMAC signals. Let us examine this phenomenon as it applies to awareness, anesthesia, and memory.

Becker [62] has clearly shown the relationship of body surface barrier potentials to alertness and anesthesia. During alert states there is a barrier potential (30 mV) between the neuraxis and the skin periphery, the neuraxis being positive in sign, and the skin being negative in sign. Anesthetic agents in the first stage of anesthesia lower this potential to zero and may even cause a reversal in sign. Hypnosis (if effective for surgery, as an example) shows the same pattern of lowering of barrier potential, as shown for chemical anesthesia.

Randt and Mazzia [63] have shown that the earliest sign of stage 1 anesthesia (Plane 1) is characterized by a spontaneous dissociation of eyeball movements, so-called ocular divergence. In this condition humans can perform simple calculations, respond to questions and other stimuli, but do not retain any memory of such mental performance. Yet, at the same time it is possible for a patient to undergo major surgery during this state. Apparently, ocular divergence is a precision measure of the titer of anesthetic molecules required to uncouple perceptive-motor acts from memory imprinting. Let us analyze this important effect.

According to Pauling's [64] theory of anesthesia, anesthetic chemical agents act by forming clathrate hydrates. For example, in the case of the inert anesthetic gas xenon, the hydrate which forms around the xenon atom has been shown to be a dodecahedron of HOH molecules. Pauling states that such "water cages" produce anesthesia by a kind of plasma membrane water control rod function which damps the electrical oscillation of the neurons. All tests of this theory since Pauling first announced it in 1961 tend to confirm his concept of perineural water cage formation in anesthesia.

In addition to the Pauling concept of perineural water cages, I wish to bring up Hydén's concept of the perineural role of glia in the memory process:

"In an acute learning situation, the modulated frequencies (time patterns) set up by the neuron are also transferred to the glia. The glia are characterized by potentials of a 500 to 1000 fold *longer duration* than those recorded from nerve cells. When the neural frequency is changed a lock-in effect brings the slow frequency of the glia in synchrony (with nerve pulse frequency), the difference being a multiple. This coupling of the frequencies of the neuron and the glia forms an information system. The glial ionic equilibrium is disturbed and substrates in the form of nucleotides are transferred from the glia to the neuron to release the repressed chromosome (DNA) region, and induce the necessary enzyme synthesis for the RNA production.

"This lock-in mechanism would, therefore, constitute the information system whereby the specific RNA was synthesized, triggered, or mediated by the glia as a regulator. As was stressed in the dicussion earlier, the glia have many features of a feedback system.

"The glia are composed of multiple, thin membranes. Such a composition is well suited for rapid processes, for example proton transfer.

"Both the glia and the neuron constitute a unit. As I see it, that is the functional unit of the nervous system.

"Modulated frequencies set up in neurons of specific areas would specify RNA and proteins. These alterations would be stable for the best part of an individual's life time. After the first chemical specification, the protein's response on the same electrical pattern that once specified the RNA would be to dissociate rapidly. A molecular fragment would be provided which will react in an activation of the transmitter substance. In view of the fast reaction, the modulated frequency could affect fluctuating charges existing between basic groups of the protein and their attached protons." [65]

Basic to our theory of memory in a brain is that the permanent spin of the proton is considered to be the seat of information. Inputs or outputs from this seat of information occur by modulating the precession frequency.[66] The macroscopic structure of the memory system is believed to be ferroelectric, as described. Ferroelectric properties have been found in RNA by Stanford and Lorey.[67] We propose the following scheme for the memory function in the central nervous system.

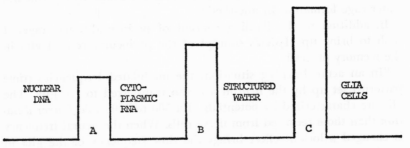

A) is the cell nucleus membrane barrier and is a conduction band semiconductor.

B) is the cytoplasmic plasma membrane barrier and is a tunnelling semiconductor.

C) is the structured water-glia interface in the perineural region— with proton-hopping semiconduction.[68]

When the nerve impulse fires across B, the sodium ion goes into the cell, and the magnesium ion is activated to damp the action of the sodium. The Mg^{++} and the electronic pulse tell the nuclear DNA proton to produce RNA.[69] As the electric pulse first started, the K^+ ion went out of the cell across B, and perturbed the water proton lattice so that a proton hops into the glia to activate RNA.[70] The DNA proton and the glia RNA proton, if activated by the same energy in coincidence, come into proton-proton spin coupling at a definite precession frequency controlled by the quantum rules of current density: magnetic field described earlier. This spin coupling is transmitted through the water structure in the peri-neural area where a third proton freed by the hydrosynthesis process is also imprinted with the precession frequency of the other two protons. By this scheme the brain becomes an enormous set of interference patterns of magnetic waves generated by the proton precession frequencies.[71] It is these interference patterns which I believe humans subjectively experience as imagings, memories, and all the other mind dynamics.

The requirement of the brain for oxygen and glucose for maintenance of consciousness, memory and structure will now be considered. Let us quickly place this question in perspective. In the biological world mammals are not capable of cracking water, i.e., hydrolysis, to obtain free oxygen and hydrogen. Only algae, bacteria and plants are capable of hydrolysis—furnishing man with oxygen, the flame of his consciousness, and with hydrogen (in glucose) as the fuel of that flame. In all of man's metabolic processes the end result is the combination of 4 H with 2 O to form $2H°H$ and of course CO_2.[72] Thus every metabolic act of the brain, every nerve cell electrical impulse is accompanied by the formation of water, hydrosynthesis.[73] The forms that such water takes in the nerve cell, and around each nerve cell, etc. is a matter of vigorous research today.[74] The announcement of polywater by Deryagin has stirred this research to the highest level in history.[75] What is emerging is a concept first formulated by McCulloch [76] which states that mind processes are mediated by crystalline water structures, and that the nerve cell is a supporting skeletal structure for such water forms.[77]

Since consciousness is maintained only by a continuous supply of oxygen, and the integrity of brain structure (largely as water crystals) is also dependent on a continuous supply of oxygen we must consider continuous hydrosynthesis as a fundamental aspect of consciousness and mind operations. The modulation of mental states by anesthetic agents, hallucinogenic drugs, trance, hypnosis, etc. in order to influence Direct Brain Action (DBA) and Direct Brain Perception (DBP) performance can best be understood in terms of crystalline water states in the brain.

6. *Direct Brain Perception*

By direct brain perception, DBP, I mean the process of obtaining new information by a person without using the channels of sense, the memory bank or deductive logic. The perception originates from a person at distance (telepathy), or is a vision of a scene beyond the range of sight (clairvoyance), or is the audition of a voice beyond the reach of the ears (clairaudience).

There are empirical psychological states, used over the centuries, to set the stage for the experience of DBP. Amongst these are self-induced trance—a dissociative state; release of cortical inhibitory states by the use of small amounts of alcohol, or other drugs; a state between waking consciousness and Stage 1, Plane 2 anesthesia; the REM state of sleep: cholineriag induced by drugs of the muscarinic group, e.g., *Amanita Muscaria.*[78] What is it that these various states and techniques have in common?

One of the keys as to how this process works can be illustrated with telepathy experiments where high scoring is controlled with negative ion inhalation, and low scoring is controlled with positive ion inhalation.[79] This effect can be rationalized by the principle of electronegativity which states that atoms have varying degrees of power to attract and hold electrons. If we saturate the respiratory air with negative ions (O_2^- and free electrons) certain atoms in the CNS* will become saturated with the maximum number of electrons they can hold. For example, the muco-polysaccharide coatings of cells will carry a high negative surface charge.[80] This will obviously create a large barrier potential. In general, we can predict that each atom will have maximum quantum orbital stability when its power of electronegativity is saturated, and this is the ground state of that atom. On a large scale this will create a condition wherein the core of each cell will be positively charged, and the cell periphery will be negatively charged.

If we induce such a state in a human subject by means of negative ion inhalation we can further stabilize these ground quantum energy level states by shielding the person from photonic and electronic perturbations within a Faraday Cage.[81] Under these conditions, namely,

a) Self-induced trance on the part of a clairvoyant,

b) Negative ion inhalation,

c) Faraday Cage shielding.

I have been able to show consistent, repeatable, statistically significant scoring in DBP tests designed as telepathy tests.[82]

It is my opinion that the quantum orbital electron stability so induced further acts by building and maintaining the proper types of water protonic structures favorable to DBP.

The techniques cited thus far all act to quench the electronic noise

* CNS = Central Nervous System

of the neuronal system. The self-imposed dissociative techniques act to shift attention to the para-neural information system—peri-neural water: glia cell system.

When the slow oscillations of this system dominate the electrical activity of the brain, the so-called alpha waves, in the frequency range from 8 to 14 Hz, the protons of the water structure are receptive to similar signals at a distance.[83] The best example of this phenomenon is the synchrony of alpha waves in identical twins by Direct Brain Action and Direct Brain Perception—or, more scientifically, proton resonance at-a-distance between two brains. The unique feature here is that protons are not to be thought of as points of energy in space, but rather as energy systems whose magnetic waves mushroom out over regions of space. We shall take up this concept in a later section.

7. *Direct Brain Action*

By Direct Brain Action, DBA, I mean the power of a person to induce a physical action-at-a-distance without the use of any known transducers, such as the muscular system. DBA is also known as psychokinesis in connection with dice tests, levitation in connection with lifting objects, poltergeists in connection with erratic movement of objects, table rapping, etc.

One of the common manifestations of DBA is in the phenomena of healing. I have already mentioned Grad's work on the induction of healing in animals, and growth induction in plants; and the transfer of healing energy from a person to water which potentiates enzyme activity. I have had occasion to study healing for a number of years in Arigó, the recently deceased Brazilian healer who did major surgery without anesthetics and without pain or shock. But the most interesting healing action I have studied was in the case of a healer, Mrs. H., who uses non-contact hand passes over a patient. This healer had previously cured a patient of a ventricular arrhythmia. The healer, Mrs. H., passed her hands over the spine of this patient, who with eyes closed, was in a prone position, covered with a white sheet. When the healer's hands passed (in the air) over the TIO to Cl vertebrae of the patient the normal asynchronous EEG waves showed an immediate high amplitude alpha wave synchrony of 9Hz. This was readily repeatable. I conclude that non-contact healer's manual passes over a patient induce a short range magnetic transmission to the hydrogen bond water protons of the brain causing them to precess in the frequency range from 7 to 14 Hz. This interpretation is compatible with the nuclear magnetic resonance frequency predicted by the Larmor equation for the parameters involved (body magnetic field of 10^{-6}

Gauss).[84-86] If the proton is in fact the universal carrier of information, per se, it would not only encode this information in quantum magnetic moments, precession frequencies, and quantum electro-dynamic resonances, but must logically do work at a distance.

Recent evidence suggests that gravity waves exist [87] with a frequency in the audio range, and detection has repeatedly occurred at 1660 Hz.[88] We have considered proton-proton spin coupling between brains at the so-called alpha frequencies. It will be recalled that protons have a not insignificant mass. We raise the very real question as to the possibility of the weak interaction between proton spin couplings, proton magnetic moment couplings and gravity waves showing in-phase locking at frequencies that are in the physiological range, i.e., from .2Hz to 30KHz, accounting for direct brain action.[89] In my experience all the DBA phenomena I have observed are very short range—a few meters at most.[90] Such short range action is compatible with the suggestion I have made.

8. *Memory in Nature*

If protons in a biological matrix are the carrier of information, per se, then protons in the cosmos as a whole would also be vehicles of proto-communication.

Hannes Alfvén has sharply reminded us that until the advent of recent space probes in peri-planetary and solar space, scientists were under the impression that deep space was a pure vacuum.[91] This impression is wrong. We now know that deep space is alive with plasmas, magnetic fields, electrostatic double layers, and currents.[92] It is estimated that about 90% of the atoms of the cosmos are made up of hydrogen atoms, and that there is on the average about one H atom per cubic cm. of space.[93] This cosmic distribution of H atoms existing as a proton matrix can be treated as a universal framework for proto-communication. Since about 63% of the human body also consists of hydrogen atoms we can look for a resonance between its protonic magnetic spin and precession systems and the protonic matrix of the cosmos as a whole. This effect would be most prominent in the peri-isolar region which we now know is alive with energetic protons streaming out from the sun.[94] The magneto-sheath of the earth is now also known to form a gigantic shock wave against this protonic flux from the sun. The entire picture is that of a mushroom cap facing the sun with the earth at the point of attachment of the stem to the cap and the stem reaching out as a tube far into space. In short all space is alive with protons so that any communication from proton to proton can occur through a chain-like coupling. These protons exist in an enormous energy range from highly energetic relativistic protons to hydrogen-bond resonant quasi-static protons.

One of the curious reasons that protons in the cosmic matrix, and protons in the bio matrix can resonate is that they can in fact, under certain conditions exist at the same thermal energy level.[95] It is a fact that at temperatures of 300°K, and in the cold of deep space, proton nuclear spin systems are like dilute ideal gases in the simplicity and universality of their thermodynamics.[96]

If one applies a static magnetic field, and an RF field to a nuclear spin system at room or body temperatures one can produce within the nuclear spin system temperatures of 1°K. This is due to 3 properties of such a system: [97]

1) In a magnetic field all the protons will precess at the same frequency.

2) Because the spin moments are all polarized opposite to the magnetic field, the energy of the system has a distinct upper and lower boundary.

3) The system is subjected to a monochrome RF frequency.

We have seen that an effect similar to 1), 2), and 3) occurs in manual alpha wave induction: DBA and DBP induction of alpha waves between twins, and in transfer of a healer's power to water hydrogen bond systems. Since these effects are due to protons in elements common to planet earth, C,O,H,N, and found in interstellar space we expect to find the same information carried throughout all nature. In fact, the phenomenon of object-reading by DBP (psychometry) is one where the object carries information which may be detected by touching and by skin-stroking. I have treated this subject extensively under the title "Memory Capacity of Objects." [98] What concerns us here is the question of the basic nature of information, per se, in nature. I have treated this question in this paper, and indicated that life begins with a proton magnetic bias in nature which produces biased levorotatory molecules. I have tried to show that proton magnetic spin properties are ubiquitous in the human sensory and memory systems, and that these extend into so-called "inanimate" nature. Julian Schwinger [99,100] has recently proposed a new theory called "A Magnetic Model of Matter." While this theory is unproven, it addresses itself directly to the questions I have raised. Schwinger points out that even though the Maxwell equations call for a symmetry between electric charge and magnetic charge, the cold fact is that no magnetic counterpart to electric charge is known. Yet the unit of electric charge is unvarying in its universality. Why? He further notes that common to all nuclear particles is isotopic spin and hypercharge which has no explanation. In addition he wonders why there exists in the universe a weak violation of charge-parity (CP) symmetry. He proposes an answer to these four disturbing questions—which are too complex to go into here. Nevertheless, he does deduce a unit of basic magnetic charge. He shows that electric charge is given by

$$e^2/hc \approx 1/137$$

and the magnetic charge becomes for ground states,

$$g^2_0/hc \approx 4(137)$$

His new charge unit which he calls the DYON is a fractional unit compared to the universal unit of electric charge now known, where

$$DYON = e_0 = \tfrac{1}{3} e$$

The same type of fractional charge has been proposed for the proton and the neutron called quarks, or partons.[101]

If these theories of fractional charge, consisting of electric charge and magnetic charge are proven, we shall have a truly scientific basis for the theory of protocommunication proposed herein.

We speculate that on a cosmic scale protons are imbedded in a magnetic field matrix which gives them spatial orientation. The cosmic gravitational field determines the lattice spacing of such protons. These two fields determine the gestalt of the proton lattice, and input and output of "information" is mediated by quantum boson, pion, electronic, and photonic pulses. This concept of a brain applies equally to the bio-domain, or the cosmic domain.

It now remains to illustrate features of protocommunication and the nature of protons which can only come from observations of precognition.

9) *Precognition*

Nineteen years ago (August 1952) this month I conducted an experiment with Eileen Garrett.[102] The target she was seeking clairvoyantly was created by big cosmic ray pulses incident upon a coincidence counter housed 0.3 miles away from her. This target source gave a purely random distribution of events. Her direct hits in calling the time of arrival of the cosmic rays were at a P level of 10^{-6}. This gave me confidence that the experimental design and procedure were valid.

One of the striking findings of this study was the precognition hits made by Mrs. Garrett, not only for their statistical significance ($P = 10^{-3}$), but for the verbal description of the "coming" event. I must state that the counter was so set that only the big cosmic (C.R.) ray events triggered the detectors. In this way during the course of the experiment the average C.R. pulse interval was about 6 minutes with a range of 1 to 30 minutes. By clairvoyant knowledge alone, Mrs. Garrett was able to see and describe the components and function of the C.R. detector. In this way we knew unambiguously when she "saw" the pen recording device, the amplifier circuits, the coincidence counter tube, the Faraday Cage in which this apparatus was housed, or the arrival of the cosmic ray showers. She was able to sense and describe the coming of a cosmic ray as long as 116 seconds before it hit the detector circuit, and then to call, within a second or two, the final movement of the pen that recorded the C.R. event. Here is a description by Mrs. Garrett of one such event starting 33 seconds before the pen recorded the event:

"I see little particles coming down. A formation of particles. The particles look like mercurial globules assembling. They have a fluid, magnetic quality. The particles gather together, they pile up in the *tube* (Note by author: The coincidence counter *tube*). The particles strike and make a sound as they hit—it has a shrill quality. The sound is transmitted into a light. NOW! The pen moves!" The Target Pen recorded the cosmic ray event at 23'05" of the experiment. Mrs. Garrett said "NOW" at 23'06" of the experiment. This is clearly both a brilliant precognition hit, and a hit synchronous in time.

I, and all my colleagues (seven of them) present at the experiments were impressed with this power of description of an event 3×10^{10} meters out in space, or about half the diameter of the sun. I personally am convinced that her mind locked onto those protons in space which were headed on a collision course for a point on a rotating planet. If all this be true how do we account for it? Let us examine some of the facts.

Interstellar space is filled with a plasma made up of magnetic fields of the order of 10^{-6} gauss, and atoms and ions such as protons making what Hannes Alfvén [103,104] has called a viscous medium. Protons moving at relativistic velocities are profoundly influenced by the magnetic field while their rest mass is not significantly altered, their total energy, particularly the magnetic component, is increased. It is my opinion that the quantum concept of a point proton is not valid under these conditions. Rather we should think of a spread out, a mushroom-shaped proton, if you will. If we accept this point of view the proton now has a frame of reference which (depending on its energy) may have a wave length that is equal to the radius of the solar system. Thus we do not have to be concerned with Einstein's limiting velocity of light, c, nor with Feinberg's velocities that exceed c. We need only be concerned with spin temperatures and plasma temperatures which determine resonant conditions between protons in the clairvoyant's brain, and those in space. Protons in interstellar space can have temperatures ranging from 1°K to 10,000°K. It would seem that the two protons in question must be at the lower end of this scale in order to be at thermal equilibrium. If this condition can be met and it is within the physiological range, I see no difficulty in bringing the bioproton and the cosmoproton sets into resonance.[105-111] It requires an extraordinary quality of perception on the part of a clairvoyant to come into resonance with such an elusive target.[112-116] Now what can we say about more long range precognition? Does the proton plasma in which all planets and life are immersed act as a giant brain?

Concluding Remarks

Let me briefly review the essential points that I want to make as a concluding statement.

In order to find some place in the greater order of nature for our personal experience of the brain as mind-qualities, I have been led by my biophysical and parapsychological researches to examine the most common unit in the universe—the proton.

I find that a magnetic basis for matter, as proposed by Schwinger, is required in order to explain 1-amino acid molecular asymmetry of life processes operating through proton magnetic asymmetry.

I find that the DNA hydrogen bond system is a suitable matrix for proton superconductivity which may account for basic bio-control mechanisms that must operate in cell division, cell growth and repair, and abnormalities such as cancer.

I find that the $C=O:H:N$ set is a good molecular basis for semi-conduction, ferroelectricity, and proton precession effects with which to build a sensory apparatus.

Biological memory finds a rational basis in the simple concept of modulated proton spin states. The same concept applied to a para-neural domain of water-glia is a possible basis for direct brain perception (DBP). However, this latter mechanism is intimately linked to the concept of a cosmic protonic plasma brain built into all of nature.

I feel that no man should put forth a serious theory without suggesting experiments that will test its validity. I want to propose, very briefly, a number of such experiments.

I believe that if the proton-proton spin coupling exists in DBP it should be possible to shield a sender from a receiver in a telepathy experiment. This may be done by placing one of the participants in an enclosure of D_2O. I predict this will stop, or attenuate DBP. A control for this experiment would place the subject in a charged

Faraday Cage Enclosure whose walls could be emptied, or filled with D_2O without perturbing the subject.

Long range precognition and detection of protons, as was described for Mrs. Garrett, can best be done by astronauts in a satellite in space. On earth we would have a clairvoyant. In space, an astronaut with a helmet that would detect when an energetic proton went through his brain. The clairvoyant would try to guess when the astronaut's brain is activated by a proton. The experiment could be reversed with the astronaut trying to guess when a person on earth had a cosmic ray event pass through his brain. This experiment would be highly important in determining proton energy levels, spin temperatures, and the role of the earth's magneto-sheath in direct brain perception.

Another experiment would involve driving two brains in synchrony using the techniques of nuclear magnetic resonance. It would be desirable to have the two brains at matching thermal equilibria, and at driving frequencies such as the alpha frequency. We would look for either increased or decreased DBP transmission between the two subjects.

The most important study would be a long term study of the life cycle of the salmon. I believe that this study could yield more basic information about geo-cosmic information imprinting than any other study of which I can conceive. The most important phase for study would be the ritual egg laying and egg fertilization.

REFERENCES

1. BAR-NUN, A.; BAR-NUN, N.; BAUER, S. H.; and SAGAN, CARL: "Shock Synthesis of Amino Acids in Simulated Primitive Environments," *Science* **168** (1970): 470–473.
2. MILLER, S. L.: "The Formation of Organic Compounds on the Primitive Earth," *Ann. N.Y. Acad. Sci.* **69** (1957): 260.
3. FOX, SIDNEY, W.: "Synthesis of Amino Acids by the Heating of Formaldehyde and Ammonia," *Science* **170** (1970): 984–86.
4. DONN, BERTRAM: "Interstellar Molecules and Chemistry," *Science* **170** (1970): 1116–17.
5. WICK, GERALD L.: "Interstellar Molecules: Chemicals in the Sky," *Science* **170** (1970): 149–50.
6. MILLER, S. L.: *Op. cit.*, ref. 2.
7. FOX, SIDNEY, W.: *Op. cit.*, ref. 3.
8. BAR-NUN, A.; BAR-NUN, N.; BAUER, S. H.; and SAGAN, CARL: *Op. cit.*, ref. 1.
9. PAULING, LINUS: *Nature of the Chemical Bond* (Ithaca, N.Y.: Cornell University Press, 1948).
10. CORRIGAN, JOHN, J.: "D-Amino Acids in Animals," *Science* **164** (1969): 142–49.
11. CONDON, E. W., (Ed.), and ODISHAW, HUGH: *Handbook of Physics*, Table 3.1. Nuclear Moment Values; section 9–93 (New York: McGraw-Hill, 1967, 2nd. ed.).
12. PAULING, LINUS, and HAYWARD, ROGER: *The Architecture of Molecules* (San Francisco: W. H. FREEMAN, 1964), Plate 45.

13. DONN, BERTRAM: *Op. cit.*, ref. 4.
14. ANDREWS, DONALD HATCH: *The Symphony of Life* (Lee's Summit, Mo.: Unity Books, 1966), p. 200.
15. YEAGER, ERNEST: "Fuel Cells," *Science* **134** (1961): 1178–1186.
16. CRICK, F. H. C.: "On the Genetic Code," *Science* **139** (1963): 461–64.
17. WICK, GERALD L.: *Op. cit.*, ref. 5.
18. ORÓ, J., and KIMBALL, A. P.: "Synthesis of Purines under Possible Primitive Earth Conditions. I. Adenine from Hydrogen Cyanide," *Arch. Biochem. Biophys.* **94** (1961): 217–27.
19. TARKOWSKI, A. K.: "Spermless Egg Activation Is Achieved in the Mouse," *Dateline in Science* **5** (1970): 1.
20. LITTLE, W. A.: "Superconductivity at Room Temperature," *Scientific American* **212** (1965). 21–27.
21. GROSS, PAUL R., and SPINDEL, WILLIAM: "Heavy Water Inhibition of Cell Division: An Approach to Mechanism," *Ann. N.Y. Acad. Sci.* **90** (1960): 345–613.
22. CONDON, E. U. (ed.), and ODISHAW, Hugh: *Op. cit.*, ref. 11.
23. SMITH, JUSTA: "Are These Healing Hands?" *Response* (publication of Rosary Hill College, Buffalo, N.Y. **11**, Spring 1968, p. 18.
24. ———: "Effect of A Homogeneous Magnetic Field on Enzymes," in *Third International Biomagnetic Symposium* (Chicago, Ill.: University of Illinois, 1967), pp. 22–25.
25. ———: "Considerations Regarding the Mechanism of the Action of Magnetic Fields of Enzymes," in *Third International Biomagnetic* Symposium (Chicago, Ill.: University of Illinois, 1967), pp. 26–27.
26. ———: *Op. cit.*, ref. 23.
27. TARKOWSKI, A. K.: *Op. cit.*, ref. 19.
28. REDFIELD, ALFRED G.: "Nuclear Spin Thermodynamics in the Rotating Frame," *Science* **164** (1969): 1015–23.
29. FLANAGAN, JAMES: "Computer Simulation of Basilar Membrane Motion and Electronic Artificial Larynx," 1965 IEEE International Convention Record, Part 12, p. 40.
30. WEISSKOPF, VICTOR F.: "The Three Spectroscopies," *Sci. Amer.* **218** (1968): 15–29.
31. HAMILTON, WALTER C., and IBERS, JAMES A.: *Hydrogen Bonding in Solids* (New York, N.Y.: W. A. Benjamin, 1968), p. 87.
32. CRICK, F. H. C.: *Op. cit.*, ref. 16.
33. LUMMIS, R. C.: "The Secret Code of Hearing," Bell Laboratories Record, September 1968, pp 261–66.
34. KANEKO, Y., and DALY, J. F.: "Activity of Acetylcholinesterase on the Endolymphatic Surface of Outer Hair Cells," *Acta Otolaryng.* **67** (1969): 602–10.
35. LUMMIS, R. C.: *Op. cit.*, ref. 33.
36. PUHARICH, H. K., and LAWRENCE, J. L.: "Means for Aiding Hearing." U.S. Patent No. 2.995.633, August, 1961.
37. ———: "Alternating Current Energy Used to Simulate Audition in Deaf Humans." Paper presented at the 35th Annual Convention Aerospace Medical Association, Miami, Florida, May 13, 1964.
38. ———: "Hearing Rehabilitation by Means of Transdermal Electrotherapy in Human Loss of Sensorineural Origin (I)," *Acta Otolaryng.* **67** (1969): 69–83.
39. REDFIELD, ALFRED G.: *Op. cit.*, ref. 28.
40. ECCLES, SIR JOHN: "The Synape," *Sci. Amer.* (Jan. 1965): 56+.
41. BAKER, PETER F.: "The Nerve Axon," *Sci. Amer.* (March 1966): 74+.
42. MAURO, ALEXANDER: "Space Charge Regions in Fixed Charge Membranes and the Associated Property of Capacitance," *Biophys. J.* **2** (1962): 179–98.
43. ECCLES, SIR JOHN: *Op. cit.*, ref. 40.
44. PAULING, LINUS: *Op. cit.*, ref. 9.

45. Hydén, Holgar: "Activation of Nuclear RNA of Neurons and GLIA in Learning," in *The Anatomy of Memory* edited by Daniel P. Kimble (Palo Alto, Calif.: Science and Behavior Books, 1965): p. 231.

46. Von Hippel, Arthur R.: "Molecular Designing of Materials," *Science* 138 (1962): 91–108.

47. Bobeck, Andrew H., and Scovil, H. E. D.: "Magnetic Bubbles," *Sci. Amer.* (June 1971); 78–90.

48. Puharich, H. K., and Lawrence, J. L.: *Op. cit.*, ref. 36.

49. Parisi, Mario; Rivas, Emilio; and De Robertis, E.: "Conductance Changes Produced by Acetylcholine in Lipidic Membranes Containing a Proteolipid from Electrophorus," *Science* 172 (1971): 56–57.

50. Puharich, H. K., and Lawrence, J. L.: *Op. cit.*, ref. 38.

51. Manfredi, A., and Bombelli, U.: "Radioacoustic Treatment of Deafness," *Atti della Fondazione Giorgio Ronchi* 18 (1963): 603–16; and *Publicazioni dell'Istituto Nazionale di Ottica, Arcetri Firenze, Serie IV*, No. 408.

52. ———: "Explanatory Notes on Radioacoustic Treatment of Deafness." Paper presented at the Seventh Congress of the International Society of Audiology, Copenhagen, August 24, 1964.

53. Puharich, H. K., and Lawrence, J. L.: "Hearing Rehabilitation by Means of Transdermal Electrotherapy in Human Hearing Loss of Sensorineural Origin (II)." Excerpta Medica International Congress Series No. 189 containing abstracts of papers read at the Ninth International Congress of Oto-Rhino-Laryngology.

54. Ingalls, Clyde, E., E.E.: "Sensation of Hearing in Electromagnetic Fields," *New York J. Med.* 67 (1967): 2992–97.

55. Gibson, T.; Stark, H.; and Evans, J. H.: "Directional Variation in Extensibility of Human Skin in Vivo," *J. of Biomechanics* 2 (1969): 201–4.

56. Puharich, H. K.; Lawrence, J. L.; and Dugot, R. S.: "Transdermal Electrostimulation of Hearing." Paper presented at the Thirteenth Annual Scientific Meeting Committe for Research in Otolaryngology, American Academy of Ophthalmology and Otolaryngology, Chicago, Ill., October 11, 1969.

57. Puharich, H. K., and Lawrence, J. L.: *Op. cit.*, ref. 53.

58. Commoner, Barry; Woolum, John C.; and Larsson, Ernst: "Electron Spin Resonance Signals in Injured Nerve," *Science* 165 (1969): 703–4.

59. Puharich, H. K., and Lawrence, J. L.: "Electrostimulation Techniques of Hearing." Technical Documentary Report, Defense Documentation Center, Virginia, December, 1964.

60. *Ibid.*

61. Nelson, F. A., and Weaver, H. E.: "Nuclear Magnetic Resonance Spectroscopy in Superconducting Magnetic Fields," *Science* 146 (1964): 223–32.

62. Becker, Robert O.: "Some Observations Indicating the Possibility of Longitudinal Charge Carrier Flow in the Peripheral Nerves." Paper presented at the Second Annual Bionics Symposium, Ithaca, N.Y., August 31, 1961.

63. Randt, Clark T., and Mazzia, Valentino D. B.: "Recent Memory Fixation in Man." Reprint from Transactions of the American Neurological Association, 1965, pp. 141–44.

64. Pauling, Linus: "A Molecular Theory of General Anesthesia," *Science* 134 (1961): 15–21.

65. Hydén, Holgar: *Op. cit.*, ref. 45.

66. Redfield, Alfred G.: *Op. cit.*, ref. 28.

67. Stanford, A. L., Jr., and Lorey, R. A.: "RNA's Function in Memory: Lingering Polar Alignment?" *Dateline in Science* 3 (1968): 1.

68. Shah, Dinesh O., and Hamlin, Roy M., Jr.: "Structure of Water in Microemulsions: Electrical, Birefringence, and Nuclear Magnetic Resonance Studies," *Science* 171 (1971): 483–485.

69. DE ROBERTIS, EDUARDO: "Molecular Biology of Synaptic Receptors," *Science* 171 (1971): 963–71.
70. RUNNELS, L. K.: "Ice," *Sci. Amer.* (December 1966): 118–26.
71. KASTLER, ALFRED: "Optical Methods for Studying Hertzian Resonances." *Science* 158 (1967): 214–21.
72. WALKER, J. L., JR.: "Unified Account of the Variable Effects of Carbon Dioxide on Nerve Cells," *Science* 167 (1970): 1502–4.
73. ROSENBERG, BARNETT, and POSTOW, ELLIOT: "Semi Conduction in Proteins and Lipids—Its Possible Biologic Import," *Ann. N.Y. Acad. Sci.* 158 (1969): 1+
74. RABIDEAU, S. W., and FLORIN, A. E.: "Anomalous Water: Characterization by Physical Methods," *Science* 169 (1970): 48–52.
75. FRANK, HENRY S.: "The Structure of Ordinary Water," *Science* 169 (1970): 635–41.
76. MCCULLOCH, WARREN S.: "The Biological Sciences in the Great Ideas Today," Encyclopaedia Britannica, Chicago, 1966, pp. 288, 334.
77. TEORELL, TORSTEN: "Electrokinetic Considerations of Mechanoelectrical Transduction," *Ann. N.Y. Acad. Sci.* 137 (1966): 403–1048.
78. PUHARICH, H. K. (ANDRIJA): *Beyond Telepathy* (New York, N.Y.: Doubleday & Co., 1962).
79. ———: *Sacred Mushroom* (New York, N.Y.: Doubleday & Co., 1959).
80. LIPPMAN, MURIEL: "A Proposed Role for Mucopolysaccharides in the Initiation and Control of Cell Division," *Transactions of the New York Academy of Sciences* 27 (1965): 342–60.
81. PUHARICH, H. K. (ANDRIJA): *Op. cit.*, ref. 78.
82. PUHARICH, H. K.: "Electric Field Reinforcement of ESP," *Int. J. Neuropsychiat.* 2 (1966): 474–86.
83. PUHARICH, H. K.; SMITH, J.; and KITSELMAN, A.: "Computers, Chance and Cholinergia," *Darshana* (India) 1 (1961): 41–43.
84. ROCARD, Y.: "Actions of a Very Weak Magnetic Gradient: The Reflex of the Dowser," *La Nature* (1963), No. 3343: 468–72.
85. WALSH, W. M., JR.: "Magnetic Resonances and Waves in Simple Metals," *Science* 171 (1971): 36–42.
86. WIGNER, EUGENE P.: "Events, Laws of Nature and Invariance Principles," *Science* 145 (1964): 995–1006.
87. WEBER, JOSEPH: "Evidence of Gravity Waves Reported," *New York Times*, June 15, 1961, p. 1.
88. WITTEBORN, FRED C.: "Data Confirm Faint Gravity Pulls Free Electrons in Magnetic Field," *Dateline in Science*, January 20, 1967, p. 1.
89. *Ibid.*
90. PUHARICH, H. K. (ANDRIJA): *Op. cit.*, ref. 78.
91. ALFVÉN, HANNES: "Antimatter and Cosmology," *Sci. Amer.* (April 1967): 106.
92. ALFVÉN, HANNES, and ELVIUS, AINA: "Antimatter Quasi-stellar Objects, and the Evolution of Galaxies," *Science* 164 (1969): 911–17.
93. ALFVÉN, HANNES: *Op. cit.*, ref. 91.
94. NESS, NORMAN F.: "Earth's Magnetic Field: A New Look," *Science* 151 (1966): 1041–52.
95. PORTER, WILLIAM S.: "Hydrogen Energy Levels: Perturbation Caused by Proton Structure," *Science* 143 (1964): 1324–25.
96. REDFIELD, ALFRED G.: *Op. cit.*, ref. 28.
97. *Ibid.*
98. PUHARICH, H. K. (ANDRIJA): *Op. cit.*, ref. 78.
99. SCHWINGER, JULIAN: "Relativistic Quantum Field Theory," *Science* 153 (1966): 949–53.
100. ———: "A Magnetic Model of Matter," *Science* 165 (1969): 757–61.
101. KENDALL, HENRY W., and PANOFSKY, WOLFGANG K. H.: "The Structure of the Proton and the Neutron," *Sci. Amer.* (June 1971): 61–77.

102. PUHARICH, H. K.: *Op. cit.*, ref. 82.
103. ALFVÉN, HANNES: *Op. cit.*, ref. 91.
104. ———: *Op. cit.*, ref. 92.
105. REDFIELD, ALFRED G.: *Op. cit.*, ref. 28.
106. CRANE, H. R.: "The g Factor of the Electron," *Sci. Amer.* (Jan. 1968): 76–85.
107. JENSEN, L. H., and SUNDARALINGAM, M.: "Hydrogen Atom Thermal Parameters," *Science* **145** (1964): 1185–87.
108. JOHNSON, CHARLES Y.; YOUNG, J. M.; and HOLMES, J. C.: "Magnetoglow: A New Geophysical Resource," *Science* **171** (1971): 379–81.
109. PORTER, WILLIAM S.: *Op. cit.*, *ref.* 95.
110. REINES, FREDERICK, and SELLSCHOP, J. P. F.: "Neutrinos from the Atmosphere and Beyond," *Sci. Amer.* (Febr. 1966): 40+.
111. ROMIG, MARY F., and LAMOR, DONALD L.: "Anomalous Sounds and Electromagnetic Effects Associated with Fireball Entry." Memorandum RM-3724-ARPA, July 1963, The Rand Corp., Santa Monica, Calif.
112. VAOLENTINUZZI, MAXIMO: "Theory of Magnetophosphenes," *Amer. J. Med. Electronics* (April-June 1962): 112–21.
113. VOLKERS, W.: "Detection and Analysis of High Frequency Signals from Muscular Tissues with Ultra-Low Noise Amplifiers." Technical Report No. TR 76, Millival Division of COHU Electronics, Schenectady, N.Y.
114. WEI, LING Y.: "Role of Surface Dipoles on Axon Membrane," *Science* **163** (1969): 280–82.
115. WITTEBORN, FRED C.: *Op. cit.*, ref. 88.
116. WIENER, N.: *Cybernetics* (New York, N.Y.: John Wiley & Sons, 1948), p. 166.

SUMMARY OF THE CONFERENCE

EMILIO SERVADIO

It would be unthinkable to actually summarize a conference such as this one, which is now approaching its end. We have been presented with a downright avalanche of names, facts and figures, and any attempt to condense all this material would be futile. My task, therefore, as I understand it, will be to try to point out some trends that seem to emerge from all the work that is being done in these intense days.

First of all, I think it was an excellent idea for all of us to get some direct, solid information about what our parapsychological colleagues are doing and pursuing East or West, North or South. Some of the information that has been offered to us was quite new and even surprising—at least to some of the participants. I, for one, was struck by the news that, in Finland, a Society for Psychical Research was founded as early as 1907; but even more, perhaps, when I learned that in California there are at least twenty-five societies for psychical research—under various names, of course!

Another important item has come out of the Conference, i.e., that most researchers in most countries (perhaps in all countries) are faced with more or less the same problems—practical and theoretical—as Dr. Ryzl has clearly pointed out in his presentation. The situation of parapsychology vis-à-vis the academic bodies and the universities raises difficulties in Japan as well as in France, in Johannesburg no less than in Stockholm. However, there are also signs everywhere that the scene is slowly changing. I'll just mention a few of these signs that were recently brought to our attention: the acceptance of parapsychological work in some British universities; university courses in Toronto, Canada; the connections—in spite of the ups and downs described by Dr. Musso—of some leading parapsychologists in Argentina with several universities; the courses in universities and other academic bodies given by prominent California parapsychologists; the work done at official or semi-official levels in Johannesburg and Capetown, also the Ph.D. obtained at Pretoria University with a thesis on ESP; the Italian doctoral degrees bestowed by some universities to students who have presented theses on parapsychological subjects, and also the oncoming Conference on Psychiatry and Parapsychology at the University of Modena, Italy; work in parapsychology done by Japanese students within their own universities; and the work which has been done and is continuing in such parapsychologically famous places as Utrecht in Holland or Freiburg in Germany, at recognized and official levels.

If we now turn to the actual work—experimental or otherwise—that has been achieved or is being done in the countries represented in this Conference, we have a prima facie reason to be favorably impressed. Here again, it would be foolish and repetitious to go into details and I shall only remind you of some landmarks in our international panorama. In England, in spite of the rather pessimistic picture given to us by Dr. West, we have the Randall experiments with small animals and the even more interesting attempts of Brookes-Smith to provoke PK effects by diverting the attention of the experimenters. In California there are Targ's ESP teaching machine and Vogel's researches on the "emotions of plants," plus, of course, the repercussions on the West Coast of the Ted Serios phenomenon—not to speak of the personal activity of Dr. Milan Ryzl. You have all heard of the various experimental endeavors of Japanese parapsychologists among others: research on correlations between ESP and skin resistance, or body temperature, or call-intervals, or other subjective or objective conditions of the subjects. In India, besides the experimental activity at Waltair, some plans have been made to study the possible relationships between psi and Yogic training. I was rather impressed by the work done in Israel, linking trends of modern experimental psychology to possible psi interferences and effects. The three main prongs of the German parapsychological fork as presented by Professor Bender—experiments on animals, on precognition in dreams, on paranormal interferences in tape recordings—are good examples of serious and painstaking work. Nothing *very* new seems to go on in Russia as we have all heard, but it appears that what is being done in Leningrad with the "electric aura," in Moscow with telepathy and speed variations, and in Sverdlovsk with finger-reading has to be taken into serious account. I do not know how many of you had an idea of the good work which is being done in South Africa, and I need only mention, besides the Bleksley "clock-waking" experiments, mass ESP, poltergeist activity, studies in ESP distortion, radiesthesia, etc., the fascinating investigation of the so-called out-of-the-body experiences such as have been described and philosophically commented on in a scholarly fashion by Dr. Poynton. Swiss parapsychologists, reasonably cautious vis-à-vis their audiences, appear to cover with a grand angular vision the ample field of their investigations. In Argentina, in spite of all the strife and difficulties that you have heard about, we see a constant deepening and refining of the statistical quantitative approach in the experimental study of ESP, also the work in progress related to the grandiose, although not yet concluded, "Antartida experiments." About Holland, besides what is being done in Utrecht by Professor Tenhaeff and his collaborators, we heard from Dr. Kappers what has been or is being achieved with psychedelic substances, inquiries on spontaneous cases, and several other lines of research. Dr. Cassoli has reported the activity of the Bologna Center of which he has always been the most dynamic promoter. He mentioned studies on precognition, on the growing of fungi, on fire-walking, on alleged cases of poltergeist activity, etc. Dr. Duplessis gave us a very impressive report on what is happening in France in at least six different experimental directions, namely psychokinesis, clairvoyance, psi phenomena connected with blindness, qualitative telepathy, quantitative studies of ESP, and induced precognition. It really seems as if parapsychology in France is going through a new Golden Age, reminding all and sundry of the glorious times of Richet, Geley, Osty and other pioneers. Needless to say, my references have been all too scanty, and I apologize for their almost telegraphic character. May I now add something Dr. Rush has mentioned in his most valuable paper, namely the Ullman-Krippner-Feldstein experiments on induced telepathic dreams, the experimental work of Douglas Dean and collaborators with plethysmographic techniques, the Osis and Turner observations on telepathy at a distance, or telepathy and time—and I am more and more convinced that I have left out plenty of my description of this extraordinary parapsychological fair.

Faced as we now are with this impressive array of facts, results, and work in progress, we ought apparently to be satisfied, convinced that we are on the right track, and that all we have to do is to go on in the same direction. But in all earnestness, we all know that this is not the case.

Elements of dissatisfaction with the present state of affairs in parapsychology have been expressed by more than one colleague. In this Conference, among others, Dr. West made it quite clear that he was far from being satisfied, and I remember very well that in a previous Conference, he remarked that the "phenomena" seemed to fade away under closer scrutiny. Similar views were expressed by others. The day before yesterday, Dr. Ryzl even more openly stated that in his opinion, phenomena seemed to be somehow disappearing, and also expressed his concern, and his feeling that no decisive step forward in parapsychology had been made in recent years.

Dr. Dommeyer's views were also significant in this respect. He condemned the "isolating" approach to parapsychology, and said that if we look at them closely, psi phenomena are socio-culturally conditioned, which is saying that we cannot and should not look at them independently of the historical and cultural frame of reference in which they take—or do not take—place. On a different occasion, as I remember, I myself said that it is not by chance that within certain historical and socio-cultural conditions, subjects and phenomena such as have been studied by Richet, Morselli or Schrenck-Notzing were taking place, whereas nowadays we have to go after them, rarified as they are, with the help of the Zener cards, random numbers, thousands of trials, and the statistical approach. It was also refreshing to hear from Dr. Dommeyer that in California new ways of dealing with psi phenomena are considered or adopted nowadays, apart and also away from the more traditional views, in such a fashion as to justify the statement that, as he put it, a parapsychological sun is now rising in the West.

However, in this very Conference we heard several statements, all showing that also the East, once more, had something to suggest and to teach. Prof. Otani recalled the noble traditions of Japan, from original shamanism to Chinkon and Shingon and, finally, to Zen and Zazen Buddhism. He also reminded us of contemporary authors such as Iritani, Suzuki, Chiba and others who are exponents of Japan's philosophy and wisdom, and whose writings certainly have definite parapsychological implications. As I said on a previous occasion, I was impressed by the personal *Erlebnis* of Professor Fukurai, who finally decided that Buddhism contained the final answer to the main questions that had first oriented him toward precise parapsychological investigations.

Dr. Prasad reminded us of the traditions of India, and recalled that in those traditions, psi occurrences had always been taken into consideration, although the Indian sages had never looked at them as something to be particularly pursued or praised.

Such considerations, it must be said, are by no means alien nowadays in Western parapsychology—even apart from what comes to us from the American West Coast. Studies about altered states of consciousness, obtained with manifold methods, with or without the use of drugs, have been made and assembled by several parapsychologists all over the world. I was extremely impressed by the fact that a prominent researcher like Dr. Rush—who is certainly neither a dreamer nor a mystic—gave due attention in his survey to Yoga practices, meditation techniques, and in general, to ways and means aimed at getting psi under the control of conscious volition. I was also in complete agreement with him when he stated that in his opinion, the views of Lawrence LeShan were to be considered with the utmost respect and attention. LeShan, as you have heard, thinks that the "world of psi" is just a "different" world, rather similar to the world of the mystics, seers, etc., also similar to the world according to the views of some modern physicists, and not necessarily less "real" than the world we perceive in our everyday experience. Here, of course, I am reminded of what Dr. Poynton had to say about reality, and the necessity of getting away from a limited, all too empirical concept of what is "real" in the usual sense of the word.

I have come to think that, perhaps, an answer to our query will come out of such views as have found expression here and there during this Conference, together with all the information about experimental activity in the well known, modern and solid Western tradition. It was after all a Western philosopher and psychologist, William James, who said that most probably, other kinds of experiences existed, unknown to us, but divided from our own usual experiences by very thin screens or barriers. And was it not William James (as quoted by Allan Angoff) who pointed out that we with our lives are like trees in the forest, with their roots underground, unaware of something uniting them—a "something" that has also been called a totally different state of consciousness, the Collective Unconscious, "cosmic consciousness," and the like?

This "different" world, or state of consciousness, or other side of things, has been hinted at by innumerable seers, men of wisdom, poets, novelists. I am reminded of the descriptions of a world "the other side of the looking-glass" in the second part of *Alice in Wonderland,* of such mysterious lands as Thule, Atlantis or Montsalvat—all symbolic descriptions of different possible ways of perceiving "reality," of seeing things in ways that seem more akin to the world of ESP, and of parapsychological experience in general, than of the empirical, "classical," scientific coordinates into which we have tried and are trying to squeeze them.

I for one have, needless to say, the greatest respect for science. I think that the "Protocommunication" of Dr. Puharich was a formidable tour de force of pure scientific thinking. It had profundity, it had splendor. And it is almost superfluous for me to state, most emphatically, that not for one moment has it come to my mind that we should relinquish science, the scientific attitude, the scientific method in parapsychology. I wish that there should be no misunderstanding on this point. However, we should not forget that science, as we know it nowadays, is the product of a certain attitude of the mind, and that, as such, it may have neglected some traditional Weltanschauungen, putting these into the same wastepaper basket where we rightly find sheer superstitions and queer beliefs of old. A modern philosopher and essayist, Titus Burckhardt, has tried to reestablish a balance in a book which I strongly recommend to your attention, *Modern Science and Traditional Wisdom.*

It has been for a long time my conviction, and I found it borne out in this Conference, that parapsychology is struggling—in a largely unconscious way—to rediscover some lost truths. Perhaps, as I said, the answer to our present dissatisfaction with our own achievements—such as has been expressed by some of us here—lies in this direction: making ourselves more aware of such truths, of the existence of another side of the coin, of the complementarity between our world this side and another world the other side of the looking-glass. This is what I wanted to say when I expressed the view, the other day, that in order to know more in parapsychology, and to get over the impasse lamented by such prominent researchers as Ryzl, or West, we should perhaps pursue inner changes in us, the observers, getting more and more familiar with the beyond in our very depths, approaching the world of psi by prodding our inner paths, by becoming "intronauts"—to use a word which was invented by a lady-poet of my acquaintance.

I mentioned a moment ago the term "complementarity." This is certainly not the same thing as the "schizoid state" jokingly mentioned by Dr. Rush to characterize the attitude a parapsychologist ought to adopt. Complementarity does not mean division: it means union of the opposites. Again, the ancient traditions with their imperishable symbols give us some cues: the Star of David—the "Mogen David"—with its two opposite triangles; the Yin-Yang of the Far East with its black and white "commas" inscribed into the circumference; and, of course, the Cross. Let us be humble, and accept the idea that we should not be unilateral, that we ought to keep in mind the *two* branches of the Cross, the *two* commas of the Yin-Yang, the *two* triangles of the Mogen David.

One of the last works of Eileen J. Garrett has a significant title: *Many Voices.* Eileen Garrett had the deepest respect for science, for her scientific collaborators, for all those who investigated her gifts with the most modern, refined, scientific means. However, although always cautiously, and never completely committed, she also had the deepest respect for those entities which she called her "controls," also for other important agencies which were contents of her particular inner world, for "voices" which spoke to her with the same "reality" quality, and the same impact, as the voices of her relatives, friends, and co-workers.

"Many Voices," as we have heard here. Not *one* voice. Many sides to our query. Once more, we have to get some inspiration from the exceptional personality that made it possible for us all to be here, exchange views, go back to our usual work more assured and with more energy.

One day, Eileen told me—and I heartily agreed—that perhaps, our whole approach in parapsychology, our constant putting an object in front of us, had to be modified, and that the old saying, "Know thyself," was just as cogent as the other, typically scientific tenet, "Know the object of thine Search."

I shall end with a quotation from a well-known scholar, a student of Eastern traditions, Sir Arthur Avalon: "If we would know what some other than ordinary experience is, we must actually shift not our speculative thought on to it but our being into it."

This, Mr. Chairman, Mrs. Coly, Mrs. Bolton, Ladies and Gentlemen, Friends and Colleagues, is the end of my effort, and the gist of what I could reap out of the magnificent orchard presented to our attention and reflection by this Twentieth International Conference of the Parapsychology Foundation. Thank you.

CLOSING REMARKS

Mrs. Coly: Ladies and gentlemen, I just wanted to thank you all again for coming—for giving us three wonderful days, fantastic days. I know that it has taken some of you away from vacations or very heavy schedules of work, and we appreciate it all the more that you could be with us. The Foundation, I am sure, is inspired to work even harder from the blue print set up by Eileen Garrett. And her good friend, Mrs. Bolton, is still with us to see that it continues that way. Thank you very much for coming.

Angoff: Mr. Chairman, Mrs. Coly, Mrs. Bolton, ladies and gentlemen: And so we come to the end of what we may call a great three-day travelogue. We have been through many lands; through all the continents—the East and the West, as our veteran colleague, Emilio Servadio, has already told you. And we have also been through many disciplines. The results have been impressive, I think you will agree. We are all richer, more enlightened for what you have presented here. You have revealed, as I anticipated when I was privileged to open these meetings three days ago—you have revealed, I say, the universality of psychical research. You have brought to us here in the mountains of southern France a wealth of data about the works of our colleagues everywhere in the world. More than that, you have brought this wealth of information to the whole world of learning, for what you said here (I must remind you) has been recorded and will be transcribed and will be made into a book that will find a much greater audience, and indeed I will confirm this as Mr. Coly, my good colleague, distributes to you the bound copies of last year's Conference. May I add my thanks to the thanks already given to you by our president. My thanks again to all of you—to our three sturdy chairmen: Hans Bender, Donald West, and Fred Dommeyer. And, of course, my thanks again to Dr. Servadio for his herculean task in giving us a summary which, I might say, is going to appear in the *Parapsychology Review*. My thanks, of course, to the President of the

Foundation, Mrs. Eileen Coly, who continues in a great and enduring tradition of achievement. And my thanks to Mr. Robert Coly, the Administrative Secretary of the Foundation, whose work at the back of the room has made it possible for all of us here to work at the front of the room. Even though they are not here, I know that Mrs. Coly would agree that we should thank our good colleagues back in our office on Fifty-Seventh Street in New York; and it is largely due to their cooperation that we got here and have done so well. Above all, our thanks to Eileen Garrett. As Mrs. Bolton pointed out when we opened our meetings, Eileen Garrett has been with us throughout these days. Please let me turn now, finally, to Mrs. Frances Bolton, our Vice-President, who has symbolized so much for so many years in psychical research. This year at these meetings, her presence, her participation has continued to excite and inspire us with particular force. It is a force, I dare say, that pervades the greater world of learning. This is a very high tribute to a gracious and devoted leader.

Mrs. Bolton, I know I speak for all of us here in this room when I say that your example enables all of us to return to our homes, our offices, our universities and our laboratories in near and distant lands on a note of high hope for the future.

MRS. BOLTON: Now our Twentieth Meeting has taken place. Parapsychology has meant a great deal to me through these years when I served in the Congress of the United States, and I'm happy to be here now that I am free, and I don't have to take orders from anybody.

Life to me—and when you get to the other side of seventy-five, and get going towards a hundred pretty fast—is a most delightful experience, because life is like a river. It flows continually—sometimes over very, very difficult rapids, through dark canyons, into light and understanding. I think that is perhaps the greatest gift that the years can give: understanding of life. There's nothing more wonderful.

But I, too, want to say something of Eileen Garrett. She did a wonderful thing when she assembled people throughout the world who were interested in psychical research. Let us continue her work. We can certainly take with us from here a new sense of strength, of courage, of endurance, and of understanding of the ways of the infinite.